The Cassava Economy of Java

The Cassava
Economy of Java

Walter P. Falcon · William O. Jones
Scott R. Pearson

John A. Dixon · Gerald C. Nelson
Frederick C. Roche · Laurian J. Unnevehr

STANFORD UNIVERSITY PRESS
Stanford, California 1984

Stanford University Press
Stanford, California
©1984 by the Board of Trustees of the
Leland Stanford Junior University
Printed in the United States of America
LC 82-42912
ISBN 0-8047-1194-1

This book is dedicated to the memory of
Sidik Moelyono
former head of the Expert Staff of BULOG

Foreword

I am honored to have been invited to write a Foreword to *The Cassava Economy of Java*. It is an important volume, both because of its methodological approach and because of its substantive findings. It also demonstrates the great potential of research collaboration among institutions within Indonesia and abroad.

A primary focus of the New Order has been on food and food policy. Indonesia's success in agriculture, especially rice, has been a central element in the growth and development of the Indonesian economy during the past 15 years. Though rice continues to dominate the diets of Indonesians and the food-policy agenda, attention to secondary crops has increased since the mid-1970's. Progress with the *palawija* crops has been slow, however, in part because the research base on these cropping systems is less well developed. Indeed, there is now a critical need for a series of commodity volumes to complement the classic studies by Leon Mears on rice published in 1959 and 1981 ([100], [101]) and the current volume on cassava.

Three methodological aspects of the cassava study seem especially important. Too often research has focused only on production or consumption. The integrated nature of this volume, stressing all components of the cassava system, offers a useful guideline to others contemplating commodity studies in Indonesia or elsewhere.

A second major methodological feature is the demonstrated usefulness of placing a single crop within the broader context of national policy. No one can deny the importance of agricultural technology, extension, and credit. What this book amply demonstrates is that decisions made in the Ministry of Trade, the Ministry of Finance, and other ministries can also have a very great impact on consumers and producers.

Third, embedding Java's cassava system squarely in the context of the world food economy adds substantially to the volume. There is considerable discussion in the press about global interdependence. One of the most interesting features of *The Cassava Economy of Java*, therefore, is its precise documentation of how European agricultural policy has, in this instance, greatly benefited cassava producers in Indonesia.

Stressing the methodological aspects of the book in no way diminishes its important substantive findings. The present and potential labor intensity in upland cropping systems will come as a welcome surprise to those who see productive employment in the 1980's and 1990's as perhaps Indonesia's greatest problem. Few would have guessed, for example, that some 20 million days of work annually, mostly for women, are now provided by the cassava starch industry. At the farm level, the potential of the upland cropping systems underscores the need for more vigorous efforts to find and fund relevant research, extension, and credit activities.

The volume highlights the importance of gaplek consumption in rural areas, especially by poorer people. It also demonstrates that middle- and upper-income Indonesians consume far more cassava (in the form of snacks, like krupuk, made from starch) than they may realize and that the domestic demand potential for cassava is not nearly so bleak as many had anticipated. And the final chapter underscores a new dilemma that Indonesians will face as incomes grow. The preliminary comments about Java's future feed-livestock economy are very sobering for all who must develop a strategy for a domestic feed industry.

Finally, the institutional partnerships exemplified by this book deserve special comment. Stanford University has made a substantial commitment of time and experienced personnel, supported financially by the Ford Foundation. In Indonesia, great efforts were also made by the ministries of Agriculture and Trade, BULOG, the Central Bureau of Statistics, BAPPENAS, and the University system. In this cooperative spirit, the decisions of the Stanford group to publish the volume in Bahasa Indonesia, as well as in English, and to provide supplemental appendixes of special relevance to Indonesian students engaged in commodity studies seem especially noteworthy.

The partnership that has produced this important volume on cassava has been impressive, and I am delighted to have been associated with the effort.

Jakarta   SALEH AFIFF

Preface

Most volumes owe their existence to a large number of people, few of whom appear as authors. *The Cassava Economy of Java* is no exception, and with seven authors working over a four-year period, the list of organizations and individuals who deserve recognition is so long that a second volume would be needed just for the proper acknowledgments. The partial listing that follows, therefore, in no way diminishes the support of literally hundreds of Indonesian producers, consumers, traders, and government officials who permitted the Stanford team to impose on them.

The origins of this volume trace to 1978, when BAPPENAS, the Indonesian planning agency, became increasingly worried about Indonesia's dependence on imported rice. Dr. Saleh Afiff, then Deputy Head of BAPPENAS, arranged for Peter Timmer and me to make a preliminary assessment of the potential of secondary food crops in solving Indonesia's food problems. It was Saleh Afiff also who later pressed for the cassava project, shepherded the necessary paperwork through the Cabinet, and chaired numerous sessions of the Indonesian Advisory Committee to the project. Without him, this book could not have been written.

The Ford Foundation also played a vital role in the research process. Theodore Smith, then Representative for the Ford Foundation and now President of the Agricultural Development Council, arranged funding for the first phase of the project as part of the Foundation's food policy initiative within Indonesia. His successor, Thomas Kessinger, arranged funding for the second phase. The Foundation also underwrote a reconnaissance survey of the cassava economy by William O. Jones.

Rector Harsono made possible Laurian Unnevehr's placement at Brawijaya University, Director-General Suhadi Mangkusuwondo assisted Gerald Nelson's placement in the Ministry of Trade, and Director Sjarifuddin Baharsjah made Frederick Roche an integral part of the Puslitbang in Bogor. Ratna Wahab of BAPPENAS had overall responsibility for coordinating the project with the Government of Indonesia.

We are also grateful to a number of Indonesians who worked directly on various components of the project. These include Aang Kanaan, Malino Pangaribuan, Murad Sulaeman, Achmad Suryana, Salyo Sutrisno, and Djumilah Zain. Their progress, promotions, and entry into advanced degree programs are a pleasant and important joint product of this research.

We are grateful as well to the management of BULOG, the national logistics agency charged with many responsibilities in the food sector. Generals Bustanil Arifin and Sukriya Atmaja, always gracious hosts, arranged for seminars, for contacts and transportation in the provinces, and for food policy short courses that complemented the cassava research. Sidik Moelyono, the late head of BULOG's expert staff, was invaluable as friend and substantive adviser.

Although most of our impositions occurred in Indonesia, we are also extremely grateful for the support at Stanford. Deborah Prentice typed innumerable drafts of the manuscript, Ellen Barker exhausted the Food Research Institute's supply of blue pencils with her editorial assistance, and Susan Maher handled the countless administrative matters that occur with a project of this size and duration. Peter Kahn, Associate Editor at Stanford University Press, greatly improved the readability of the manuscript, and to him specifically and the Press generally we are greatly indebted.

Finally, we are indebted to the assistance of several referees. James Cock, S. K. Hahn, B. T. Kang, John Lynam, Leon Mears, Edgard Normanha, and Delane Welsch commented on the entire manuscript; Anne Peck made major contributions to the consumption chapter; and Martin Wijler offered important insights on European trade issues.

Although *The Cassava Economy of Java* could not have been completed without the assistance of those mentioned here, they should not be held responsible for the final draft. We only hope that they, and other readers, find it a useful contribution to understanding the world's fifth-largest country.

W. P. F.

Contents

Tables

Figures

Abbreviations and Exchange Rates

Abbreviations of Indonesian and international organizations and
  programs

BAPPENAS	Badan Perencanaan Pembangunan Nasional, the national planning agency
BIMAS	Bimbingan Massal, a farm input program
BULOG	Badan Urusan Logistik, the national logistics agency
CBS or BPS	Biro Pusat Statistik, Central Bureau of Statistics
CIAT	Centro Internacional de Agricultura Tropical, Cali, Colombia
CRIA	Central Research Institute for Agriculture
FAO	Food and Agriculture Organization of the United Nations, Rome, Italy
IITA	International Institute for Tropical Agriculture, Ibadan, Nigeria
IRRI	International Rice Research Institute, Los Baños, Philippines
KCK	Kredit Candak Kulak, a credit program for small village traders
KIK	Kredit Investasi Kecil, a program of small investment credits
KMKP	Kredit Modal Kerja Permanen, an intermediate credit program for working capital
Susenas	Survei Sosial-Ekonomi Nasional, the national household expenditure survey

Value of American dollar (U.S.$1.00) in Indonesian rupiahs

August 1971 to November 1978	Rp 415
1979 (annual average)	Rp 623
1980 (annual average)	Rp 627
1981 (annual average)	Rp 632
1982 (annual average)	Rp 661
after March 30, 1983	Rp 970

Units of physical measurement
  Metric except where otherwise specified.

The Cassava Economy of Java

1. Cassava and Java

*Scott R. Pearson, Walter P. Falcon, and
William O. Jones*

Cassava is a tropical root crop and the world's cheapest source of food calories.[1] It is consumed as a staple food by perhaps 400 million people in the humid and semi-humid tropics of Africa, Asia, and the Americas. Java is an equatorial island of 132,000 square kilometers, about the size of Greece, inhabited by 90 million people.[2] It might seem to follow logically that cassava would have an important place in the food system of Java, one of the most densely populated and poorest regions of the world. But the inhabitants of Java eat five times as much rice as cassava and rely on rice for half their total calories. Moreover, cassava has been regarded as an inferior foodstuff since its introduction into Java during the nineteenth century.

What, then, motivates a group of economists to carry out a detailed study of a secondary, nonpreferred staple food? The answer begins with rice—the starting point for almost any food policy investigation in Indonesia. Yields and total production of rice increased on Java by more than 50 percent during the 1970's, largely as a result of the introduction of high-yielding varieties, chemical fertilizers, production credit, and improved water control. Though annual rice production will probably continue to increase, it will do so at a slower rate than in the early days of the Green Revolution. At the same time, Indonesian demand for rice, both on Java and elsewhere, continues to grow. Increases in rice consumption are fueled by an expanding population and rapidly rising incomes. In several recent years (although not in 1980 and 1981) Indonesia imported more rice than any other country in the world.

The original motivation for this study, therefore, was to investigate whether increases in cassava production are technically and economically feasible, and, if so, whether they might reduce rice imports.

[1]Cassava is also known as *manioc, tapioca, mandioca,* and *yuca.* On Java it is called *ketela pohon, ubi kayu, singkong,* and *kaspe.* (See Normanha [110]).

[2]The Indonesian archipelago contains 3,000 islands and 150 million people. This study focuses principally on the island of Java but occasionally also on southern Sumatra.

Preliminary reconnaissance in 1978 suggested that the technical efficiency of cassava production might be increased through the adoption of improved varieties and practices, but little was known about how cassava is grown and marketed on Java. It was not at all clear whether such innovations would lower production costs or increase either output or the amounts offered for sale. A great deal of new information about cassava consumption, however, was becoming available from a series of household expenditure surveys conducted by the government after 1963.

There was also hope that improved cassava policy might further growth and equity objectives. Cassava is a central component of many rain-fed intercropped farming systems, mostly in the hilly areas of Java, which are typically marginal agricultural areas inhabited by poor people. These farming systems have received less attention by government food crop programs, which have concentrated almost exclusively on irrigated rice production.

Cassava differs from other Indonesian staples in that it is extremely perishable and must be quickly consumed or transformed into a storable product. The fresh root is eaten as a staple near where it is grown and as a delicacy in the cities. One of its two storable products, starch, is consumed primarily in snacks and small cakes; the other, dried peeled pieces called *gaplek*, serves as poor people's food in Indonesia and animal feed in Western Europe.

The economics of Indonesia's cassava system therefore entailed investigation of processing, consumer preferences, and the export market—as well as of farm production and marketing. Studies were accordingly undertaken in 1979/80 of cassava cultivation on Java (F. C. Roche), internal marketing (L. J. Unnevehr), cassava processing and export marketing (G. C. Nelson), and domestic consumer demand (J. A. Dixon).[3] The production study relied heavily on intensive surveys of current farm practices in three principal cassava-growing areas, and the internal-marketing study depended on interviews with farmers, merchants in rural areas, and others further up the marketing chain. Processors and international traders were interviewed in Java, southern Sumatra, Thailand, and Western Europe about the starch and gaplek trades. More general questions about the consequences of market imperfections, the impact of gov-

---

[3] Three of these detailed studies formed the basis of Ph. D. dissertations at Stanford University (Nelson [105]; Unnevehr [151]; and Roche [123]); the fourth is available as a report of the International Food Policy Research Institute (Dixon [40]).

ernment policies, and changes in the world economy were considered in a series of discussions with Indonesian policymakers.

Principal Themes

Four principal inquiries are pursued in this book: (1) How efficiently does the existing system produce, process, and market cassava? (2) What is the potential for expanding the capacity of the existing cassava system? (3) What markets exist for expanded supplies of cassava? (4) How do current government policies affect cassava, and how might they be improved?

Efficiency, the ability of an economic system to generate the most output for given resources, is important throughout the cassava system, but is especially important in the marketing sector. Marketing inefficiencies cause farmers to receive too little and consumers to pay too much, and they also distort and reduce the efficiency of production. Hence, the study of marketing and production efficiency is an important precursor to expanding output. Expansion of capacity depends on investments to relieve physical constraints (such as inadequate roads), to finance research to develop improved technical packages for farmers, or to find cheaper and more attractive product forms for consumers. Whether an expansion occurs in firms of greater or less labor intensity has implications for employment and income distribution. The government, in effect, determines the most profitable technique through its set of policies affecting the industry. Increased productivity will not lead to increased production unless there are economic uses for cassava products. Examination of the potential demand for cassava in all of its uses, therefore, also becomes an essential part of the analysis. Efficiency, capacity, and markets are related; all three are influenced by government policy, either through measures that change the prices of outputs and inputs or through measures that regulate production and consumption. With few exceptions, however, the government of Indonesia has chosen to permit the cassava system to operate independently of specific government actions.

Cassava policy is but one dimension of Indonesian food policy. The costs of inputs and the prices of other foods influence cassava through substitutions in production and consumption. There is a need, therefore, for understanding how cassava fits into the complete food system on Java and how policies affecting other food crops have important cross effects on cassava. This point underlies much of the policy discussion in the chapters on the individual components of the cassava system, and it is at the core of the food-policy analysis in the concluding chapter. A second key element of policy lies largely outside the control of the Indonesian government. The determination of world prices for internationally traded cassava products is a fascinating story that requires more detail about the commodity and a broader view of cassava in the world food economy.

Cassava in the World Food System

Plant characteristics peculiar to cassava impose common features on its use wherever it enters into the world food system.[4] Cassava will grow in marginal soils and tends to be associated with rain-fed, intercropped farming systems. Cassava can be harvested at any time between 6 and 24 months (or even later) after planting. Time of harvest can therefore be adjusted to time of need or time of best market price, and this characteristic has made cassava popular as a famine-relief crop in high-risk tropical farming areas. It also reduces price risks and adds a measure of stability to farming systems like those on Java. This advantage is enhanced by the fact that harvesting constitutes a large part of the cost of growing cassava; in some parts of the tropics where land is cheap, cassava fields are planted speculatively to be harvested only when prices exceed harvest costs.

Marketing and consumption are strongly influenced by the cassava roots' bulkiness, perishability, and toxicity. Fresh cassava roots contain less than one-third as much food energy per kilogram as threshed cereal starchy staples and are therefore much more costly to transport to market or processing plants.[5] They begin to deteriorate as soon as they are harvested and spoil within two or three days unless subjected to expensive cold storage or wax coating. Usual practice, therefore, is to transform them at once into dried forms. Fresh roots contain hydrocyanic acid (HCN), and care must be taken to remove it by soaking, crushing, fermenting, or drying. This combination of characteristics explains why cassava tends to be favored by farmers who consume most of what they grow, and it determines the kinds of marketing and processing systems that are required for commercial production.

[4] See Cock [21, 21a] for a summary assessment of cassava's role in the tropics.

[5] Some cassava clones have up to 40 percent dry matter and contain 1,200 to 1,600 calories per kilogram.

TABLE 1.1. *World Cassava Production, 1980*

	Production		Area under cultivation		Yield
	(000 tons)	*(percent)*	*(000 ha)*	*(percent)*	*(tons/ha)*
Brazil	24,554	20%	2,056	15%	11.9
Thailand	13,500	11	1,015	7	13.3
Indonesia	13,300	11	1,420	10	9.4
Zaire	12,500	10	1,880	13	6.6
Nigeria	11,000	10	1,200	9	9.2
India	6,500	5	370	3	17.6
Tanzania	4,600	4	940	7	4.9
China	3,174	2	243	2	13.1
Mozambique	2,800	2	600	3	4.7
Colombia	2,640	2	241	2	10.9
Rest of world	27,566	23	3,961	28	7.0
World total	122,134	100%	13,926	100%	8.8

SOURCE: FAO, Production Yearbook, Vol. 34, 1980.

Of an estimated world total of 122 million tons of fresh root production in 1980, Africa, Asia, and Latin America contributed roughly equal shares. The five leading producer countries—Brazil, Thailand, Indonesia, Zaire, and Nigeria—accounted for nearly two-thirds of total world output of cassava (Table 1.1). Reported yields in Indonesia increased by a quarter during the 1970's and reached 9.4 tons per hectare by 1980—somewhat higher than the world average of 8.8 tons, but considerably below yields in Thailand, Brazil, and India.

International diversity in the role cassava plays in commodity systems stems from its multiple end uses. Primary end uses are as fresh and dried food, animal feed, and starch for food and industrial purposes. Indonesian cassava is used in all of these ways, with direct consumption as food being most important. Thirty-five percent is consumed on farms, 30 percent is marketed as food, 25 percent is sold to starch factories, and 10 percent is exported.

None of the other leading cassava producers closely approximates Indonesia's pattern of end uses. Brazil feeds more than one-third of its cassava to its own livestock, consumes one-fourth in the form of *farinha de mandioca* (a precooked food product), and utilizes smaller amounts for fresh or dried food, starch (including minor exports), and alcohol. Almost all cassava produced in Thailand is exported as animal feed or starch. Zaire uses almost all of its crop as a domestic foodstuff, about half of it processed. Nigeria, like Zaire, uses cassava as a human foodstuff, much of it processed into *gari*, a prepared product similar to farinha de mandioca. Small amounts are fed to livestock and made into starch.

From the perspective of cassava's role in the food system, Indonesia most resembles Brazil and Nigeria, which have the largest populations in Latin America and Africa, respectively. In all three of these nations, cassava now provides between 200 and 300 calories per capita per day, or between 8 and 13 percent of total calorie consumption. As these countries achieve higher per capita incomes, trade-offs between food and nonfood uses and between domestic and foreign demand will become increasingly important.

Historically, exports have provided important outlets for Java's cassava products. Starch was the first cassava product to be traded internationally in significant amounts. The cassava industry of Indonesia (then the Netherland Indies) developed at the turn of the twentieth century. It exported an annual average of 260,000 tons of cassava products from 1934 to 1938, accounting for more than 80 percent of world exports. The Second World War and Indonesia's war for independence interrupted cassava trade, and Indonesian exports did not return to prewar levels until the late 1960's.

A dramatic shift in the international trade of cassava products occurred during the late 1960's and 1970's, when cassava pellets for animal feed replaced starch as the dominant product traded internationally. High grain-price policies pursued by the European Community favored substitution of cassava pellets for grain in European feed mixtures. In recent years, the Community has accounted for 90 percent of the world's cassava imports, and in 1978 it absorbed a peak volume of 6.5 million tons, valued at more than $600 million. Despite the fact that Thailand has dominated recent trade, Europe's effect on Indonesia has been and will continue to be significant. International developments thus figure prominently in the discussions of domestic processing, marketing, and price formation.

Reader's Guide

This book is concerned with the prospects for and implications of expanding the cassava system on Java. Chapter 2 begins by analyzing the principal cassava-producing systems in upland areas of southern Java, where cassava is mainly intercropped with cereals and legumes. Expansion of cassava production depends on the availability in the countryside of yield-increasing technology and on the existence of government policies that provide suitable incentives for cassava producers.

Profits at the farm level are directly influenced by prices in markets for cassava products and by the costs of preparing and distributing those products. Four succeeding chapters are therefore devoted to an economic examination of current and prospective end uses. Demand for fresh and processed cassava for direct human consumption is analyzed in Chapter 3, focusing on income level and regional differences. Consumers' behavior in response to changes in their incomes and in cassava product prices relative to prices of other foodstuffs is central in determining whether expanded cassava output will further food policy objectives on Java. Chapter 3 also introduces a discussion of the desirability of expanding the number of end uses for cassava, including admixtures and new storable products. The manufacture and trade of starch are discussed in Chapter 4. Cassava starch is an important source of food on Java, perhaps three-fourths of it being used in making food products, mostly *krupuk*, a popular snack. Effects of industrial policy on industry structure, choice of technique, and employment are also treated. The export market for gaplek pellets is analyzed in Chapter 5. The focus broadens to include Thailand, the world's largest exporter of cassava products, and Europe, where farm and trade policies exert great influence on gaplek demand. Chapter 6 contains an analysis of marketing efficiency and of the capacity of the market to expand operations in response to an increased supply of and demand for cassava products. It integrates the components of the cassava system through examination of domestic and international price determination for cassava products. Price policy is discussed in the broader context of Indonesia's food policy in Chapter 7. Options for government policy in advancing growth, equity, security, and nutrition objectives are analyzed in the light of the economic constraints and opportunities anticipated for the 1980's.

2. Production Systems

Frederick C. Roche

Cassava has been grown on Java for more than 150 years, although the exact date and manner of its introduction are unknown. Prior to the Second World War, cassava-producing estates covered extensive areas. Java was the world's major exporter of cassava starch, whose production came more or less equally from smallholders and large plantations. The latter were disbanded after Indonesia gained independence from the Dutch in 1949, so today all cassava is produced by smallholders. Cassava is cultivated throughout Java, but it is especially important in the island's marginal upland areas.

This chapter assesses current and potential costs and returns to cassava production on Java. The first section analyzes production trends during the 1970's, describes Java's main cassava production systems, and reviews the agroclimatic and socioeconomic characteristics of the regions where cassava is produced. Because the ways cassava is grown, the productivity of the crop, and the end uses it is put to vary considerably by region, the second section reports detailed information from field surveys conducted in three of the major producing regions. The third section shows the potential benefits to be gained from improving cassava cropping practices in the surveyed areas, and estimates the farm-level costs of and returns to these improvements, which vary significantly among the three regions and entail very different levels of public resources. The fourth section analyzes economic and institutional factors that influence the adaptability and regional distribution of improved cassava technologies. Estimates of returns to improved cassava cropping practices are analyzed for sensitivity to relative price changes for inputs and outputs. The chapter concludes with a discussion of policy alternatives for Indonesian decision makers, especially for the development of Java's previously neglected upland agricultural systems.

An Overview of Cassava Production on Java

Cassava has been an important food crop on Java since the early years of this century. In the 1920's a much smaller population (about 40

TABLE 2.1. *Cassava Area, Production, and Yields, Java and Indonesia, 1951–81*

Year	Area (million ha)		Production (million tons)		Yields (tons/ha)	
	Java and Madura	Indonesia	Java and Madura	Indonesia	Java and Madura	Indonesia
1951	.75	.87	5.3	7.1	7.1	8.2
1952	.77	.93	5.1	7.5	6.6	8.1
1953	.87	1.04	6.5	9.0	7.5	8.7
1954	.87	1.07	6.4	9.6	7.4	9.0
1955	.88	1.08	6.5	9.4	7.4	8.7
1956	.90	1.12	6.4	9.1	7.1	8.1
1957	.99	1.22	7.2	10.1	7.3	8.3
1958	1.08	1.34	8.1	11.3	7.5	8.4
1959	1.19	1.46	9.0	12.7	7.6	8.7
1960	1.14	1.42	8.6	11.4	7.5	8.0
1961	1.14	1.48	8.4	11.2	7.4	7.6
1962	1.14	1.45	8.1	11.4	7.1	7.9
1963	1.28	1.56	8.7	11.6	6.8	7.4
1964	1.26	1.58	9.1	12.3	7.2	7.8
1965	1.40	1.75	9.7	12.6	6.9	7.2
1966	1.17	1.51	8.3	11.2	7.1	7.4
1967	1.18	1.52	8.3	10.8	7.0	7.1
1968	1.16	1.50	8.8	11.4	7.6	7.6
1969	1.14	1.47	8.2	10.9	7.2	7.4
1970	1.09	1.40	8.0	10.5	7.3	7.5
1971	1.10	1.41	8.1	10.7	7.4	7.6
1972	1.13	1.47	7.9	10.4	7.0	7.1
1973	1.06	1.43	8.1	11.2	7.6	7.8
1974	1.16	1.51	9.6	12.9	8.3	8.5
1975	1.02	1.41	9.3	12.3	9.1	8.7
1976	1.00	1.35	8.8	12.2	8.8	9.0
1977	.99	1.36	9.1	12.5	9.2	9.2
1978	1.01	1.38	9.5	12.9	9.4	9.3
1979	1.02	1.44	9.9	13.8	9.7	9.6
1980	1.00	1.41	9.8	13.7	9.8	9.7
1981[a]	.99	1.40	9.9	13.7	10.0	9.8

SOURCES: 1950 to 1962 from Indonesia [77]; 1962 to 1974 from Leon A. Mears, "Indonesia's Food Problems," *Pelita II/11* 24, no. 2 (June 1976); 1975 to 1981 from Indonesia [77].
[a]Preliminary estimate.

million in 1930) produced about 6 million tons a year on 700,000 hectares of land and exported from 150,000 to 500,000 tons of dried products. World depression, the Second World War, and Indonesia's war for independence seriously disrupted production and exports, but by 1950 production was approaching prewar levels.

Two distinct production trends for cassava can be identified between 1951 and 1981 (Table 2.1). Both area planted to cassava and production on Java rose until 1965, with yields varying from 6.6 to 7.6 tons per hectare around a mean of 7.2 tons. Area planted dropped in 1966 and declined slightly thereafter though yields remained steady at around 7.3 tons until 1974. In 1974 yields rose abruptly to 8.3 tons per hectare, and in 1975 to 9.1 tons per hectare. They remained at about that level through 1980.[1]

Factors Contributing to Declining Cassava Areas

Various phenomena, all difficult to quantify precisely, have led to the reduction in cassava areas on Java. Major irrigation construction and rehabilitation programs that were undertaken throughout Indonesia during the 1970's permitted irrigated rice to be substituted for rain-fed crops like cassava and extended the period of irrigated cultivation in existing fields. Evidence on the areas affected by these programs is inconsistent, but since Java is nearing the point of full exploitation of irrigable land,[2] the impact of new irrigated areas on cassava plantings will be smaller in the future.

The government's afforestation (*penghijauan*) efforts in the uplands of Java have also reduced the amount of land available for cassava. Steep and highly eroded areas are being retired from continuous cultivation as residents are moved into newly opened farmland off Java. No reliable data exist on the progress of the afforestation program, and laws proscribing cultivation of officially retired land have not been well enforced. In the cassava-producing uplands of West and South Central Java, however, annual crops on steep hillside terraces have been replaced occasionally by shrubs and young trees. Because cassava is a particularly important crop where soil and topography constraints are most severe, successful afforestation efforts will have a significant impact on cassava plantings.

Relatively high prices for competing staple crops have also affected cassava areas on Java. Rural prices for cassava declined relative to the prices of other major staples throughout much of the 1970's (Figure 2.1). The sharp fall from 1973 to 1974 was caused by an export ban on cassava products in effect from July until November of 1973, and the continued low levels of the next year reflected the huge harvest of 1974, when areas harvested were at a peak for the decade (the 1973/74 rainy season began late in many areas of Java, which probably led farmers to delay late 1973 harvests until the next year in hopes of price increases). During the period 1976–79, land in soybeans increased considerably and the area in peanuts and corn was greater

[1] There are problems with the data on reported yields, and national estimates are far from precise, but the increase in yields seems real, especially since fertilizer use has been up, as reported in a later section.
[2] The progress of irrigation development in Indonesia has been studied most closely by Nyberg and Prabowo [113] and Booth [12]. Montgomery and Sugito [102] examine intercensal (1963–73) changes in land classified as irrigated and rain fed.

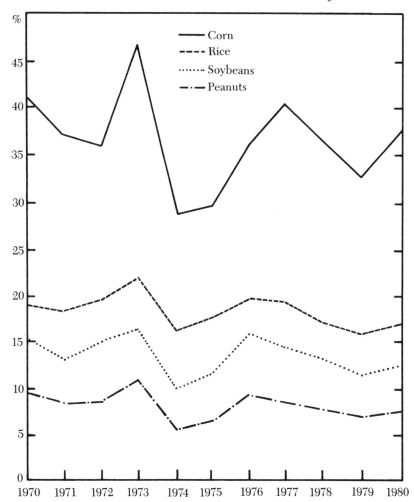

s o u r c e : Indonesia [77], *Statistical Pocketbook of Indonesia.*

Figure 2. 1. Cassava Prices as Percentages of the Prices of Other Major Food Crops, Rural Markets, Java and Madura, 1970–80

than the 1968–80 average (Indonesia [76]).³ The devaluation of the rupiah in late 1978 and the rise in European gaplek prices during 1979 increased rural cassava prices on Java, but no changes in trends for cassava and other staple crops are yet visible in the area statistics.

Over the past ten years there have also been extensive plantings of perennial cash crops—principally clove and citrus—in Java's uplands. Farmers are attracted by the high prices and low current costs

³These relationships probably reflect marginal substitutions in lowland areas.

TABLE 2.2. *Application of Chemical Fertilizers to Cassava, Corn, and Upland Rice, Java and Madura, 1970–79*
(kg/ha)

Year	Cassava	Corn	Upland rice
1970/71	6.2	30.3	14.2
1971/72	7.8	38.0	65.1
1972/73	8.1	45.1	46.5
1973/74	6.6	34.6	40.4
1974/75	8.8	49.8	45.9
1975/76	12.6	53.6	58.0
1976/77	18.2	58.1	66.8
1977/78	17.4	69.7	83.0
1978/79	21.7	71.2	82.3

SOURCE: Indonesia [78].
NOTE: These figures are derived from a large random sample of interviews with farmers conducted annually by the Central Bureau of Statistics on production costs and returns. The results are averages over all farmers sampled (both users and nonusers of fertilizer). The published figures do not distinguish among the specific types of inorganic fertilizer used. However, urea and TSP predominate in Java and Madura; potassium and compound fertilizers are considerably less widespread.

of production. Typically, seedlings are planted in rain-fed fields surrounded by the normal pattern of cassava and annual intercrops. In later years, as the young trees grow and their canopies enlarge, the areas planted to annual crops decrease. Statistics on acreage are scarce, but the frequency of this cropping system in Java's uplands suggests that tree-crop plantings have resulted in a small but significant decline in the areas planted to cassava and other upland crops. Farmers in all three of the field survey areas had recently planted trees in this manner. Plantings were most extensive in the Garut survey area (West Java), where 26 of 34 farmers had planted tree crops within the last five years. Several of these farmers reported that the trees had replaced cassava or cassava intercropping patterns on significant portions of their land.

Factors Contributing to Higher Cassava Yields

The major source of the growth in average cassava yields thus far has been the increased use of chemical nutrients on cassava and other upland crops (Table 2.2) made possible by the development of fertilizer marketing channels—both public and private—since the early 1970's. Fertilizer pricing policy has also allowed the real prices of urea and triple super phosphate (TSP) to decline over the decade. Average doses of chemical nutrients on cassava more than tripled between 1970 and 1978, with a particular surge in the last three years. Nonetheless, the average rate of use in even that last three-year period—about 19 kilograms per hectare—was low. Application rates on corn and upland rice also increased greatly over the decade and are considerably higher than for cassava. Because most of Java's cassava is intercropped with cereals and legumes rather than planted in pure stands, cassava appears to benefit from the fertilizer used on its companion plants.

It is not clear why yields increased during the 1970's. Indeed, it is not certain that they did, since national estimates are far from precise. Nevertheless, increasing use of fertilizers generally on cassava in the 1970's created a strong presumption that the increase in yields was real and due in large part to increased fertilizer applications, especially on mixed stands. There is no evidence of widespread changes in the varieties of cassava grown on Java during the period.

Although agronomists at research centers in South America and Africa[4] have been engaged in efforts to create improved varieties of cassava, they have had no consistent success along the lines of the Green Revolution technology developed for wheat and rice beginning in the late 1960's. Indonesian agronomists have a small cassava improvement program under way, but new varieties have not been released on a large scale, and agricultural extension programs and farm credit programs for cassava have been limited (Indonesia [82]).[5]

One of the new approaches being studied is the so-called Mukibat cassava, a system that grafts cassava planting material (*M. esculenta*) onto trunks of treelike ceara rubber (*M. glaziovii*).[6] Despite its high potential yields, the Mukibat's long growing period (much longer than normal cassava) and its poor taste and low starch content are likely to prevent its widespread acceptance by farmers.

The Agroclimatic Environment

At present, about 95 percent of Java's cassava is grown on rain-fed soils (*tegal*), most of which are deep and fine textured.[7] Throughout

---

[4]These organizations include the Centro Internacional de Agricultura Tropical (CIAT) in Colombia, the Instituto Agronomico de Campinas in Brazil, and the International Institute for Tropical Agriculture (IITA) in Nigeria.

[5]*BIMAS* (*Bimbingan Massal*, or "Mass Guidance") is the Indonesian term for agricultural extension programs, especially for irrigated rice, which offer production credit to farmers for the purchase of fertilizer and other inputs.

[6]The Faculty of Agriculture at Brawijaya University in East Java has published a number of studies on this form of cassava production arising from its ongoing Cassava Research Project. For a summary, see Brawijaya University [17]. The nature of Mukibat cassava and its initial development are described in Bruijn and Dharmaputra [18].

[7]The distinction between rain-fed and irrigated soils is not straightforward in Indonesia because land types are classified by their capacity for flooded rice production. *Tegal* refers to soils over which water movement is uncontrolled (that is, no bunds). The term *sawah* refers to both irrigated and rain-fed soils that are bunded to collect standing water for wet rice production. Approximately 52 percent of Java's agricultural land is classified as tegal, and the remainder consists of various forms of sawah (Indonesia, [71]).

Java, population pressure has led to the cultivation of hillsides that might better be returned to natural forest. Erosion is a serious problem. Inadequate terracing of tegal plots and poor drainage channels combine to make soil runoff highly visible during the intense rainy season. In most of Java's uplands, the tegal soils are sufficiently deep and well developed to make their complete destruction by erosion a distant concern. However, where annual topsoil loss is heavy, the productivity of these soils is seriously diminished. At the same time, upland erosion has led to silting problems in many downstream irrigation systems, making costly rehabilitation necessary.

In a small but significant share of the rain-fed uplands, steep slopes, erodible soils, and improper land use have resulted in severe erosion damage. Exact data on the extent of Java's truly "critical lands" are not available,[8] but they are concentrated largely in the upland areas along the south central coast. Because cassava is unique in its ability to grow under such adverse soil conditions, it tends to be a major crop on land of this type. Hence, both the production and the consumption of cassava in these areas make up disproportionately large shares of the totals for Java, as will be discussed below. But a dilemma lies in the fact that though cassava tolerates poor soils, it can also accelerate erosion because of its limited canopy cover during its early growth and because of the soil movement involved in its harvest. Cassava alone is not the problem—all annual cropping on this land contributes to erosion. The real source of the problem is the extreme pressure of people on the land in rural Java, a pressure that will be an intractable problem for many years to come. And while it is, cassava will inevitably be a major crop on soils where little else will grow.

Cassava is less important in the irrigated and rain-fed sawah areas of Java. Where water supplies are adequate throughout the year, sawah soils are almost always planted continuously to rice or to a multi-year rotation of rice and sugarcane. However, on sawah that receives sufficient water for only one flooded paddy crop a year, lesser staple crops (*palawija*) with lower water requirements are planted following the rice harvest to grow on late-season rains, residual soil moisture, and irrigation water. This second type of sawah constituted 54 percent, or about 1.4 million hectares, of the the total land area classified as sawah during the 1973 Agricultural Census and amounts to

---

[8] The Indonesian Directorate of Land Use defines "critical lands" only on the basis of slope (>50 percent), ignoring soil type and existing forms of land use.

approximately one-fourth of Java's total agricultural land. Legumes and corn are the crops most commonly planted after the rice harvest.[9] However, from an agronomic standpoint, the better-drained soils of this class of land possess the greatest short-run potential for profitable increases in cassava production.

Annual rainfall is abundant on Java, ranging from a minimum of about 160 centimeters (about 62 inches) to more than 300 centimeters (almost 120 inches). Over much of the island, however, this rainfall is highly seasonal, and the lack of capacity to store water means that food crop cultivation is limited to the rainy season. Average annual rainfall declines both from west to east and from south to north on Java; the length and intensity of the dry season increase in the same manner (see Figure 2.2). On purely rain-fed land in the island's southwestern quadrant, for example, the wet season is generally long enough for two nonrice crops a year. By contrast, on Java's northern plains, in much of East Java, and throughout Madura late-season plantings are risky unless supplementary irrigation water is available.

Patterns of Land Ownership and Use

According to the 1973 Agricultural Census, the more than 8.6 million farms on Java and Madura occupy a total area of only some 5.5 million hectares. It is likely that more than 90 percent of the farmland operated by smallholders is planted to food crops domestically consumed; the production of export crops such as rubber and coffee is more important on the Outer Islands.[10] The median farm size in 1973 was approximately 0.4 hectare, and few farms were larger than five hectares. Nonetheless, significant inequality exists in the distribution of land. Farms larger than two hectares amount to less than 5 percent of all farms, yet occupy almost one-quarter of total agricultural land (Table 2.3). It has been estimated that the nearly landless constitute about 10 percent of all rural households in West and East Java, and about 25 percent in Central Java and the province of Yogyakarta (Montgomery and Sugito [102]).[11] Almost three-quarters of Ja-

[9] Official crop statistics indicate that only about 5 percent of Java's cassava is planted on land classified as "sawah," whether fully or partially irrigated (Indonesia, [76]).

[10] The Central Bureau of Statistics reports total numbers of trees, but not the corresponding occupied areas (Indonesia [71]). Hence it is difficult to estimate the exact shares of land planted to industrial versus food crops.

[11] Montgomery and Sugito's estimates are derived from the 1973 Agricultural Census. The "nearly landless" are defined as households working less than 0.05 hectare of sawah or 0.1 hectare of tegal, or 0.075 hectare of the two land types combined. Using both the Agricultural Census and the 1971 Population Census, White and Makali [162] estimated that more than 31 percent of Java's agricultural laborers are primarily wage laborers.

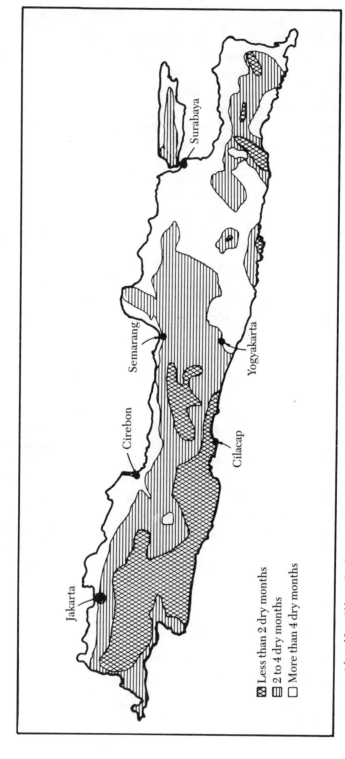

Jakarta

Cirebon

Semarang

Surabaya

Yogyakarta

Cilacap

⊠ Less than 2 dry months
⊞ 2 to 4 dry months
☐ More than 4 dry months

SOURCE: Adapted from Oldeman [114]. Dry months are defined as having less than 10 centimeters of rain.

Figure 2.2. Average Number of Consecutive Months Per Year with less than 10 Centimeters of Rainfall, Java and Madura

va's farms are operated entirely by their owners. Pure tenancy is rare and is concentrated in the smallest farms. A substantial number of farmers rent or are share tenants on parts of their holdings; partial tenancy rates tend to be highest in the largest farm-size classes.

Despite the minuscule size of most of Java's farms, the employment of nonfamily labor is considerable on farms of all sizes (Table 2.4). Although hiring labor is less common on smaller farms, labor is used more intensively there than on large holdings. As the figures in Table 2.5 suggest, small farmers use fertilizer more intensively as well. These structural and land-use characteristics have important implications for agricultural development on Java. First, despite considerable inequality in land distribution, the prevalence of small farms and hired labor suggests the potential for widespread adoption of labor-intensive technologies, thus increasing employment opportunities for the poorest rural classes.[12] Second, many of Java's farmers appear to operate holdings too small to meet their families' staple food requirements. Nonfarm income is accordingly important throughout rural Java in providing the wherewithal to make up the difference. But such work is usually low-paying, and because income levels are low, the capital necessary to buy seed and fertilizer may have to be provided by farm credit programs in many areas of Java to encourage widespread adoption of the more expensive new crop technologies.[13]

Cassava Cropping Systems

On densely populated Java, cassava is usually intercropped with grain and legumes rather than planted in pure stands.[14] In West Java, upland rice, corn, peanuts, and soybeans are most commonly intercropped with cassava; in Central and East Java, where rainfall is less

[12] William Collier and his associates have concluded generally that the new rice technologies have had, on balance, a positive impact on employment opportunities for Java's poorest rural groups. See, for example, Collier et al. [25]. Hayami and his associates have supported Collier's conclusions and demonstrated the positive distributional implications of the divisible seed and fertilizer inputs when they are accompanied by improved irrigation. See Hayami et al. [65] and Kikuchi et al. [94]. It is also widely reported that wealthier rural groups have had greater access to the government institutions responsible for disseminating improved agricultural inputs. See, for example, Sinaga et al. [126].

[13] For excellent village-based studies that demonstrate the many income-earning activities of rural-household members, see White [161] and Hart [64]. In addition, Stoler [133] documents the important contributions of homestead gardens to family consumption.

[14] The 1973 Agricultural Census figures for Java indicate that, of the farms on which cassava, upland rice, and corn were harvested, 54, 63, and 52 percent, respectively, contained stands of these crops interplanted with annual or perennial crops. Both the census figures and field observations suggest that the intercropped shares of the total areas planted to these crops will probably be even higher (Indonesia [80], vol. 2, tables 2 and 3, pp. 18–19, 40–41).

TABLE 2.3. *Percent Distribution of Land by Farm Size, Java and Madura, 1973*

Farm size	Farms	Farmland	Sawah as pct. of total farmland	Distribution of farms by tenancy status		
				Wholly owned	Part tenant[a]	Pure tenant[a]
0.1 to <0.3 ha	32.5%	9.9%	46.0%	76.0%	20.0%	4.0%
0.3 to <0.5 ha	20.4	12.4	50.4	72.2	25.1	2.7
0.5 to <0.75 ha	16.4	15.5	49.3	73.2	24.6	2.2
0.75 to <1.0 ha	8.4	11.2	48.7	72.0	26.5	1.5
1.0 to <2.0 ha	13.0	26.8	45.7	70.8	28.0	1.2
2.0+ ha	4.7	23.8	48.0	66.9	32.4	0.7
All farms[b]	100.0%	100.0%	47.8%	73.4%	23.7%	2.9%

SOURCE: Derived from Indonesia [80], vol. 1, table 7, pp. 204–7, and table 8, pp. 230–33.
[a]The census tables do not distinguish between specific forms of tenancy such as cash rental and share tenancy.
[b]Includes farms of less than 0.1 ha.

TABLE 2.4. *Percent Distribution of Employment by Farm Size, Java and Madura, 1973*

Farm size	Percent of farms employing:		Number of regular workers per unit			
	Regular hired labor[a]	Seasonal hired labor[b]	Total regular labor per farm[c]	Family labor per hectare[d]	Hired labor per hectare[d]	Total regular labor per hectare
0.1 to <0.3 ha	14.3%	58.6%	2.04	8.61	2.22	10.83
0.3 to <0.5 ha	17.5	69.7	2.36	4.64	1.46	6.10
0.5 to <0.75 ha	20.3	70.8	2.59	3.11	1.18	4.29
0.75 to <1.0 ha	23.0	73.8	2.81	2.26	0.95	3.21
1.0 to <2.0 ha	26.9	75.2	3.10	1.39	0.68	2.07
2.0 to 15.0 ha	38.4	79.8	3.91	0.77	0.51	1.28
All farms[e]	19.3%	66.5%	2.47	2.87	1.06	3.93

SOURCE: Derived from Indonesia [80], vol. 7, tables 6.1 and 7.1, pp. 53, 73.

[a]Regular hired labor is defined as full-time workers for at least the entire crop season preceding the 1973 Census. The number of hours worked per day or days worked per week is unstated.

[b]Seasonal hired labor is defined as part-time workers in specific farm activities paid either by wage or in kind during the crop season preceding the census. The total number of workers and total hours or days worked are unstated.

[c]Includes both family and hired labor working full-time.

[d]Farm size categories are more highly aggregated here than in the census tables. Per-farm and per-hectare figures are averages over all farms (both users and nonusers of regular labor) divided by the midpoints of the disaggregated farm size categories and then weighted by the total number of farms in each size category.

[e]Java averages include farms of less than 0.1 hectare.

TABLE 2.5. *Percent of Farms Using Fertilizer, and Average Application Rates, Java and Madura, 1973*

	Percent of farms using:			
Farm size	Only chemical fertilizer	Only organic manures	Chemical fertilizers alone or with manures	Average rate of chemical fertilizer use[a] (kg/ha)
0.1 to <0.3 ha	47.7%	15.7%	55.8%	211.9
0.3 to <0.5 ha	56.6	17.5	66.7	197.7
0.5 to <0.75 ha	55.8	19.2	66.5	185.4
0.75 to <1.0 ha	57.4	21.2	69.4	180.5
1.0 to <2.0 ha	55.2	22.9	67.0	167.4
2.0 + ha	57.0	22.0	68.8	156.9
All farms	52.4%	18.1%	62.2%	178.9

SOURCE: Derived from Indonesia [80], vol. 7, table 4, p. 33.
NOTE: The published figures do not distinguish types of chemical fertilizer or the specific crops fertilized. Urea and TSP make up the great bulk of total chemical fertilizer consumption, and in 1973 irrigated rice was the major crop receiving chemical nutrients.
[a]Rates of chemical fertilizer averaged only over users of chemical nutrients.

abundant, cassava is commonly intercropped with corn and legumes only. Where market channels are well developed and microclimates permit, cassava is often interplanted with high-value vegetable crops. Cassava lends itself to intercropping because of the flexibility with which it can be planted and harvested, and because of its ability to grow well in dry periods when other crops do poorly. Where cassava is planted in pure stands, it is usually because poor soils and low or unreliable rainfall hinder other crops. In southern Java's isolated uplands, for example, farmers intercrop cassava in their better plots but plant it in pure stands otherwise. Since little fertilizer is used in these isolated regions, some farmers follow a multiyear rotation of intercropped cassava/pure-stand cassava/fallow to restore soil fertility. Finally, in areas of newly opened forest, pests such as termites and wild pigs often seriously damage noncassava crops.

In the irrigated lowlands and the better-endowed and more intensively cultivated rain-fed areas, other factors enter into the decision on growing cassava. Because cassava requires relatively little labor and has no specific harvest age, it is a convenient crop when alternative income-producing activities compete for the farmers' time—in particular, off-farm job opportunities and the labor demands of irrigated rice. Another consideration is the proximity and strength of markets for cassava. It is a common pure-stand cash crop near urban centers where demand is secure, marketing information is plentiful, and marketing costs are fairly low. By contrast, in more isolated areas where market linkages are weaker and nonfarm job opportunities fewer, farmers are more reluctant to specialize.

Seasonality in Cassava Cropping Systems. The seasonality of rainfall dictates that first plantings of cassava occur early in the wet season to ensure that subsequent crops can be established before the dry season arrives. For cassava, which does not mature at a specific age, decisions on harvesting are constrained by the farmer's need to prepare land and plant again early in the next rains. When the cassava is to be sun dried into gaplek, harvesting must occur well before the heavy rains begin.

In intercropping systems, the timing of cassava planting is probably bounded by two additional considerations. If planted too long before the intercrops, cassava will shade them. If planted too late, the cassava will suffer from excessive competition for water and nutrients (Zandstra [169]). Regardless of the planting system, cassava does best when established under plentiful rainfall; the plant can tolerate drought except during its early growth period (Onwueme [115]). As a result, almost 75 percent of Java's cassava is planted during the early wet-season months of October through January (Indonesia [76]).[15] Exceptions to this pattern are confined largely to areas where late-season plantings (February through May) are possible either because the wet season is longer (as in southern West Java) or because supplemental irrigation water is available. Less than 10 percent of Java's cassava is planted between May and September (Figure 2.3).

The need to clear and prepare the land for new crops at the beginning of the wet season imposes an upper limit on the age of cassava at harvest—10 to 11 months for early-season plantings and 6 to 7 months for cassava planted later on. Unless subjected to moisture stress, cassava roots continuously accumulate weight from three months after planting. Hence, yields for early-season cassava are significantly greater than for late-season cassava. Farmers only rarely allow late-season cassava to grow well into the rains before harvesting, because the greater water requirements of the staple cereal crops take precedence.

A lower limit on cassava's age at harvest is set by the minimum time needed to produce roots of economic size. Although this depends on cassava variety, prices, the growing environment, and cultivation practices, harvesting rarely begins before six months. Hence there

---

[15] The specific months vary from year to year depending on when the wet season begins.

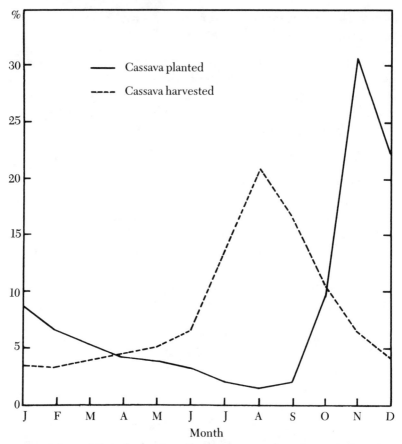

SOURCE: Indonesia [76], *Production of Annual Food Crops*, 1977, 1978, and 1979. The figure shows an average for these years.

Figure 2.3. Percent of Cassava Planted and Harvested by Month for an Average Year, Java and Madura

exists a speculation period of roughly five months before the field must be replanted when farmers can wait to harvest their crop until prices are favorable.[16] Because this period occurs mainly during the dry season, the opportunity cost of land—one measure of the real cost of this storage—is low. When asked about the decision to harvest, farmers generally reply that they wait as long as possible before harvesting unless they have a pressing need for food or cash.[17]

[16] Farmers can continue to speculate after harvesting by storing gaplek for periods up to several months.

[17] In areas of Central and East Java, however, where the dry season is more pronounced, it is not uncommon for farmers to claim that their cassava must be harvested at some particular

About 70 percent of Java's cassava is harvested during the five months of June through October (Indonesia [76]). Harvesting begins later in the year as one moves from west to east across Java because of differences in seasonal rainfall patterns. Within agroclimatic domains, cassava harvesting generally begins and ends within a two- to three-month period. Cassava cannot be stored long either fresh or as gaplek. This seasonality affects the cassava starch and export industries, which would benefit if harvesting could be spread out over more of the year. Contractual arrangements between farmers and traders often specify harvest times in advance, but because planting is seasonal, these arrangements cannot eliminate annual peaks and troughs in harvesting. In a few parts of West Java, starch factories and farmers make agreements mediated by village officials to stagger planting and harvesting times across blocks of farmers. However, these arrangements are only possible where rainfall permits planting throughout much of the year and where planting is in pure stands.

Of the 30 percent of Java's cassava that is harvested outside the June to October period, perhaps one-sixth is grown at higher elevations where orographic precipitation permits pure-stand plantings most of the year, and another third comes from late-season plantings on either sawah or tegal that are harvested during November or December. The remaining off-season harvesting consists of cassava taken periodically in small quantities to be sold or consumed on the farm.

Technology in Cassava Cropping Systems. Except for fertilizer use, cassava production practices on Java are traditional. Improved cassava planting material has been released only in very tiny pockets of Java. The most commonly planted varieties are the so-called "bitter cassava" varieties (high in hydrocyanic acid [HCN]), because they are more resistant to pest problems. "Sweet cassava" varieties, which contain less HCN, are generally used when the crop is to be consumed fresh. Cassava stalks are typically saved for two to four months between harvest and replanting, but cuttings do not receive special treatment before planting. As a result, many cuttings often fail to germinate and must be replanted.

---

age—usually 9 or 10 months—for optimal starch content. The limited scientific evidence indicates that starch reserves in the roots are used for new leaf formation after the plant experiences a prolonged dry period. Hence, farmers in Java's drier regions may harvest cassava in advance of the new rains to avoid the resulting decline in starch content. See Toro and Atlee [142].

Field observations suggest that the use of inorganic fertilizer is now widespread, particularly in cassava intercropping systems. As indicated earlier by the data in Table 2.2, however, average application rates on cassava are low. Urea and TSP are the most commonly used fertilizers, in part because the distribution of alternatives is limited in many upland areas. Application rates vary considerably and are generally highest in more commercial areas and intercropping systems; they are lowest in remote areas and when cassava is planted in pure stands. Many currently used cassava varieties respond well to fertilizer applications, but their absolute yield potential may be low. Variations in fertilizer use (particularly of urea) are strongly associated with cassava yield variability throughout most of Java.

Fertilizer use and cassava yields tend to be lowest in the steeper upland areas with their highly eroded and infertile soils. The better-endowed lowlands have been the primary recipients of government agricultural research, extension, and credit programs. The development of fertilizer distribution channels occurred first in these areas and has only recently spread to the uplands. Farmers in Java's upland areas are poorer than those in the lowlands precisely because their soils are poorer; crop sales produce little cash for fertilizer purchases or loan payments.

Although the incidence of cassava pests and disease is high at times, the resulting damage appears to be minor. The red spider mite (*Tetranychus urticae*) and cassava ash disease (*Oidium manihotis*) are common dry-season problems, but are probably of minor economic importance overall. Cassava bacterial blight (*Xanthomonas manihotis*) is reputed to be a serious problem in parts of northern Java, but is less important in the southern uplands where cassava cultivation is most extensive. Cassava root-rot problems caused by soil fungi are reported on heavy-textured, poorly drained soils, but overall losses are again rather small. By contrast, pest and disease problems are often severe for the grains and legumes with which cassava is intercropped. Crop failures are not uncommon for soybeans, upland rice, and peanuts, and yields of these crops vary much more than those of cassava. Few upland farmers use pesticides, and those who do rarely apply the full recommended doses. Though improved upland cropping systems could undoubtedly be developed through varietal improvement and pest and disease control, the necessary institutional mechanisms to do so are just being established in Indonesia.

A Regional Mapping of Cassava Production on Java and Madura

The preceding discussion of climate, land types, and cropping systems provides useful criteria for creating a typology of reasonably distinct cassava-producing regions on Java and Madura. Both the predominant cassava cropping systems and the end uses of cassava are influenced by variations in seasonal rainfall and by soil and topography. Cassava's relative importance is demonstrated in Figure 2.4 by plotting harvest areas of cassava as percentages of the total harvest areas of the major food crops.[18] It can be seen from the figure that cassava is a minor crop in Java's northern lowland plains, which are extensively covered by irrigation systems. Approximately 60 percent of total production is concentrated in the area of southern Java extending from Sukabumi Kabupaten in West Java to Malang Kabupaten in East Java. The topography of this area is often steep, and irrigation systems are typically small. The island of Madura is also an important cassava-producing area.

Table 2.6 shows the five cassava-producing regions distinguished on the basis of the criteria previously discussed. The first region, hereafter referred to by the shorthand form "West Java," is centered in Ciamis and Tasikmalaya Kabupatens in southern West Java and extends west to Sukabumi and east to Purbolinggo. The dry season is relatively short here, and the upland soils, although erodible and of low natural fertility, are generally quite deep. It thus appears that this region's rain-fed cropping systems can be profitably intensified. Direct human consumption of cassava is low and limited almost exclusively to fresh root forms. Surface water for starch factories is abundant, and most of this region's cassava is used fresh for starch production.

Extensive cassava production continues in the coastal and inland districts extending from Banjarnegara to Madiun and referred to in the regional scheme as "Central Java." Soils and topography are similar to those of the first region, but the longer dry season means that corn replaces upland rice as the principal intercrop with cassava. Cassava is again produced largely for market, here usually in the form of gaplek; limited surface water supplies constrain the possibilities for starch production in all but a few localities. Direct human

[18] These crops include irrigated and rain-fed rice, corn, soybeans, peanuts, and sweet potatoes in addition to cassava. The exclusion of harvest areas of tobacco, sugarcane, and tree crops does not introduce a large bias into the results.

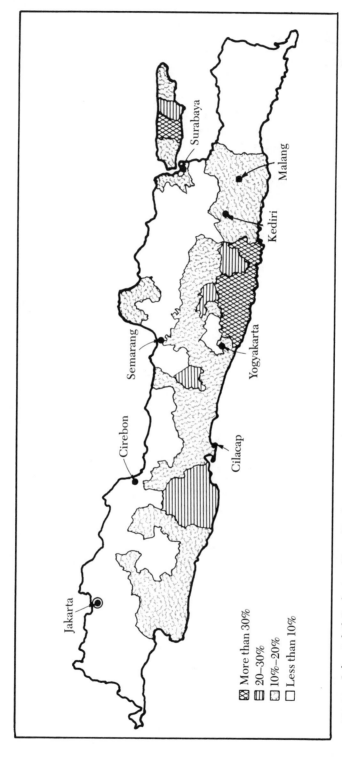

SOURCE: Indonesia [76], *Production of Annual Food Crops on Java and Madura*, vols. for 1977, 1978, and 1979. The major food crops include rain-fed and irrigated rice, corn, soybeans, peanuts, and sweet potatoes in addition to cassava.

Figure 2.4. Cassava Harvest Areas as Percentages of Total Harvest Areas of Major Food Crops, Java and Madura, 1977–79

TABLE 2.6. *Characteristics of the Five Major Cassava-Producing Regions of Java and Madura*

	West Java	Central Java	South-Central Java	East Java	Madura
Cassava as a percent of total major food crops harvested[a]	15%	18%	35%	14%	24%
Range of cassava yields (*tons/ha*)					
Official data, 1977–79	10–12	9–11	7–9	10–11	7–9
Field surveys, 1979/80	6–20	5–12	2–10	10–40	4–8
Level of soil erosion	High	High	Severe	Moderate to high	Moderate
Principal intercrop with cassava	Upland rice, legumes	Corn	Upland rice, corn	Corn	Corn
Principal end use of cassava	Starch	Gaplek sales	Staple food	Gaplek sales, staple food	Staple food, gaplek sales
Direct human consumption of cassava					
Quantities	Low	Low to moderate	High	Moderate to high	High
Form	Fresh	Fresh, gaplek	Gaplek	Gaplek	Fresh, gaplek

SOURCES: Data on cassava production and yields are from Indonesia [76], volumes for 1977, 1978, 1979; on erosion, principal intercrops, and end uses from field interviews with farmers during 1979/80; on quantities and forms of consumption from Indonesia [75], Susenas VI.

[a]Major food crops are irrigated and rain-fed rice, corn, soybeans, peanuts, and sweet potatoes, in addition to cassava.

consumption of cassava is somewhat higher than in the first region and is more equally divided between fresh roots and gaplek.

The third region—lying along the southern coast from Gunung Kidul in Yogyakarta Province to Trenggalek in East Java—constitutes the center of cassava production and consumption on Java. This South-Central region is steep and often very eroded, and this fact combined with a highly seasonal pattern of rainfall severely constrains both current and future productivity of rain-fed cropping systems. Average crop yields are generally very low. Gaplek is the preeminent starchy staple, and average marketed shares of cassava are probably the lowest on Java. Where soils permit, cassava intercropping systems are often extremely complex and intensive. However, in much of the region only cassava or intercropped cassava and corn can be grown profitably. Because of the limitations on agriculture, average farm incomes are low.

The fourth region, East Java, contains several kabupatens—especially Kediri and Malang—where cassava yields are the highest on Java. Soils are of well-developed volcanic material and highly fertile. Although rainfall is seasonal, much cassava is planted during the late rains on partially irrigated sawah. Farmers are more commercially oriented than in other parts of upland Java and apply much more chemical fertilizer. Most cassava in this area is processed into gaplek and ultimately exported, but gaplek is also an important staple food for the poorer rural groups. Small- and medium-scale starch firms are an alternative market where water supplies permit their operation.

Finally, cassava production is extensive throughout most of the island of Madura, the fifth region. Average yields are low because most of the crop is planted during the late rains and grows in an exceptionally arid dry-season environment. Cassava's drought tolerance is a key factor underlying its importance in Madura's agriculture. End uses are about equally divided between sales of gaplek for export and direct human consumption of cassava, both fresh and dried.

Production and Consumption of Cassava in Three Regions of Java

Village-level surveys were conducted in three different producing regions to understand the role of cassava in various farming systems. The survey villages were selected to include Java's predominant cassava cropping systems, but though the villages were selected purposively, sample respondents were selected in random draws. Farmers were interviewed individually and asked about household composition, sources of income from farm and other activities, and plot-specific costs and returns in crop production. The surveys were timed to coincide with periods of land preparation and planting of rain-fed crops at the beginning of the 1980–81 crop year.[19] Rainfall and cropping patterns in the three areas of Java are illustrated in Figures 2.5, 2.6, 2.7, and 2.8.

West Java: Garut

Almost all agricultural land in Garut has been terraced. Local soils are deep and well developed, but natural fertility is only moderate. One basic cassava intercropping pattern is predominant on

---

[19] For a complete description of the survey results, see Roche [123].

the rain-fed soils of Garut—as it is throughout the uplands of West Java. (See Figure 2.5.) Just prior to the onset of the heavy rains, upland rice, corn, and in some places legumes are planted. After three or four weeks, cassava cuttings are planted at near pure-stand density. When the cereals and legumes have been harvested, the field is left with a dense cover of cassava, which is harvested at an age of nine to 11 months.

Farmers with larger holdings frequently follow multiyear rotations, and cassava is generally the last crop planted before the fallow period. Farmers who have irrigated sawah in addition to rain-fed plots use improved rice varieties, pesticides, and high levels of inorganic fertilizer (urea and TSP), and consequently average yields of the two annual rice crops are high. Rice is the predominant staple in the local diet, and consumption varies little by season. Small quantities of cassava are also consumed, but cassava is mainly a cash crop in Garut. Several small-scale starch factories operate nearby, and large quantities of fresh roots are shipped out for processing.

South-Central Java: Gunung Kidul

The second survey site is surrounded by domelike hills and narrow valleys. About 40 percent of the total area is severely eroded and has extremely thin soil on unterraced hillsides where only cassava and corn can be grown profitably. Corn is planted first, at the beginning of the rainy season, and the cassava that follows about a month later is left for up to 20 months before harvest. Terraced hillsides make up another 30 percent of the village land area, and there legumes are interplanted with the cassava and corn, and soils are often cultivated continuously. These crops are rarely fertilized, and yields are very low. The remaining 30 percent of the survey area consists of level valley soils that are deep and intensively cultivated. Upland rice and corn are sown before the rains begin, and cassava, legumes, and more corn are planted after the start of the wet season. Peanuts or soybeans are planted before the sharp decline of rainfall in April. The cassava is harvested in July and August at an age of eight to ten months and made into gaplek. Although gaplek is the main dietary staple, sales of gaplek are an important source of income as well.

East Java: Kediri

The Kediri survey area contains both lowland soils and hillside terraces. The level lowland soils are highly productive when inorganic

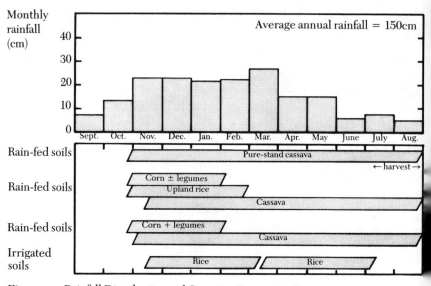

Figure 2.5. Rainfall Distribution and Cropping Patterns in Garut

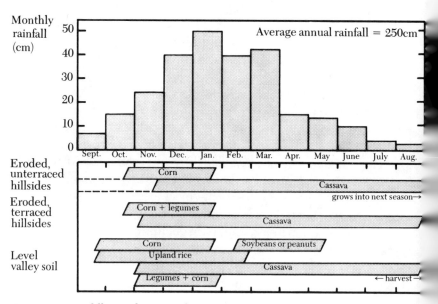

Figure 2.6. Rainfall Distribution and Cropping Patterns in Gunung Kidul

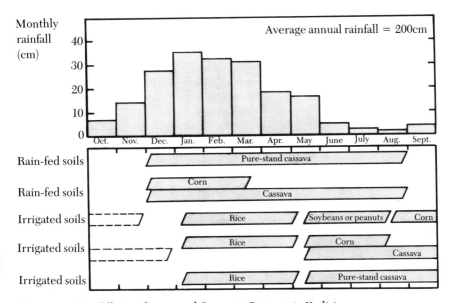

Figure 2.7. Rainfall Distribution and Cropping Patterns in Kediri

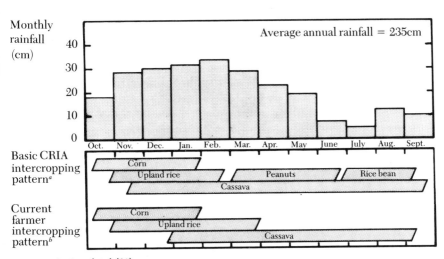

SOURCE: Inu Ismail et al. [86].
  [a] Improved crop varieties and cultivation practices.
  [b] Traditional varieties at CRIA's test site in Lampung Province, Sumatra.

Figure 2.8. Current and Improved Cassava Intercropping Patterns, Lampung

fertilizer is used; by contrast, the terraced hillsides have become seriously eroded and are considerably less productive. As in much of Central and East Java, cassava is intercropped with corn on rain-fed land. On irrigated soils, flooded rice is always the first crop of the wet season, followed by palawija plantings—non-rice staples and legumes. Intercropped corn and cassava is the most profitable late-season combination. Cassava yields are very high.

Kediri is a more prosperous area than the two other survey sites. Cassava is almost exclusively a cash crop, and a thriving small-scale starch industry in local villages provides a steady demand. The diet of wealthier families farming lowland soils is based on rice, supplemented by eggs and meat. For poorer farm families living on the eroded uplands, however, corn and gaplek are the basic staples.

Comparison of the Survey Areas

The effects of agroclimatic and socioeconomic characteristics on income levels in the three regions are shown in Tables 2.7 and 2.8. The differences between land owned and operated in Garut and Gunung Kidul reflect the fact that some land there is left fallow. By contrast, fallow periods are rare in Kediri, and many farmers rent land to supplement their own holdings, which is why more land is operated than owned there. Gross family income is much higher on average in Kediri than in Gunung Kidul or Garut, reflecting the productivity of Kediri's lowland soils. Livestock and tree-crop sales and nonfarm employment contribute significantly to family income in all three areas. The gross value of food crop output is smallest in Gunung Kidul, despite the large average farm size, because the soil is poor. Cassava sales constitute a major share of the total value of food crop sales in all three areas (Table 2.8). Cassava sales amount to about a third of total gross family income in Kediri, and a smaller but still significant share in Garut. Cassava's predominant role as a cash crop in these two regions is evidenced by the high ratios of sales to total production. Sales are smallest in Gunung Kidul, where cassava is the major calorie source.

The Gunung Kidul families are poor in both relative and absolute terms, in large part because their land is poor. Because the soil is depleted, cassava plays a major role in farming; because of poverty, it is an important foodstuff. The welfare implications of increased cassava productivity could be substantial in Gunung Kidul. However, because agroclimatic constraints are particularly binding in this area,

TABLE 2.7. *Summary Indexes for Garut, Gunung Kidul, and Kediri*

Index	Garut	Gunung Kidul	Kediri
Average no. of hectares owned per family	0.92	2.25	1.23
Average no. of hectares operated per family	0.86	1.65	1.32
Average gross family income, 1979/80 (Rp 000)	352.8	219.1	827.0
Percent of income from:			
Food crop production	63.2%	59.7%	56.4%
Other agriculture[a]	14.7%	25.6%	18.9%
Nonfarm sources[b]	22.1%	14.7%	24.7%
Food retained for own consumption (kg/capita/year)[c]			
Rice	107.4	21.8	79.7
Corn	9.2	18.9	27.6
Cassava	43.5	253.5	61.0
Legumes	2.5	10.6	0.2
Average 1979/80 cassava yields[d] (ton/ha)	8.1	4.1	14.6
Average cassava production cost (Rp 000/ton)	21.4	16.4	15.4
Percent of labor force primarily dependent upon farm wages for income	49.8%	13.5%	39.0%

SOURCES: For Garut, Nurmanaf [112]; for Gunung Kidul, village secretary's estimate; for Kediri, village records for 1979.

[a]Includes livestock, tree crops, and land rental.

[b]Includes home industries, agricultural wage labor, other off-farm employment, and pensions.

[c]Figures are for an "adult equivalent," and children under six are considered half an adult equivalent. The forms of the food are as follows: rice = milled rice; corn = dry seed corn; cassava = fresh roots; legumes = soybean equivalent valued at Rp 270/kg.

[d]Yields on different land types are weighted by the estimated proportion of each land type in the total survey area.

the development of improved cropping practices is likely to be difficult, particularly on the eroded hillsides. Average farm incomes are higher in Garut. Cassava productivity is low, but not as low as in Gunung Kidul. Soil constraints are fewer and land use is less intensive. Thus, there is greater agronomic potential for profitably intensifying rain-fed cropping systems in areas like Garut. The Kediri area is much more prosperous than the others. The lowland soils are highly productive under present practices. Farmers on irrigated land enjoy more flexibility in cropping decisions than those on season-bound rain-fed soils. On the whole, there is likely to be less need here than elsewhere for institutional intervention to improve cropping practices on lowland soils. However, productivity is considerably lower on Kediri's upland terraces, and farm families there are noticeably

TABLE 2.8. *Shares of Food Crops in Total Value of Production and Income, Garut, Gunung Kidul, and Kediri*

	Garut	Gunung Kidul	Kediri
Percent of total food crop value from:			
Rice	64.2%	16.3%	22.3%
Corn	3.7	9.2	12.2
Cassava	25.8	41.0	60.1
Legumes	3.7	32.7	4.2
Other food crops	2.6	0.8	1.2
Total	100.0%	100.0%	100.0%
Marketed Percentages of:			
Rice	28.2%	1.3%	31.6%
Corn	40.9	16.3	61.8
Cassava	88.9	36.3	96.3
Legumes	37.8	55.2	98.4
Total food crop output	53.4	37.8	81.6
Cassava sales as a percent of total crop sales	43.0%	39.9%	70.4%
Cassava sales as a percent of average gross family income	14.5%	8.9%	32.7%
Value of total cassava production as a percent of gross family income	16.3%	24.5%	34.0%

SOURCES: Same as for Table 2.7.

poorer, as the dietary role of ampas (a by-product of starch production) suggests. Thus, the potential welfare impact of cropping system improvements on those soils is substantial.

Households primarily dependent on agricultural wages for income constitute large percentages of all households in the Garut and Kediri areas. As the appendix tables on current costs and returns to crop production show, a substantial share of labor in the Garut and Kediri areas is hired. The family incomes shown in Table 2.7 are averages of farm families; average incomes of the families of wage laborers are undoubtedly much lower. Hence the introduction of improved technologies in these two areas could have important implications for the poorest families if the new methods are sufficiently profitable to warrant greater labor use.

Finally, as the field survey results have demonstrated, the intercropping of cassava is the most productive and currently most profitable system, allowing as it does the harvesting of crops throughout the year. Intercropping is common on Java because it is particularly suited to farmers for whom very small landholdings must produce the bulk of staple foods. Whether in pure stands or intercropped, cassava forms the basis of cropping systems in many upland areas of Java. Cassava suffers from relatively few of the pest, disease, and water-stress problems that cause substantial yield variability for the other upland crops. Because marketed shares of cassava production are generally higher than those of the other crops, cassava is often the single most important source of cash income from food crop production, even in areas where its importance as a dietary staple is greatest.

Potential Costs and Returns to Improved Cassava Practices

Despite the lack of improved varieties of cassava to match those developed for wheat and rice beginning in the 1960's, there is substantial evidence that changes in cultivation practices can result in highly profitable productivity gains with current cassava varieties. Primary among these changes is the greater use of inorganic fertilizer. Research in Indonesia has also shown that the overall productivity of cassava intercropping systems can be profitably improved. But because this research has been conducted largely in areas of the country other than the varied upland agroclimates of Java, tests of varieties, fertilizer mixes, and cultivation practices must be made at specific upland Java sites in order to develop locally adapted recommendations. This section reviews recent Indonesian agronomic research on cassava cropping systems and discusses potential improvements to productivity in the three survey areas.[20]

Nutrient Requirements and Fertilizer Responsiveness of Cassava

Cassava produces large amounts of dry matter per unit of land; as a result, the crop extracts considerable soil nutrients during the course of its growth. However, cassava's direct nutrient uptake is not excessive per ton or per calorie when compared with that of alternative starchy staple crops (Table 2.9). Cassava extracts more potassium and calcium than rice and corn, but less nitrogen. All three crops remove roughly similar amounts of phosphorus and magnesium.[21]

[20] Most of the following discussion is based on research conducted in Indonesia by the Central Research Institute for Agriculture (CRIA).

[21] Indirect nutrient removal through erosion is similar for cassava and corn, but less for upland rice. Comparative erosion factors for these and other upland crops are presented in PRC Engineering Consultants [122]. For other works on nutrient removal, see the literature cited in Jones [88] and Howeler [68].

TABLE 2.9. *Soil Nutrients Removed by Cassava, Rice, and Corn*

	N	P	K	Ca	Mg
Nutrients per ton harvested dry matter: Economic yield (kg)					
Cassava (unpeeled roots) (1)[a]	2.2	1.6	15.2	1.95	1.11
Cassava (unpeeled roots) (2)[a]	7.0	1.6	12.3	1.83	1.02
Rice (paddy)	9.6	2.2	4.4	0.44	1.09
Corn (grain)	15.0	2.9	3.5	0.10	0.80
Nutrients per ton harvested dry matter: Total plant (kg)[b]					
Cassava (unpeeled roots) (1)[a]	7.5	2.8	27.1	9.18	2.97
Cassava (unpeeled roots) (2)[a]	14.7	3.2	17.5	5.49	2.37
Rice (paddy)	18.6	4.3	21.8	4.35	2.46
Corn (grain)	25.9	5.4	17.7	1.90	2.20
Nutrients per 1,000 Kcal. in edible portion: Economic yield (grams)					
Cassava (peeled roots) (1)[c]	0.8	0.6	5.7	0.73	0.42
Cassava (peeled roots) (2)[c]	2.6	0.6	4.6	0.69	0.38
Rice (milled rice)[d]	3.9	0.9	1.8	0.18	0.44
Corn (grain)[e]	4.3	0.8	1.0	0.03	0.35
Nutrients per 1,000 Kcal. in edible portion: Total plant (grams)					
Cassava (peeled roots) (1)[c]	2.8	1.0	10.1	3.45	1.11
Cassava (peeled roots) (2)[c]	5.5	1.2	6.5	2.06	0.89
Rice (milled rice)[d]	7.5	1.7	8.8	1.75	0.99
Corn (grain)[e]	7.4	1.6	5.1	0.54	0.63

SOURCES: Cassava (1) from Nijholt [109]; cassava (2) from Howeler [69], which represents averages over trials conducted separately by different researchers throughout the world; rice from Grist [61]; corn from Sprague, ed. [128]; calorie conversion ratios from FAO [53].

[a]Assumes 3 kg fresh unpeeled cassava yield 1 kg dry unpeeled roots.

[b]Total nutrients removed in stems, leaves, and roots, or grain per ton of economic root or grain dry matter. Excludes roots in soil for rice and corn.

[c]To account for weight loss in peeling, it is assumed that 3.75 kg unpeeled fresh roots yield 1 kg edible dry cassava. This conversion ratio is likely to be rather high, thus upwardly biasing the apparent nutrient removal of cassava. One kg edible portion dry cassava converted to 3,330 Kcal.

[d]Assumes that rice is 68 percent of paddy and that 1 kg milled rice contains 3,660 Kcal. food value.

[e]Assumes 3,490 Kcal. in 1 kg grain corn.

In cassava, potassium is largely accumulated in the roots and stems, whereas nitrogen is accumulated mainly in the leaves. Calcium, phosphorus, and magnesium are used primarily in the stems. The rate at which these nutrients can be absorbed indirectly affects root yield; where cassava is continuously cultivated, yields tend to decline sharply when these extracted nutrients are not replaced. Nonetheless, cassava will continue to produce better than alternative crops on highly infertile soils.[22] The nutrients retained in the stems and leaves can be returned to the soil if these parts of the plant are ground up. This is done by machine on some cassava estates in

[22]There is some evidence that cassava utilizes nitrogen and potassium more efficiently in the production of leaf and stem dry matter than other staple crops under conditions of nutrient stress. Cassava may also possess the unique ability to regulate its growth rate when external nutrient supplies are limited. See Edwards et al. [45].

Indonesia's Lampung Province, in southern Sumatra, but is generally not done on Java, in part because cassava leaves are typically used for food and fodder there.[23] Large quantities of farm manure are applied in cassava cropping systems, but the nutrient-to-weight value of manure is low. Inorganic nutrients in the form of chemical fertilizers are the best means of maintaining soil fertility and achieving good cassava yields.

Although cassava's general response to fertilizer has been demonstrated in agronomic trials throughout the tropics, the effects of specific nutrients have varied widely both within and across countries. In a comprehensive review of the literature, Howeler [70] concluded that phosphorus is the main nutrient limiting cassava yields in most of South America, whereas nitrogen and potassium deficiencies are more common in parts of Asia and Africa. Soil and land-use characteristics are the primary factors underlying relative nutrient response, but Howeler also cited evidence that cassava varieties differ in their tolerance of specific nutrient deficiencies and soil acidity conditions.

Research on Java by Dutch scientists during the colonial period indicated that cassava responded mainly to potassium, and that nitrogen applications were unwarranted.[24] In more recent trials, however, cassava has most consistently responded to nitrogen, and the effects of potassium and phosphorus have varied. Tables 2.10 and 2.11 present regression estimates of fertilizer response in CRIA trials of two cassava varieties in several areas of Java. These results— although from a limited number of sites—are consistent with results of fertilizer trials on cassava conducted in a much wider set of Java's agroclimatic domains.[25]

In his authoritative study of East Central Java's soils, Dames [34] concluded that nitrogen, and to a lesser extent phosphorus, were the major limiting soil nutrients. Although some of the soils in Indonesia are known to be endowed with a high reserve of available potassium

---

[23] Because cassava leaves and stems—in contrast to those of rice and corn—are not usually returned to the soil, a more rigorous comparison of relative nutrient removal by these crops is that of cassava as a total crop to the economic yields of rice and corn. By these criteria, cassava removes more potassium, calcium, and magnesium per hectare, but roughly similar quantities of nitrogen and phosphorus (Table 2.9).

[24] Howeler [70] cites Koch et al. [95], Nijholt [109], and den Doop [36].

[25] Fertilizer trials of cassava in Indonesia generally have not included chemical analyses of the soils to determine their inherent fertility, although the intercept terms (yields with no fertilizer applied) in the regressions shown in Tables 2.10 and 2.11 are an indicator of inherent fertility.

TABLE 2.10. *Effects of Fertilizer on the Gading Cassava Variety, Latosol Soils of Java, 1976/77, 1977/78, and 1978/79* (t-statistics in parentheses)

	Bogor, West Java			Wonogiri, Central Java			Gunung Kidul, Diy.	
	1976/77	1977/78	1978/79	1976/77	1977/78	1978/79	1977/78	1978/79
Intercept	102.88	83.55	76.37	169.09	110.60	50.62	53.42	11.76
	(13.33)**	(11.61)**	(6.84)**	(14.33)**	(10.15)**	(8.34)**	(5.34)**	(1.64)
N 60 kg/ha	75.37	49.83	66.70	62.59	87.65	96.17	66.45	57.66
	(10.55)**	(7.48)**	(6.45)**	(5.73)**	(8.69)**	(17.11)**	(7.18)**	(8.71)**
N 120 kg/ha	115.43^a	81.76^a	140.58^a	91.43^a	123.24^a	136.22^a	90.52^a	90.98^a
	(5.61)**	(4.79)**	(7.15)**	(2.64)**	(3.52)**	(7.13)**	(2.60)**	(5.03)**
P$_2$O$_5$ 30 kg/ha	-2.41	7.09	6.46	-3.28	5.24	-4.57	-0.61	-1.96
	(0.34)	(1.06)	(0.63)	(0.30)	(0.52)	(0.81)	(0.07)	(0.30)
P$_2$O$_5$ 60 kg/ha	6.08	5.32	-6.92	-1.26	22.34	-0.47	0.19	1.55
	(0.85)	(0.80)	(0.67)	(0.12)	(2.21)*	(0.08)	(0.02)	(0.23)
K$_2$O 50 kg/ha	1.87	9.39	23.25	19.31	19.37	11.72	67.39	34.80
	(0.26)	(1.41)	(2.25)*	(1.77)$^+$	(1.92)$^+$	(2.08)*	(7.28)**	(5.26)**
K$_2$O 100 kg/ha	-0.53	3.56	3.54	13.49	13.78	19.82^a	97.03^a	36.19^a
	(0.07)	(0.53)	(0.34)	(1.24)	(1.37)	(1.44)$^+$	(3.20)**	(0.21)
R^2	.785	.679	.723	.509	.693	.895	.747	.758
F$_{6,74}$	45.15	26.06	32.13	12.77	27.90	105.68	36.36	38.65

SOURCE: CRIA, unpublished experimental results. Dr. Suryatna Effendi at CRIA kindly permitted the author to use these data. This analysis builds upon the earlier work of Wargiono et al. [155], pp. 38–61.

NOTE: The estimates of nutrient main effects were derived from a regression model with dummy variables equal to 1 for the indicated nutrient levels and equal to o otherwise. Hence, the intercepts are average cassava yields across replicate plots receiving no fertilizer, and the coefficients on nutrients indicate the change in yield for each nutrient level averaged over all plots at that level. Estimation of a continuous quadratic response model was inappropriate because of the limited number of fertilizer levels. Nutrient interaction terms were generally insignificant and were thus dropped from the model. The significance levels for the second and most of the highest nutrient levels (for example, N at 60 and 120 kg/ha, respectively) were obtained from standard two-tailed t-tests: t_{n-7} equals main effect (N = 60) divided by standard error.

**Denotes coefficient significant at .01 level.
*Denotes coefficient significant at .05 level.
$^+$Denotes coefficient significant at .10 level.
^{a}Indicates that the following one-tailed test was undertaken of highest-level nutrient effects to examine the null hypothesis of no difference between second- and third-level effects: t_{n-7} equals main effect (N = 120) minus main effect (N = 60) divided by standard error. This latter test is shown in the table only for those cases where both second- and third-level main effects were significant at 90 percent confidence or above. In all other cases, the t-test given in the NOTE above is shown.

TABLE 2.11. *Effects of Fertilizer on the Adira I Cassava Variety, Farm Trials, Java, 1979/80*

(t-statistics in parentheses)

	Tasikmalaya (Andosol)	Garut (Andosol)	Yogyakarta (Regosol)	Jepara (Latosol)	Bogor (Latosol)	Wonogiri (Latosol)
Intercept	52.31 (2.38)*	78.87 (4.42)*	1.81 (0.08)	132.28 (7.63)**	123.84 (4.82)**	153.16 (6.22)**
N 60 kg/ha	117.38 (6.01)**	24.18 (1.53)	116.75 (6.11)**	70.01 (4.55)**	102.59 (4.50)**	75.71 (3.47)**
N 120 kg/ha	145.10[a] (1.42)[+]	24.74 (1.56)	168.61[a] (2.71)**	94.98[a] (1.62)[+]	128.97[a] (1.16)	102.45[a] (1.22)
P_2O_5 30 kg/ha	−1.27 (0.07)	36.79 (2.33)*	31.61 (1.65)	4.90 (0.32)	−0.99 (0.04)	19.92 (0.91)
P_2O_5 60 kg/ha	−8.26 (0.42)	40.80[a] (0.25)	−8.57 (0.45)	31.52 (2.05)*	−1.27 (0.06)	−3.89 (0.18)
K_2O 50 kg/ha	−0.62 (0.03)	−8.95 (0.57)	26.58 (1.39)	−11.03 (0.72)	−19.64 (0.86)	19.97 (0.91)
K_2O 100 kg/ha	−0.13 (0.01)	−12.78 (0.81)	35.19 (1.84)[+]	−3.81 (0.25)	2.58 (0.11)	24.92 (1.14)
R^2	.609	.237	.719	.573	.486	.430
$F_{6,38}$	9.89	1.96	16.22	8.52	5.98	4.77

SOURCE: CRIA, unpublished results of trials conducted in farmer fields with supervision provided by local extension workers. J. Wargiono at CRIA kindly permitted the author to use these data. The method for presenting t-statistics and significance levels is the same as that used in Table 2.10.

NOTE: Tasikmalaya, Garut, and Bogor are in West Java; Yogyakarta is in Yogyakarta Province; and Jepara and Wonogiri are in Central Java.

**Denotes coefficient significant at .01 level.

*Denotes coefficient significant at .05 level.

[+]Denotes coefficient significant at .10 level.

[a]Indicates that the t-test and significance level relate to the hypothesis of no difference between second- and third-level main effects.

(Williams and Joseph [163]), many weathered, leached, and eroded soils have low potassium reserves. As the results in Table 2.10 suggest, potassium could be a critical factor limiting cassava yields in highly eroded soils like those found in Gunung Kidul. The reasons for cassava's variable response to phosphorus are unclear, but may be related to the low requirement for this nutrient in comparison to potassium and nitrogen, and also to an association with mycorrhiza.[26] Small-scale tests of the fertilizer requirements and responsiveness of local cassava varieties have been conducted in many areas of Java in recent years. The results have shown that local varieties respond well to moderate fertilizer applications, so that the use of fertilizer can be profitable even at low cassava prices.[27]

The economically optimal levels of nitrogen will probably vary within the range of 70 to 135 kilograms per hectare, depending on cassava variety and soil conditions. Excessive application of nitrogen must be avoided because it promotes growth of cassava tops at the expense of roots. Indonesian agronomists have recommended potassium (K_2O) doses of between 50 and 100 kilograms per hectare for cassava, depending on soil type (Effendi [46]). Future research in the uplands of Java should attempt to validate these recommendations, because potassium fertilizers are expensive per kilogram of nutrient and are not always available on Java. Because cassava needs little phosphorus, the current recommendation of 30 to 45 kilograms of P_2O_5 per hectare is probably reasonable. Little research has been undertaken in Indonesia on the response of cassava to application of the secondary and minor nutrients. Of potential importance are calcium and magnesium, which the crop extracts in significant quantities, and also sulphur and zinc, which are known to affect cassava yields in other parts of the tropics. The international research centers working on cassava (CIAT and IITA) do not now have specific recommendations on these nutrients, perhaps because they are usually applied in sufficient amounts in the forms of farm manure, wood ash, or TSP, the most commonly used phosphate fertilizer (Howeler [68]).

In trials of local varieties in farmers' fields, cassava yields of 10 to

[26] In a personal communication, John Lynam at CIAT cites new research indicating that continuous cultivation may reduce the soil's content of the mycorrhizal fungi that live symbiotically with plant roots and facilitate plant uptake of phosphorus. The results of laboratory experiments of mycorrhizal associations with cassava roots are contained in Howeler [69].

[27] Profitability is also affected by government subsidies on fertilizer prices, which are examined in the next section.

TABLE 2.12. *Fertilizer Field Trials on Local Cassava Varieties,*
Central and East Java
(tons/ha)

District (No. trials)	Fertilizer recommendation (kg/ha)			Control yield (tons/ha)	Expected yield increase (tons/ha)	Value of increase (000 Rp/ha)	Cost of fertilizer (000 Rp/ha)	Net return (000 Rp/ha)	VCR[a]
	N	P$_2$O$_3$	K$_2$O						
Wonogiri	90	30	0	6.3	4.9	98	21	77	4.6
(18)	135	30	0		6.3	126	29	97	4.3
Sragen	135	30	30	2.2	7.6	152	33	119	4.6
(6)	135	45	30		7.9	158	36	122	4.4
Sukoharjo	135	45	60	6.9	7.5	150	39	111	3.8
(8)									
Karanganyar	135	45	0	2.9	6.2	124	32	92	3.9
(8)	135	90	0		7.5	150	40	110	3.7
Boyolali	90	45	0	7.9	5.4	108	24	84	4.5
(11)	135	45	0		6.2	124	32	92	3.9
Total Sura-	90	45	0	5.7	4.5	90	24	66	3.8
karta (51)	135	45	0		5.9	118	32	86	3.7
Total Ma-	90	45	0	6.0	5.8	116	24	92	4.8
diun (17)	135	45	0		6.9	138	32	106	4.3

SOURCE: FAO [55].

[a]VCR = Value-to-cost ratio, or the value of the added cassava yield divided by the cost of fertilizer. Prices for 1979/80 are used.

25 tons per hectare were obtained in West Java within the above ranges of fertilizer use. Most yields were between 12 and 15 tons at a harvest age of 9 or 10 months (Indonesia [81]). In marginal areas of Central and East Java, similar trials also demonstrated the profitability of fertilizer, although yields were lower, ranging from 10 to 14 tons (FAO [54]) (see Table 2.12). More carefully controlled experiments with a number of the local varieties that are commonly planted on Java have generally produced yields ranging from 15 to 30 tons per hectare, depending upon soil type (Table 2.13) (CRIA [30]; Effendi et al. [46]; Warigono et al. [154]). Although the experimental levels of fertilizer dose were, in most cases, too few to calculate precise optimums, the gross incremental value-to-cost ratios arising from fertilizer use were frequently greater than 10:1 and seldom less than 3:1. These results imply that farmers can expect to obtain between 10 and 35 kilograms of cassava for each kilogram of fertilizer used at these levels of application.

Indonesia's root-crop agronomists have for several years been experimenting with two promising new cassava varieties, Adira I and Adira II, which are crosses of clones from Brazil and Maluku in In-

TABLE 2.13. *CRIA Fertilizer Field Trials on Cassava at Java Test Stations*

	Fertilizer dosage (kg/ha)			Actual yield (tons/ha)	Control yield (tons/ha)	Avg. return to fertilizer[a] (Rp output/ Rp fert)
	N	P$_2$O$_5$	K$_2$O			
Latosol						
West Java	90	30	50	17.1	7.7	7.7
West Java	105	30	50	24.7	13.8	8.2
Central Java	90	30	50	23.9	10.6	10.9
Yogyakarta	90	30	50	19.8	7.5	10.1
East Java	90	0	60	31.5	20.9	10.2
Alluvial						
West Java	67.5	45	45	11.8	6.0	5.2
Central Java	105	30	90	14.7	8.1	4.2
Andosol						
East Java	75	45	45	22.7	16.8	5.0
East Java	75	30	50	36.5	21.3	13.9
Regosol						
Yogyakarta	105	30	100	11.3	2.7	5.3

SOURCE: These are a few examples taken from various editions of the annual progress reports of the root crops division of CRIA. These results are summarized in Effendi et al. [46]. The fertilizer dosages and yields are those calculated to be economically optimal over the sample plots.

[a] In 1979/80 relative prices.

donesia. Adira I is sweet (HCN content of 27.5 mg/kg in fresh root), nonbranching, and can be harvested after seven months. Adira II is bitter (124.0 mg HCN content), branching, and requires a longer growing period. Both are somewhat resistant to cassava bacterial blight and red spider mite (CRIA [33]). In addition, they appear to be very productive with moderate levels of fertilization, and average yields of 22 tons are expected under recommended cultivation practices. Adira I has been tested most widely throughout Java and exhibits strong response to nitrogen on Latosol and Regosol soils; unfortunately, the results have been mixed on the Andosol soils that cover much of the island. Results of potassium and phosphorus applications are inconsistent. Hence, more fertilizer tests on well-defined benchmark soils are needed. In any event, the Adira cultivars have not always produced the highest yields in comparative trials with local varieties (CRIA [31]).

The relationship between fertilizer dose and cassava's HCN content has not been consistently demonstrated in the literature, but it does appear that HCN in both roots and leaves tends to increase with increased levels of nitrogen (Howeler [70]). However, past research also indicates that agroclimatic conditions and age at harvest can strongly influence HCN content within individual varieties. As Chapter 3 demonstrates, current cooking and processing practices on Java are adequate to detoxify cassava prior to consumption, so increases in HCN content resulting from fertilizer use can easily be compensated for.

Recommended Cassava Cultivation Practices

Aside from application of fertilizer and choice of variety, there are two principal ways in which cultivation practices might profitably be changed: treatment of cassava cuttings prior to planting, and method of fertilizer application.[28] The practice of removing cassava leaves prior to root harvest also seems to affect root yields, but this would be harder to change because leaves are used for food and fodder.

CIAT strongly recommends an inexpensive practice of careful handling and storage of planting material and treatment with fungicide to promote more rapid plant germination and reduce disease risks (Lozano et al. [97]). Even more important than treatment, though, is the careful selection of planting material.[29] Farmers on Java do not now treat cuttings and typically store planting material under adverse temperature and humidity conditions for periods of two to five months. As a result, many cuttings fail to sprout and must be replanted. CRIA has not yet undertaken any work on this problem.

Field observations suggest that farmers often broadcast fertilizer without incorporating it into the soil. Although cassava's root system is concentrated in the upper 10 centimeters of soil, so that deep placement of fertilizer is not necessary (Howeler [70]), fertilizer broadcast on steep hillsides can be lost with soil runoff. CRIA recommends that fertilizer be dibbled close to the base of the cassava plant for maximum efficiency.

Preharvest leaf removal may explain part of the difference between experimental cassava yields and farm yields. The reduction in photosynthetic area may lessen starch accumulation and root yields. James H. Cock at CIAT reports, however, that the effect of leaf removal on root yield depends on varietal characteristics and can even be positive for more vigorous cassava varieties (personal communication).

---

[28] There are few significant differences between agronomic recommendations and general farmer practice in farm operations such as land preparation, planting, weeding, and timing of fertilizer application. In most cases, the manner and timing of these operations are determined by the competing requirements of the other crops in intercropping systems. Because cassava pest and disease problems are relatively minor, there is less need for specific control practices on Java than in other areas of the world. More thorough and regular weeding has been found to increase yields elsewhere in the world, but this is less of a concern on Java, where all fields are kept nearly weed free.

[29] James Cock of CIAT, personal communication.

Improvements in Cassava Intercropping Systems

Because most of Java's cassava is intercropped, agronomic research on cassava intercropping systems is more relevant to Java's upland agriculture than is research on cassava production alone. Thorough research on cassava intercropping has been carried out by CRIA in the transmigration areas[30] of Sumatra and, more recently, by CRIA and the International Rice Research Institute in Kalimantan, Borneo. This research has focused on the improvement of intercropping systems similar to those of Garut and Gunung Kidul and has included basic economic evaluation. Figure 2.8 compares the current form of land use and CRIA's basic intercropping system at one of the Sumatran test sites.[31]

The elements of the CRIA systems are fivefold: first, crop varieties are selected for their suitability under local conditions; second, an earlier-maturing upland rice variety allows early planting of a legume crop during the latter part of the wet season; third, the field spacing of crops is designed to reduce competition for sunlight; fourth, fertilizer and pesticide use is increased substantially, and recommended doses for each crop are developed; and fifth, mulches are used to retard weed growth and to conserve soil moisture during the drier season. As a result, substantial improvements in productivity and net farm income are achieved (Table 2.14). Average yields expected under this system and obtained under current procedures are as follows, in tons per hectare (CRIA [32]):

Crop	Expected	Current
Corn	2.0	0.8
Rice	2.3	1.9
Cassava	24.0	10.0
Peanuts, rice, and beans	1.2	—

Although many aspects of the CRIA system are familiar to cassava farmers on Java, results obtained on the level, red-yellow podzolic soils of southern Sumatra may not be replicable on the more erosion-prone upland soils of Java. Rainfall is also more seasonal on Java,

---

[30] This refers to government-sponsored colonization areas in the Outer Islands.

[31] Although CRIA agronomists have experimented with a number of variants, the improved cropping system shown in Figure 2.8 has been the most consistently successful. See CRIA [29]. For an analysis of several years of the Sumatran intercropping research, see McIntosh and Effendi [98].

TABLE 2.14. *Current Farmer Practices Compared with the CRIA Improved Intercropping System, Lampung Province, Sumatra, 1977/78*

	Current practices for intercropped cassava, corn, and upland rice	CRIA's selected varieties and cultivation practices
Annual labor use (*man-days/ha*)[a]	278	672
Fertilizer (*kg/ha*)		
Urea	90	460
TSP (triple super phosphate)	225	470
ZK	0	149
Manure	0	0
Lime	0	200
Pesticide		
Furadan 3G (*kg/ha*)	0	30.0
Surecide (*lt/ha*)	1.6	4.8
Zinc Phosphide (*kg/ha*)	1.0	0
Nonlabor cash costs (*000 Rp/ha*)[b]	39.5	161.7
Yields (*00 kg/ha*)		
Cassava	109.1	198.9
Rice	24.3	36.9
Corn	6.3	25.5
Peanut	–	9.7
Rice Bean	–	2.8
Total output value (*000 Rp/ha*)[b]	545.4	1,197.4
Profit (*000 Rp/ha*)[c]	380.8	733.3

SOURCE: Inu Ismail et al. [86].

NOTE: The patterns are two variants of current and improved practices at the Sumatran test site, chosen because they reflect present farm practices and CRIA's most successful intercropping system.

[a]The CRIA report does not distinguish between tasks performed by men and women.

[b]Outputs and nonlabor inputs are valued at the approximate prices prevailing in the cassava study's survey areas during 1979/80.

[c]Deducts all labor and nonlabor costs from total output value. Both hired and family labor are valued at Rp 450 per man-day, or the average wage paid to male and female laborers in the Garut survey area during 1979/80.

making it impractical to introduce the dry-season legume crop grown on Sumatra. Different pests and diseases and problems of varietal adaptability further complicate the direct transfer of CRIA's Sumatran systems. Nonetheless, these difficulties should not be insurmountable. The agricultural scientists principally responsible for developing CRIA's Sumatran systems believe that their results, with the exception of the dry-season crop, could be duplicated or suitably modified for much of Java. This transfer, however, requires site-specific field trials in order to derive appropriate varietal, fertilizer, and pesticide recommendations.

Returns to Improved Cropping Practices in the Survey Areas

Based upon the above research, current land-use practices, and apparent potential productivity, estimates have been made of the

TABLE 2.15. *Measures of Increased Profitability for Improved Cassava Cropping Practices*

Cropping system	Increase in cash costs[a] (000 Rp/ha)	Increase in gross value of output (percent)	(000 Rp/ha)	Increase in Profit I[b] (percent)	(000 Rp/ha)	Increase in Daygain[c] (percent)	Costs of cassava production (000 Rp/ton)	Change in production costs (percent)
GARUT								
Pure-stand cassava, local varieties, current fertilizer package	25.3	51.7%	78.4	41.1%	39.5	13.7%	23.5	−16.1
Pure-stand cassava, Adira I variety, CRIA fertilizer package	29.8	111.1	168.4	120.1	115.5	46.1	18.2	−35.0
Intercropped cassava, CRIA package	116.7	121.1	377.8	73.7	154.4	9.8	11.4	−29.2
GUNUNG KIDUL								
Intercropped cassava, lowland fertilizer use, terraced hillsides	16.8	36.6	35.6	12.3	11.2	4.8	15.7	+7.9
Intercropped cassava, CRIA package, level soils	65.7	45.1	198.0	30.7	110.8	11.1	10.4	−25.4
KEDIRI								
Pure-stand cassava, Adira I variety, lowland rain-fed soils	16.2	20.2	74.0	20.5	42.3	2.9	17.6	−8.1
Pure-stand cassava, Adira I variety, terraced hillsides	13.3	30.1	56.0	31.1	33.1	13.0	17.9	−12.6

[a]Increase in nonlabor cash input costs over costs of corresponding current cropping system.
[b]Net returns to land, family.
[c]Net returns to land and total (family and hired) labor.

costs and returns to improved cassava cropping practices in the survey areas.[32] These improved practices principally involve greater use of inorganic fertilizer and the introduction of crop varieties selected by CRIA, rather than any drastic changes in cropping systems. Three changes in practices are examined for Garut. The first is the combination of the current fertilizer credit package for cassava with local varieties planted in pure stand; the second combines the Adira I variety with CRIA's recommendations on fertilizer and cultivation practices; the third introduces the cassava intercropping system developed on Sumatra and includes planting a legume crop late in the rainy season. For Gunung Kidul, it is assumed that current lowland fertilizer quantities are applied to the local intercrop varieties planted on terraced hillsides and that CRIA's intercropping system replaces current practices on level soils. For Kediri, pure-stand plantings of Adira I are assumed both on the better lowland rain-fed soils and on the less fertile hillside terraces. Prices used for inputs and outputs are those prevailing in the survey areas during the 1979/ 80 crop year. A number of indexes comparing estimated costs and returns to current and improved practices are presented in Table 2.15.

The gross value of output is increased by all of the improved cropping practices. Gains are greatest in Garut, reflecting the low productivity of current cropping systems there. The smallest percentage gains in value of output occur with the introduction of Adira I in Kediri. The introduction of fertilizer on Gunung Kidul's hillsides produces only a modest increase in output, because of the constraint imposed by severe soil erosion. The increase in output value on Gunung Kidul's level soils is larger, but considerably less than with the CRIA intercropping system in Garut, reflecting the current high intensity of farming in Gunung Kidul. The incremental nonlabor cash costs of the new intercropping system are considerably greater than for pure-stand cassava alone, making the added value of output in the pure-stand systems highest per rupiah of added nonlabor cost.

Increases in net returns of labor and nonlabor cash costs (Profit I in Appendix Tables B.2–B.7) are also substantial and exhibit a similar

---

[32] Because of the differences in agroclimatic conditions between the agronomists' research area and the survey areas, these results are tentative and need verification. For present purposes, where the agronomists' results provided little guidance in estimating required inputs and expected outputs, an attempt was made to be liberal with the former and conservative with the latter. Perhaps the estimates are too conservative. As James Cock points out, "If yields in Kediri are already 14.5 tons per hectare, then you should be able to push them up to 20 to 25 tons per hectare" (personal communication).

TABLE 2.16. *Returns to Labor Under Improved Production Practices*

Cropping system	Percent increases in labor use			Increases in Profit II[a]	
	Total	Male	Female	*(percent)*	*(000 Rp/ha)*
GARUT					
Pure-stand cassava, local varieties, current fertilizer package	19.5%	24.3%	10.0%	157.5%	(22.7)
Source of increase[b]		C/E	E		
Pure-stand cassava, Adira I variety, CRIA fertilizer package	24.4	34.3	4.4	695.8	(100.2)
Source of increase		C/E	E[c]		
Intercropped cassava, CRIA package	72.9	69.2	80.8	117.8	(116.4)
Source of increase		A/C/E	B/E[c]		
GUNUNG KIDUL					
Intercropped cassava, lowland fertilizer use, terraced hillsides	14.6	14.6	14.6	31.0	(9.7)
Source of increase		E	E		
Intercropped cassava, CRIA package, level soils	23.0	37.1	7.5	41.2	(106.4)
Source of increase		B/C/E[c]	E[c]		
KEDIRI					
Pure-stand cassava, Adira I & CRIA rec's., lowland rain-fed soils	14.5	10.0	224.2[d]	20.3	(36.5)
Source of increase		C/E	C		
Pure-stand cassava, Adira I & CRIA rec's., terraced hillsides	13.1	10.0	82.9[d]	54.2	(29.8)
Source of increase		C/E	C		

[a]Increases in returns to land and management input after deduction of family labor input valued at prevailing agricultural wage rates. The absolute values of these increases are contained in parentheses.

[b]Major labor activities requiring greater labor input: A—land preparation; B—planting; C—fertilizer and pesticide use; D—weeding; E—harvesting.

[c]The assumptions made to derive these estimates result in a substantial decline in weeding labor input, reducing the net increase in total labor use.

[d]This percentage increase is very large, but begins from a small base of female labor input in this cropping system.

pattern in all three regions. They are largest in Garut for cropping systems using new crop varieties and smallest in Garut and Gunung Kidul for practices involving increased fertilizer use alone. The percentage increases in returns to land and total labor input (Daygain) vary widely and do not show a clear pattern across regions and cropping systems.

Significant gains in total labor use should be expected as well, particularly with CRIA's intensified intercropping system (Table 2.16).

These gains are greater for men than for women in most of the improved systems. Increases in net returns to land and management (Profit II) are also large in most cases. Cassava production costs decline in almost all cases with improved practices.[33] The lowest production costs are with CRIA's intercropping system.

In summary, there is considerable potential for increasing the productivity of most of the survey area cropping systems, but these tentative results must be verified by field testing on Java. The gains in productivity would be profitable by any measure at the prevailing prices in these regions. In addition, significant gains in employment would result, particularly with the introduction of the intensive cassava intercropping system. This would increase cash input costs substantially, but the gains in output and farm income would more than outweigh the higher costs. Potential returns to the new cropping practices vary among the survey areas. In general, returns would be highest where present practices are least intensive. Percentage gains in output and labor use will most likely be lower overall where returns are already high.

Economic and Institutional Considerations

Significant gains both in cassava output and in the total productivity of upland cropping systems are possible. For cassava alone, the minimum increase depends on the response of current varieties to fertilizer, whereas larger increases will depend on new varieties. The differences between test plot results and the yields possible on farmers' fields are assumed to be relatively small. If yields of the Adira varieties are in fact lower under farm conditions, the potential for increasing cassava productivity on Java will be reduced. This is an unresolved empirical matter that agronomic research and extension work will have to settle.

Whether local or improved varieties are chosen, considerably more inorganic fertilizer will have to be used. Increased use depends on relative prices, farmers' knowledge, the availability of farm capital, and access to land, fertilizer, and credit. The rate of adoption of new cassava varieties will be limited by the capacity for multiplication and distribution of planting material and by extension activities. These factors are particularly important for new cassava intercrop-

---

[33] The exception in Gunung Kidul occurs because of restrictive assumptions about the effects of fertilizer on crops other than cassava in this system.

ping systems and the more general issue of improving Java's upland agricultural systems.

Price Incentives to Producers

Relative prices of inputs and products are major determinants of resource allocation in agriculture. The price of cassava rose relative to prices of other food crops during 1979/80, but the aggregate production figures do not show any corresponding increase in harvested area. Java's cassava hectarage increased slightly between 1978 and 1979, but harvested areas are estimated to have declined somewhat in all of the major provinces during the 1979/80 crop year.

Indonesian domestic rice price policies also affect incentives to cassava growers. Government buffer-stock operations reduced seasonal fluctuations in rice prices and kept domestic rice prices below world prices during much of the 1970's. Because Indonesia's poorer consumers tend to substitute cassava for rice when rice prices are high, these policies reduce seasonal and average cassava prices. A government program also exists to support prices received by rice farmers. However, because cassava cannot be grown under flooded or excessively moist soil conditions, the substitution of cassava for rice on sawah is not practical. Hence, the impact of rice price policy on cassava production is principally through substitutions in demand rather than supply.

A significant increase or decrease in total cassava area in response to price changes on Java cannot be expected. Most cassava is grown in upland intercropping systems, and the competition in these systems imposes some rigidity in crop substitution. For example, the density and canopy cover provided by cassava plantings could not be increased without reducing yields of the intercropped cereals. At the same time, however, cassava's drought tolerance and pest and disease resistance provide elements of stability in rain-fed cropping systems. As a result, much cassava will be grown on Java even when its price is low.

Expansion of cassava areas on Java will be confined to partially irrigated sawah where greater flexibility exists for crop substitutions during the late season. For example, cassava alone or intercropped with corn is a highly profitable alternative to the common legume-corn sequence on this land type in Kediri. The survey results from Kediri suggest that increased cassava areas would most likely entail smaller areas planted to soybeans, peanuts, and possibly corn. The growth of cassava areas in similar regions of Java will depend on farmer expectations about prices. Even in Kediri, where the local demand for cassava is strong, the adjustment to price increases has been far from complete. The declining price trend for cassava during the 1970's—perhaps compounded by the shock of the 1974 export ban on cassava products—may make farmers skeptical about prospects for the crop.

Most cassava is produced farther from its market on the rest of Java than in Kediri. Added transport costs reduce the farm-gate price relative to prices of alternative crops for which value-to-weight ratios are higher. The result is an effective increase in the price at which cassava becomes the most profitable alternative.

Price relationships between products and factors constitute a second major determinant of supply responsiveness by their effect on yields. The key variable input affecting cassava yields is fertilizer, prices of which are heavily subsidized by the Indonesian government. Urea and TSP were sold domestically for Rp 70 per kilogram in 1979/80, or roughly 60 percent of the prevailing world price.[34] At farm-level prices for cassava averaging Rp 20 per kilogram, this implies that farmers should apply urea up to the point where the last kilogram produces 3.5 extra kilograms of cassava. If the fertilizer subsidy were terminated and the world price prevailed, the optimal input-output ratio for cassava would be 1:6 rather than 1:3.5.

Although it could be argued that the optimal input-output ratios for all crops would be affected by such a change, an increase in fertilizer prices could have a greater impact on cassava than other crops. The legume crops that compete with cassava for late-season land require less fertilizer and are often not fertilized at all. More important, cassava tends to be the last crop fertilized, perhaps because farmers have traditionally allocated their limited fertilizer supplies to more profitable crops, although recent prices and the response of cassava to fertilizer warrant greater use than most farmers practice.

Tables 2.17 and 2.18 compare estimated returns to various cropping systems under 1979/80 cassava and fertilizer prices with what returns would be if fertilizer prices were not subsidized and cassava prices fell to 80 percent and 67 percent of 1979/80 prices.[35] On irri-

[34] During 1979/80, the appropriate world price for urea and TSP was about US$200 per ton (FOB Palembang, Sumatra). This compares with the domestic subsidized price of $114 per ton at the prevailing exchange rate.

[35] The 80 percent level brings the 1980 cassava price more or less back into line with the average cassava-to-corn price ratio that prevailed in Java's major corn- and cassava-producing provinces from 1970 to 1979. The fall to 67 percent of the 1979/80 price might occur as a result of extreme changes in international markets for cassava. See Chapter 5.

TABLE 2.17. *Effects of Cassava and Fertilizer Prices on Gross Output, Fertilizer Costs, and Profits, Kediri Survey Area*
(ooo Rp/ha)

	Cropping pattern		
	Intercropped cassava and corn	Soybeans-corn	Peanuts-corn
Gross output[a]			
1979/80 prices	461	302	296
Prices 80% of 1979/80	387	–	–
Prices 67% of 1979/80	337	–	–
Fertilizer costs[b]			
1979/80 domestic prices	28	20	17
World prices	48	34	29
Profit I[c]			
1979/80 prices	290	142	84
(A) Prices 80% of 1979/80	215	–	–
(B) Prices 67% of 1979/80	165	–	–
(C) World fertilizer prices	270	128	72
(A) plus (C)	195	–	–
(B) plus (C)	145	–	–
Profit II[d]			
1979/80 prices	270	114	45
(A) Prices 80% of 1979/80	196	–	–
(B) Prices 67% of 1979/80	146	–	–
(C) World fertilizer prices	251	100	33
(A) plus (C)	176	–	–
(B) plus (C)	126	–	–

[a]Assumes "normal" yields of all crops.
[b]Assumes application rates of Kediri, 1979/80.
[c]Returns above all cash costs, labor and nonlabor.
[d]Returns to land and management input after deducting family labor valued at local farm wage rates from Profit I.

gated soils in Kediri, high cassava yields make intercropped cassava and corn superior to either of the legume-corn sequences at all assumed price levels (Table 2.17), although the profit margin declines significantly at lower cassava prices. A very low cassava price coupled with productivity-increasing technological developments for soybeans could reverse the relative profits of these two systems. At all cassava prices, the assumed world price for fertilizer tends to reduce the relative profitability of the cassava system because of its greater fertilizer requirement.

Summary comparative figures for the rain-fed systems are presented in Table 2.18. For pure-stand cassava in Garut, the Adira I variety with CRIA cultivation practices is more profitable at each of the assumed cassava prices than the alternative system using local varieties. The BIMAS fertilizer package for the local varieties would probably not be attractive to farmers if the price of cassava were to fall back to pre-1979/80 levels. Both the current and the improved cassava intercropping packages show significantly greater profits than the pure-stand systems. The CRIA intercropping package is superior to current practices in all cases and should appeal to farmers even at very low cassava prices.

TABLE 2.18. *Profitability of Current Versus Improved Cropping Practices, Garut, Gunung Kidul, and Kediri*
(000 Rp/ha)

| | Profits at varying percentages of the 1979/80 cassava price | | | | | |
| | Profit I[a] | | | Profit II[b] | | |
	at 100%	at 80%	at 67%	at 100%	at 80%	at 67%
GARUT						
Current pure-stand cassava practice	96	64	43	9	−22	−43
Pure-stand cassava, local varieties, current fertilizer package	122	76	46	23	−23	−53
Pure-stand cassava, Adira I variety, CRIA practices	188	124	82	90	26	−15
Current intercropped cassava practice	203	170	149	93	59	38
CRIA package for intercropped cassava	314	253	214	165	105	65
GUNUNG KIDUL						
Current practice, intercropped cassava, terraced hillsides	90	81	75	31	22	16
Lowland fertilizer use, intercropped cassava, terraced hillsides	90	73	63	29	13	2
Current intercropped cassava practice, level soils	349	319	299	246	216	196
CRIA package for intercropped cassava, level soils	422	364	327	315	257	220
KEDIRI						
Current pure-stand cassava practice, lowland soils	197	124	76	171	97	50
Pure-stand cassava, Adira I variety, lowland soils	222	134	77	190	102	45
Current pure-stand cassava practice, terraced hillsides	95	57	33	43	6	−18
Pure-stand cassava, Adira I variety, terraced hillsides	113	64	33	58	10	−22

[a]Returns above all (labor and nonlabor) cash costs.
[b]Returns to land and management input after deducting family labor valued at local farm wage rates from Profit I.

In Gunung Kidul, the use of fertilizer on terraced hillside soils was shown to be somewhat profitable at 1979/80 relative prices (Table 2.15). If the world fertilizer price were to prevail, however, this practice would not be attractive even at 1979/80 cassava prices. With the price of fertilizer high and that of cassava low, the greater profitability of the CRIA intercropping package might not be sufficient to induce adoption in view of the large increases over current practices for cash input costs.

In Kediri, use of the world price for fertilizer reduces the profitability of the Adira I variety. At a cassava price of 80 percent or less of the 1979/80 level, the Adira I package would be little more remunerative than current practices. Data limitations prevented examination of returns to improved intercropping of cassava and corn on this area's rain-fed soils. This system is now more profitable and more common in Kediri than pure-stand cassava.

In this analysis, input-output coefficients are assumed to be fixed. In reality, of course, marginal adjustments would be made in fertilizer doses as relative prices change. An important empirical question is whether the Adira I variety is superior to the local varieties of the survey areas at all levels of fertilizer use. If so, this variety would dominate in all cassava systems regardless of price.

Delivery, Demonstration, and Extension

Very real constraints prevent introduction of the improved varieties and cultivation practices that would be highly profitable for Java's farmers. In particular, institutions responsible for delivering many of the package inputs to farmers must be expanded.

Agronomic work on cassava is a secondary activity in Indonesia's agricultural research institutions. Because budgets for cassava research are limited, necessary site-specific field trials have not been undertaken to test the superiority of new varieties and to develop precise fertilizer recommendations for them and for existing varieties. In addition, there are no existing programs for the multiplication and distribution of cassava planting material. Moreover, most of the new varieties will require chemical fertilizer for high yields; as a result, local demonstration efforts will be necessary to develop fertilizer recommendations and demonstrate the payoff that farmers can expect. Finally, special efforts may be needed to make potassium fertilizers available in areas where trials indicate that inadequate soil potassium limits yields.

The problems of delivering and demonstrating materials are especially serious for the cassava intercropping packages. CRIA's existing breeder seed production programs for crops other than irrigated rice are very small and unable to support any widespread introduction of these cropping systems. The National Directorate for Agriculture (Dinas Pertanian) is responsible for growing and distributing commercial seed, but only small programs are currently operating for secondary crops. These shortcomings are not an immediate concern, because CRIA intercropping packages still must undergo field testing on Java to develop locally adapted varietal, fertilizer, and pesticide recommendations. However, the lack of seed distribution programs will be a binding constraint on any serious effort to develop rain-fed cropping systems.

The initial adoption of CRIA intercropping packages will require a considerably greater amount of farm-level assistance on the part of agricultural demonstration and extension workers than would be the case for improved pure-stand cassava alone. Once the components of these packages have been successfully tested and distribution channels developed, farmers can take care of much of the rest by themselves.[36] Appropriate extension activities will often require additional training of agricultural field staff in upland cropping system practices. Field observations support the view that Indonesia's extension workers, while typically young, intelligent, and highly motivated, are unfamiliar with these complex systems. The additional training need not be prohibitively expensive or time consuming. CRIA, for example, has had success with three-week sessions for the field workers assigned to its testing sites in southern Sumatra.

Access to Resources: Land, Farm Capital, and the Need for Farm Credit

Share-tenancy arrangements will act as a disincentive for the use of cash inputs by tenants unless landlords share the cost. Moreover, the great majority of Java's farms are so small that lack of farm capital will be a common constraint to intensifying land use. The seasonal nature of capital availability in the survey areas could not be determined, but annual estimates can be made from the national household expenditure survey (Table 2.19). When average expenditures for food and basic necessities are deducted from the median family incomes of the sample families, the amount available for investment

---

[36] The selected cereal and legume crops of the CRIA intercropping systems do not require the use of hybrid seed that must be repurchased each season.

TABLE 2.19. *Estimates of Annual Rural Family Income Above Expenditures for Necessities, Garut, Gunung Kidul, and Kediri, 1978*
(000 Rp)

	Garut	Gunung Kidul	Kediri
Income	365	125	605
Expenditures			
Food	268	96	369
Other necessities[a]	63	22	129
Total	331	118	498
Income above expenditures on necessities	34	7	107

SOURCE: Derived from Indonesia [75], Susenas VI, expenditures in rural Java.
[a]Housing, fuel, light, water, clothing, taxes, and insurance. Excludes durable goods, jewelry, parties and ceremonies, and miscellaneous goods and services.

can be estimated. This surplus income is relatively high in Kediri, implying that farmers should have little difficulty paying for the improved farm practices. The same is less likely to be true for the improved pure-stand cassava systems in Garut, and highly unlikely for Gunung Kidul. Even in Gunung Kidul, however, some families would probably find the funds if they were reasonably sure of a profitable return.

The data presented earlier in Table 2.15 made it clear that cash input costs and demands on available farm capital will be much greater for the CRIA intercropping system than for improved pure-stand cassava. When incremental cash costs of the CRIA intercropping system are compared with estimates of surplus income for the Gunung Kidul and Garut families, it is apparent that these costs would be excessively high for many families in these two areas if they had to be borne out of pocket.[37] However, the estimated incremental revenues from improved intercropping would generate enough cash income after the cropping season to repay these costs. In the absence of alternative private sources of financing, a government-sponsored farm credit program will be a prerequisite for widespread adoption of the CRIA intercropping packages.

Government loan programs for irrigated rice historically have lost money in the lowlands, and similar programs might fare even worse in the riskier rain-fed uplands.[38] These unambiguous financial losses

[37] CRIA agronomists recognize the problem of these high costs and are attempting to reduce them, in part by more finely tuned recommendations for fertilizer use. At the same time, seed and fertilizer are highly divisible inputs. Hence, adoption of individual components of the package rather than the complete system is an alternative and would reduce farm capital requirements.
[38] The disappointing record on repayments of farm credit loans is documented in People's Bank of Indonesia [120].

TABLE 2.20. *Marketing of Basic Staple Crops by Per Capita Income Quartiles, Garut, Gunung Kidul, and Kediri*
(Percentage marketed out of total production)

Quartile[a]	Cassava	Rice	Corn	Total output
GARUT				
I	82.9%	1.2%	30.0%	29.3%
II	88.3	16.3	26.7	58.4
III	90.3	43.0	76.3	56.0
IV	93.6	50.7	53.8	67.5
Average	88.9%	28.2%	40.9%	53.4%
GUNUNG KIDUL				
I	26.7%	0.0%	7.1%	25.5%
II	30.3	0.0	13.3	40.1
III	36.4	0.0	28.3	38.5
IV	51.6	5.0	17.9	47.2
Average	36.3%	1.3%	16.3%	37.8%
KEDIRI				
I	90.0%	7.1%	37.1%	74.5%
II	88.5	35.8	66.3	76.0
III	97.5	35.3	55.2	83.7
IV	100.0	54.2	88.7	92.3
Average	96.3%	31.6%	61.8%	81.6%

[a]Quartile I contains the bottom 25 percent of families ranked by per capita income, Quartile IV contains the top 25 percent of families.

must be weighed against benefits that are difficult to measure. If the BIMAS program has served to temporarily ease farm capital constraints so that longer-term sustainable surpluses have been generated, the program has made a very important contribution to both agricultural and rural development at a relatively low cost per family.

Cassava is an essential component of the CRIA intercropping systems because it can generate enough profit to repay capital loans. In many parts of Java, cassava is mainly a cash crop. In areas where gaplek consumption is currently high, the nature of consumer demand for this commodity should, over time, result in reduced consumption as both total production and incomes rise.[39] In Table 2.20, figures from the surveys are presented showing the relationship between income level and marketed shares of the basic staple crops. To the extent that farmers grow a crop they will sell in significant quantity, the CRIA systems should generate cash returns sufficient to repay production loans.

Because superior crop varieties are a major component of the im-

[39] The nearer-term effects, however, might involve an increase in absolute consumption by rural Java's poorest social groups. Chapter 3 contains a discussion of rural income elasticities for various staple foods.

proved cassava intercropping systems, it will be essential to forge links between credit programs and programs for distributing seeds and cuttings. There must also be additional links between input and credit systems and local demonstration and extension efforts. Demonstration activities will be central in the development of local recommendations on varieties and cultivation practices, and extension activities will similarly be essential in fostering their successful adoption. All these steps will contribute to the capacity for loan repayment.

Because cash input costs for improved pure-stand cassava are considerably lower than those for the CRIA intercropping package, the demands on farm capital and institutional resources in improving pure-stand systems should be lower as well. In Kediri, incremental cash costs would probably not prevent adoption of the Adira I recommendations, and little institutional intervention would be necessary other than demonstration plots to test the superiority of this new variety. Extension services would be more important in Garut, where farmers do not fertilize pure-stand cassava because they do not believe it is profitable. At the same time, there is a greater need for farm credit, although this would require a considerably simpler program than the intercropping package.

Availability of Farm Labor

Even on densely settled Java, seasonal peaks in labor demand occasionally limit the intensity of cassava intercropping practices. One example can be drawn from Garut, where the rush to plant the second irrigated rice crop reduces the labor available for planting the late-season legume crop of the CRIA system. Farmers allocate their labor in proportion to the profit they expect from alternative activities. If the improved cropping practices are shown to be sufficiently profitable, farmers will offer the higher wages necessary to attract labor. Even if the late-season legume crop proves not profitable enough to attract labor away from irrigated rice, productivity on rain-fed soils would increase with improved practices for early-season upland rice, corn, and cassava.

In many areas of Java, off-farm employment often competes for farmers' time. For example, cassava is often planted as a pure-stand cash crop near cities, and such farming is a part-time activity. Though the intensive CRIA intercropping systems may not be feasible in such a situation, it should still be possible to increase productivity by using more fertilizer and improved cassava varieties. This would also be true in more remote areas where cassava is planted in pure stands on more extensive holdings.

Risk and Cassava System Improvements

At the beginning of an agricultural season, when farmers cannot be sure of yields or prices, cassava yields are less uncertain than those of other upland food crops. If the relative price of cassava remains high and stable, land areas planted to cassava will probably increase on Java's better soils, and this could have a significant impact on total output. A return to the lower cassava prices of the late 1970's would inhibit this expansion because the farmers who would contribute to any outward shift in the supply curve, given the current technology of cassava production, would be commercially oriented and most sensitive to relative price movements. Movements along the production function—particularly those caused by fertilizer use— should be similarly affected by relative prices. However, the effects of fertilizer used on the noncassava crops in intercropping systems make the net price-response elements of these movements very difficult to disentangle.

The government, not farmers, will bear the initial risks of price downturns because it must bear the costs of promoting improved cassava technology. Even if demonstrations make yield increases certain, farmers will not adopt a cassava technology that requires high fertilizer use unless prices warrant it. Price variability is a lesser concern for cassava intercropping systems. Price support programs are well established for rice, and prices of legume crops are high and tend to be stable. However, variation in the yield of these crops is considerably greater than that of cassava, and this variability may be the principal risk factor inhibiting adoption of the CRIA intercropping packages.

The variation in rainfall toward the end of the wet season introduces significant risk into the late-season legume crop plantings in many areas of Java. In addition, the potential losses from pest and disease damage, to which the rice and legume crops are especially prone, increases in direct proportion to the costs of these systems. The actual risks of these losses should be reduced if CRIA's control recommendations are followed; however, very few upland farmers are now practicing anything more than the most rudimentary forms of pest control, and, as a result, these recommendations introduce an unknown into the decision to adopt.

Demonstration and extension will be important to evaluate new production systems and to provide feedback to those engaged in research and making policy. Local agricultural field workers will have to test the stability of the CRIA packages where late-season rainfall is variable. Alternative crops with lower water requirements could be substituted in areas where the basic CRIA recommendations prove risky. Similarly, local field workers will have to test and report on the site-specific adaptability of the CRIA recommendations on varieties and pest and disease control. Indonesia has developed successful programs for irrigated rice and, in so doing, has created a model that should be readily applicable to rain-fed farming systems.

Conclusions

Average cassava yields on Java are currently low, but could be increased significantly in many parts of the island. Yield potential, however, varies by region:

	Garut	Gunung Kidul	Kediri
1. Potential average cassava yield (tons/ha)	16.0	6.6	17.5
2. Current average cassava yield (tons/ha)	8.1	4.1	14.6
3. Yield "gap" (1–2)	7.9	2.5	2.9
4. Yield gap as percent of current yield	97.5%	61.0%	19.9%

Yield potential appears highest in Kediri, where productivity is already high.[40] Absolute yield potential will likely be lower in areas like Garut, where the gap between current and potential yields is greatest. In areas like Gunung Kidul, cassava yield increments could be large as a proportion of current yields, but absolute yield potential is low because of agroclimatic constraints.

The public costs of increasing yields of cassava and its companion intercrops will also vary among regions. Costs would be low in Kediri, where the current cassava cropping systems are comparatively simple and local farmers are responsive to profitable new technologies. In Garut, public costs would be greater. Some agronomic research would probably be required for the local adaptation of CRIA's complex intercropping systems, and large-scale demonstration, ex-

---

[40]The figures shown in the tabulation are weighted averages of current yields and yields under improved practices on the different land types in the survey areas.

tension, and credit programs would be needed. Public costs would be higher still in Gunung Kidul and might well entail substantial research. In view of the predominant role of rice in the food economy and the need to allocate limited research resources between rice and upland crops, it may be difficult to fund such work.

Increasing the efficient production of cassava for both domestic food supply and export at minimum cost to the government requires concentrating on areas such as Kediri and, to a lesser extent, Garut. Such concentration would have positive distributional effects within regions if the emphasis is on cassava intercropping, because gains in labor intensity would accrue to small farmers and hired laborers.

By contrast, a desire to reduce regional income inequalities implies concentration on areas such as Gunung Kidul and Garut. Government costs would increase in direct proportion to regional distributional benefits, but Java's poorer agricultural areas would also become more efficient cassava producers. The marginal productivity of fertilizer should be relatively high in these areas. The opportunity costs of land are low in Gunung Kidul and areas like it, and wage rates are low as well. Hence, the efficiency-equity trade-off in the benefits of greater cassava productivity will most likely be minor. The principal choice is between government costs and regional distribution of the benefits of greater productivity.

Given these considerations, a number of alternative approaches are possible. In view of recent relative prices, greater use of inorganic fertilizer on cassava should be profitable for farmers in many parts of Java. Such an increase would be in keeping with the trend toward higher application rates on all the major rain-fed crops. Marginal allocations of new land to cassava will occur in areas such as Kediri as long as relative prices remain attractive. Hence, a modest program for cassava alone might involve little more than demonstration efforts with current cassava varieties, particularly in areas with the agronomic potential of Kediri. The provision of price outlook information by radio or the extension services could be a useful supplement to these efforts. Finally, potassium fertilizers should be made available in cassava-producing regions where soils are deficient in this nutrient.

A more active approach to cassava would require greater field testing of the agronomists' new varieties. If the higher profits of these varieties can be demonstrated under farm conditions, multiplication and distribution programs could begin. Cooperation between CRIA and international centers such as CIAT may produce more rapid multiplication methods as well as techniques for treatment of cassava planting material. Field tests of relatively simple cassava-corn intercropping systems would also be appropriate in East and Central Java.

Since the Adira I variety is nonbranching, it should fit easily into current upland intercropping systems; distribution of this variety could be widespread on Java. Because new fertilizer recommendations will typically represent a departure from current farmer practice, extension and demonstration efforts are particularly important in areas such as Garut. As long as these programs focus on cassava, however, there is little need for additional training of extension personnel.

A third level of program effort would be motivated by a serious desire to develop upland cropping systems. This would require concentrating on intercropping rather than on single commodities. At this stage, the widespread testing and local adaptation of the CRIA intercropping packages would be warranted. The prerequisites for broadly based adoption of these packages—programs for multiplication, training, extension, and credit—will require substantial investment in human and physical resources.

To minimize program costs, field testing should logically begin in less intensive areas like Garut, where agroclimatic factors are not excessively limiting. Because Garut is typical of large parts of the uplands of West and Central Java, the distributional benefits of improved cassava intercropping systems could be widespread if the program requirements are satisfied. Some of the package components used in these areas should be profitable in Java's poorest agricultural regions as well. Areas like Gunung Kidul are not extensive on Java, so distributional concerns need to be heavily weighted in order to justify programs focusing exclusively on such areas.

3. Consumption

John A. Dixon

Cassava supplies nourishment to Indonesians in many forms. For some it is an important staple, whereas for others it is only an ingredient in processed foods. It serves also as a vegetable and snack, is eaten fresh and dried, and can be used as a substitute for many foods. This chapter explores cassava's diverse food uses and analyzes how they are affected by economic policy.

The Edible Forms of Cassava

The cassava plant has two edible parts, the roots and the leaves. The roots are the primary source of fresh and processed foods. Leaves are eaten fresh in small quantities, mostly in rural areas. Cassava roots are consumed in a variety of ways that reflect the degree of processing required to prevent spoilage and to treat the roots for different levels of toxic hydrocyanic acid (HCN). Cassava contains a cyanogenic glucoside from which HCN is liberated by enzyme action when the cell walls break down after harvest. The HCN content varies with location, variety, and growing conditions, ranging from less than 50 to more than 100 mg/kg of HCN in fresh roots (Bolhuis [11]). The less toxic varieties, sometimes called sweet cassava, can be made safe to eat by boiling, steaming, or deep-fat frying. Sweet varieties can also be fermented to produce *tape*, a snack or side dish. More poisonous varieties, so-called bitter cassava, must be detoxified by retting (soaking), grating, or drying (Coursey [26]).

On Java, bitter varieties are often made into *gaplek* by sun drying roots that have been peeled and sliced. If drying is done properly, gaplek contains only 12 to 16 percent moisture and can be stored for several months. Gaplek flour, made by pounding the dried chips, is used as a substitute for wheat flour or starch in baked goods. A rice-like product, *tiwul*, is made by moistening the gaplek flour slightly and heating it in a flat pan until it beads into tiny kernels, which are then steamed. A similar dish, *oyek*, is prepared by grating roots, cooking the mash with steam, drying the product, and then reconstituting it with steam.

Cassava starch is made by peeling and grating fresh roots, then filtering out the starch and drying it. In contrast to gaplek flour, starch does not contain fiber or other impurities. Most cassava starch is used in food manufacturing in Indonesia. Cookies and cakes use starch as an ingredient, and *krupuk*, a fried chip commonly served as a snack, is made almost entirely of cassava starch. Moderate quantities of cassava starch are also used in home kitchens on Java and in the baking industry. (See Chapter 4.)

Cassava and Nutrition

Cassava supplies food energy mostly from the roots, which are easily digested and provide calories but little protein. The data in Table 3.1 show the caloric value and protein content of the major starchy staples available in Indonesia. Fresh cassava compares poorly with rice and corn, but this reflects the high moisture content of fresh roots. The figures for gaplek show that cassava's caloric value is similar to that of grains on a dry-weight basis. Nonetheless, its protein content is significantly lower.

The leaves of the cassava plant, eaten as a vegetable or condiment, are a reasonably good source of protein. They also provide the following vitamins and minerals per 100 grams (United States and FAO [150]): calcium, 144.0 mg; iron, 2.8 mg; thiamine, 0.16 mg; riboflavin, 0.32 mg; beta-carotene equivalent, 0.08 mg; niacin, 1.8 mg; and ascorbic acid, 82.0 mg. Cassava leaves are consumed primarily in rural areas. Data from the 1978 Susenas VI expenditure survey (Indo-

TABLE 3.1. *Calorie and Protein Composition of Rice, Corn, and Cassava*

| | Composition per 100 grams edible portion | | | Protein (grams per 1000 calories) |
	Water (percent)	Calories	Protein (grams)	
Rice				
Brown	13.5%	354	7.6	21.5
Milled, polished	11.8	366	6.4	17.5
Corn (grain)	13.6	349	9.1	26.1
Cassava				
Fresh root	65.5	135	1.0	7.4
Dried chips (gaplek)	12.0	349	0.5	1.4
Cassava leaves (fresh)	81.0	60	6.9	115.0

SOURCE: United States and FAO [150].

nesia [75]) show an average weekly consumption of 110 grams per capita in rural areas but only 30 grams in urban areas.

Neither the roots (because of their composition) nor the leaves (because very few are eaten) supply a significant portion of recommended daily protein allowances. Because of this and other issues, the relationship between cassava-based diets and nutrition is still a source of concern. The main nutritional problems in Indonesia are protein-calorie malnutrition (PCM), vitamin A deficiency, goiter, and anemia (Sanders [124]; Soekirman [127]; Djumadias [42]), many of which are prevalent in areas dominated by cassava cultivation and consumption—although low income, rather than cassava itself, is largely to blame. Gunung Kidul Kabupaten near Yogyakarta is one such area. In extensive field studies conducted between 1957 and 1959, Bailey [6] found PCM to be common and both calorie and protein intake levels to be very low. In 1958/59, the average daily measured intake of calories was only 1,350 kilocalories, and of protein an astoundingly low 15.6 grams.[1] Nutrition in Gunung Kidul has improved since that time, but the area still contains many people who are undernourished (A. G. van Veen et al. [152]).

The relationship between cassava consumption and nutritional status on Java remains unclear. Cassava-based diets in Indonesia are traditionally mixed ones, with legumes and vegetables (including cassava leaves) providing a large share of required protein, vitamins, and minerals. Edmundson [44] has shown that this mixed diet may actually improve the quality of protein consumed, and M. S. van Veen's analysis [153] has shown its potential for preventing vitamin A deficiencies. In addition, Indonesians seem to be aware of the nutritional limitations of cassava and try consciously to adjust for them. A study of the connection between anemia in pregnant women and consumption patterns (Mortoatmodjo et al. [103]) found the rate of anemia to be lowest in Gunung Kidul, a cassava-consuming region, and highest in Indramayu, where the diet was based mainly on rice. The authors ascribed this result to the more varied diet in Gunung Kidul—especially legumes and vegetables—as compared to other areas. Despite the fact that the inhabitants of Gunung Kidul were the poorest of the groups studied and had the lowest calorie and protein intake, their consumption of calcium and vitamins was the highest.

[1] Estimates of energy and protein "requirements" changed in the 1960's and 1970's. Since 1973 the requirements for an average male weighing 65 kg are said to be 2,600 kcal and 37 grams per day (FAO, [53a]).

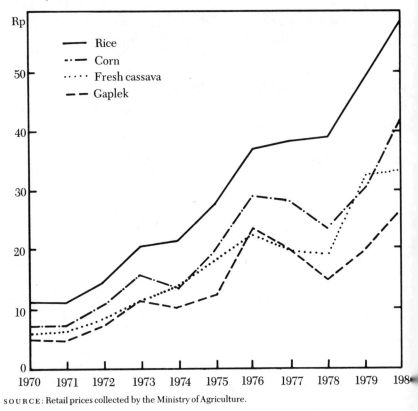

SOURCE: Retail prices collected by the Ministry of Agriculture.

Figure 3.1. Retail Prices for 1,000 Calories of Staple Foods, Rural Java, 1970–80

The relationship between cassava and nutrition remains confusing primarily because cassava, especially in the form of gaplek, is a food of the poor. Cassava is a significantly cheaper source of calories than rice, and gaplek has been the cheapest source of calories during the entire decade of the 1970's (see Figure 3.1). The dried forms are eaten in large quantities only by poor people, who switch to fresh cassava and rice as their income permits. Because of its cheapness, then, cassava helps remedy inadequate calorie intake, the main nutritional problem in Indonesia.

The toxicity of cassava is an additional concern. Goiter and mental disorders have been attributed by a few researchers to chronic toxin buildup from cassava-based diets in parts of Africa (Nestel and MacIntyre, eds. [106]). However, by contrast with Africa, where cassava provides 40 to 50 percent of total calories in some places, cassava in Indonesia contributes less than 10 percent of total calories on average and rarely more than 30 percent among even the poorest classes in a few specific areas. Moreover, Barbara Chapman [19] has found evidence linking the high incidence of goiter in a highland village of Java not to cassava consumption but to the substitution of monosodium glutamate for a traditional fish-flake condiment in food preparation. This evidence, combined with the fact that cassava is detoxified with the usual food-preparation practices, suggests that HCN toxicity should not be a major concern on Java.

Cassava in the Staple Food System

Food balance sheets published by the Indonesian government for the period 1968 to 1979 provide one view of the importance of cassava in Indonesian diets.[2] These estimates provide a useful perspective on the relative importance of major commodities and on changes in their position over time (Table 3.2).

Rice, corn, and cassava are the major sources of food calories in Indonesia. Rice is the most important, consistently providing more than 70 percent of the starchy staple calories and more than 50 percent of total calories. In every year except 1976, corn was the second most important calorie source, with cassava a very close third, each providing about 10 percent of total calories. In urban areas, virtually all staples were purchased. Purchases of staples were also important in rural areas. Sixty-three percent of all rice consumed was purchased in 1976, as was 60 percent of corn. Of total cassava consumed in rural areas, about 43 percent was purchased, although the percentage varied by form. Only 34 percent of fresh roots were purchased, whereas the corresponding figure for gaplek was 51 percent.

The starchy staple ratio, the proportion of total calories that the starchy staple foods represent, ranged from 74 percent to 77 percent during the period. These ratios are among the highest in the world. Other countries at about this level include Burma (80 percent), China (74 percent), Thailand (71 percent), Guinea (74 percent), and Zambia (73 percent) (FAO [56]). Prior to the Second World War, Java's estimated starchy staple ratio was 84 percent (Bennett [10]).

---

[2] Food balance sheet calculations are at the national level and reflect availabilities of major foodstuffs. Annual domestic production of each commodity is adjusted for annual international trade flows, stock changes, nonhuman consumption, losses, and waste. When converted to calories and divided by the total population, figures in the food balance sheets report average energy available daily to each person.

TABLE 3.2. *National Food Balance Sheet Estimates of Daily Per Capita Consumption, Selected Years 1968–79*
(Calories)

Staple food	1968	1970	1972	1974	1975	1976	1977	1978	1979
Milled rice	952	1,070	1,068	1,140	1,127	1,165	1,212	1,237	1,269
Corn									
Grain	258	203	165	202	201	175	206	260	231
Fresh ears	49	49	49	49	49	22	22	6	7
Cassava									
All forms	193	153	144	176	181	204	203	199	182
Starch[a]	1	1	2	4	3	9	4	5	4
Sweet potatoes	50	45	41	46	45	42	42	35	36
Sago and sago flour	39	39	40	39	13	7	7	7	10
Wheat flour	32	33	24	47	38	48	38	40	59
Total starchy staples (A)	1,574	1,593	1,533	1,699	1,654	1,663	1,730	1,784	1,798
Total all foods (B)	2,035	2,097	2,052	2,248	2,150	2,231	2,314	2,417	2,443
Starchy staple ratio (A/B)	.77	.76	.75	.76	.77	.75	.75	.74	.74

SOURCE: Indonesia [73].
[a]Figures shown may be seriously underestimated. See Chapter 4.

TABLE 3.3. *Regional Per Capita Consumption of Major Staples, by Urban and Rural Areas, Java and Madura, 1976 and 1978*
(kg/year)

	Jakarta	West Java	Central Java	Yogyakarta	East Java[a]
			1976		
Urban areas					
Rice	112.3	120.0	101.7	96.5	98.8
Corn	0.1	0.3	1.0	0.1	2.1
Cassava (fresh root equivalent)	4.4	5.3	12.0	10.4	10.9
Fresh cassava	(3.7)	(5.1)	(11.4)	(7.0)	(9.0)
Gaplek	(0.1)	(0.0)	(0.2)	(2.9)	(0.2)
Starch	(0.6)	(0.2)	(0.4)	(0.5)	(1.7)
Rural areas					
Rice		149.1	93.0	77.2	78.8
Corn		0.4	16.0	3.8	31.8
Cassava (fresh root equivalent)		28.5	50.1	108.2	81.9
Fresh cassava		(26.8)	(22.3)	(18.9)	(26.3)
Gaplek		(0.8)	(21.1)	(80.2)	(43.5)
Starch		(0.9)	(6.7)	(9.1)	(12.1)
			1978		
Urban areas					
Rice	104.8	120.5	90.8	89.4	93.9
Corn	0.1	0.2	0.6	–	3.8
Cassava (fresh root equivalent)	5.7	8.1	9.9	7.9	12.4
Fresh cassava	(4.7)	(8.1)	(9.5)	(6.4)	(10.6)
Gaplek	(0.0)	(0.0)	(0.1)	(0.7)	(1.3)
Starch	(1.0)	(0.0)	(0.3)	(0.8)	(0.5)
Rural areas					
Rice		141.1	82.3	67.4	74.7
Corn		0.6	24.5	11.3	32.9
Cassava (fresh root equivalent)		25.3	64.2	96.3	79.3
Fresh cassava		(23.3)	(25.0)	(23.5)	(20.8)
Gaplek		(1.2)	(21.3)	(68.6)	(57.2)
Starch		(0.8)	(17.9)	(4.2)	(1.3)

SOURCE: Indonesia [75]. The 1976 data are from special computer runs done on Susenas V data by the Central Bureau of Statistics. Calories per day were converted to kilograms per year on the basis of the following ratios: rice, 3,600 cal./kg; corn, 3,200 cal./kg; cassava (fresh), 1,095 cal./kg. The 1978 data are unpublished tabulations prepared by the Central Bureau of Statistics in Jakarta based on the Susenas VI survey.
[a]Includes the island of Madura.

Thus, the trend appears to be toward a lower ratio, although the change has been slow.

Regional Variations

The national food balance sheets mask significant regional variations in the consumption of starchy staples.[3] By contrast, household

---

[3] See Farnsworth [49] for a general appraisal of food balance sheets as a basis for analyzing food availability.

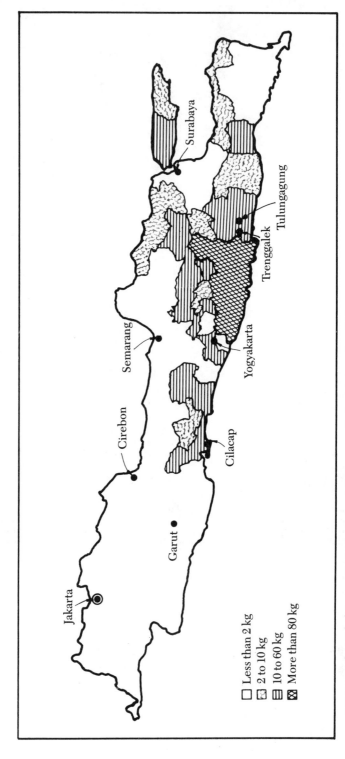

Less than 2 kg

2 to 10 kg

10 to 60 kg

More than 80 kg

SOURCE: Indonesia [75], Susenas VI. There were no areas with consumption levels between 60 and 80 kg.

Figure 3.2. Annual Per Capita Consumption of Dried Cassava (Gaplek), Java and Madura, 1978 (fresh root equivalent)

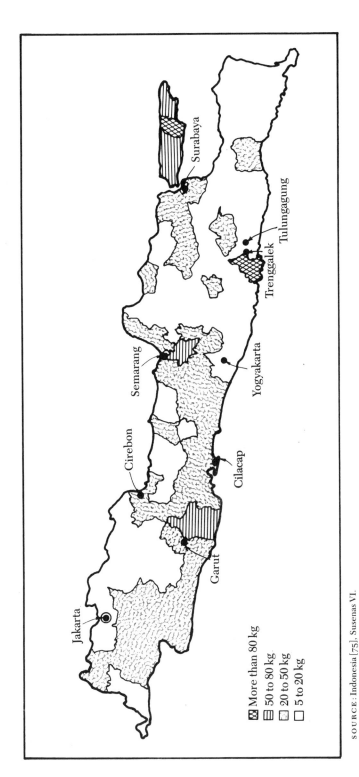

Labels on map: Jakarta, Cirebon, Semarang, Surabaya, Tulungagung, Trenggalek, Yogyakarta, Cilacap, Garut

⊠ More than 80 kg
⊞ 50 to 80 kg
▨ 20 to 50 kg
☐ 5 to 20 kg

SOURCE: Indonesia [75], Susenas VI.

Figure 3.3. Annual Per Capita Consumption of Fresh Cassava, Java and Madura, 1978

expenditure data from the Susenas surveys are location specific and, when disaggregated, provide insight into regional diversity of consumption patterns.[4] Provincial aggregates of urban and rural consumption from the two most recent surveys are shown in Table 3.3. Clear regional patterns and urban-rural contrasts emerge in these totals. The diets of urban dwellers throughout Java are based on rice; some cassava is also consumed, mostly as fresh roots, but virtually no corn is eaten. Regional differences are pronounced in rural areas: rice consumption is higher than average in West Java; corn and cassava consumption are greatest in Central and East Java; and cassava consumption levels are highest in Yogyakarta.[5] Finally, the form in which cassava enters the diet also varies regionally. Cassava in rural West Java is almost entirely consumed in the form of fresh roots, whereas gaplek is more important in Yogyakarta and East Java.

Disaggregation of the province-level data by kabupaten reveals these differences even more clearly (Figures 3.2 and 3.3). Generally, cassava consumption is greater in southern Java than along the northern coast. Fresh root consumption is particularly high on Madura, near Trenggalek, and south of Garut and Semarang. Dried cassava consumption is greatest in the region between Yogyakarta and Trenggalek.

Seasonal Variations

Cassava is an important food for the poor and provides calories for all income groups in seasons when other foods are less available and more expensive. The comparisons of annual average prices of food calories shown in Figure 3.1 suggest cassava's potential importance as a source of inexpensive calories. Figure 3.4 extends these comparisons by showing average seasonal price patterns for the major staples in one region, East Java. Seasonally, rice prices rise from a harvest low of 88 percent of average in May to a late-season high of 112 percent of average in January, a rise of 27 percent, despite BULOG's price-stabilizing policies.[6] Seasonal price variation is less for corn, ranging from 92 to 105 percent of average, a change of 14 percent, with the low occurring in March. Both fresh cassava and gaplek show insignificant seasonal price changes, although gaplek prices are low-

---

[4]The Susenas surveys are described in Appendix C.

[5]This province includes Gunung Kidul, where Bailey [6] found cassava contributing as much as 64 percent of all calories in the diet in 1960.

[6]BULOG (Badan Urusan Logistik) is the national logistics command charged with many responsibilities in the food sector.

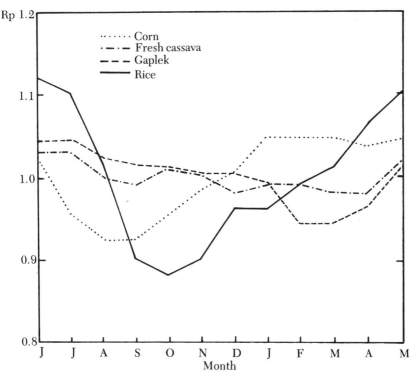

SOURCE: Retail price data collected by the Ministry of Agriculture. Indexes are monthly prices as a proportion of a 12-month centered moving average.

Figure 3.4. Average Seasonal Price Indexes for Staple Foods in East Java, 1971–79

est during the heaviest harvest months of September and October. These seasonal changes, averaged across a period of years, show cassava's price advantage to be greatest in the last quarter of the year, whereas corn is relatively cheapest in the first quarter.

Seasonal consumption patterns are apparent in the four rounds of Susenas VI (Indonesia [75]) and confirm the importance of these relative price changes for consumption (Table 3.4). Total calories derived from the three principal starchy staples vary little by season. However, the composition of those calories changes markedly during the year. Rice consumption is at or above its average in all quarters except January through March, the quarter immediately preceding the rice harvest. Corn is then a relatively cheap calorie source, and increased corn consumption offsets the reduced consumption of rice. Corn consumption declines markedly in the re-

TABLE 3.4. *Seasonal Consumption of Starchy Staples, Java and Madura, 1978*

	Percentage of average annual calories consumed in:				Annual average calories[a]
	Jan.–Mar.	Apr.–May	July–Sept.	Oct.–Dec.	
Rice	89.9%	106.5%	104.0%	99.4%	964
Corn	176.7	88.7	62.0	74.0	150
Sweet potatoes	110.0	100.0	60.0	130.0	10
Cassava	88.7	79.2	108.2	124.5	159
Fresh	(80.6)	(93.5)	(121.0)	(103.2)	(62)
Gaplek	(95.4)	(69.0)	(103.4)	(131.0)	(87)
Starch	(72.7)	(72.7)	(63.6)	(181.8)	(11)
Total	101.3%	102.2%	100.5%	95.9%	1,283

SOURCE: Indonesia [75], Susenas VI survey.
[a]Per capita daily calorie consumption, on an annual average basis.

maining three quarters, but consumption of fresh cassava increases in the third quarter as rice prices begin their seasonal increase and cassava's price advantage is at its greatest. Finally, increased gaplek consumption in the fourth quarter makes up corn and rice deficits. Cassava in fresh and dried forms is thus a primary substitute for rice for about half of the year.

Income Variations

Additional evidence on the economic importance of cassava is derived from data on consumption by income classes provided by the four major Susenas surveys (Figure 3.5).[7] In each quadrant, weekly per capita consumption of the major starchy staples is plotted against income for both urban and rural consumers. The consistency of the relationships—commonly called Engel curves—from survey to survey is impressive. Rice consumption increases rapidly with income among the poorest groups, slows among middle-income consumers, and increases little if at all among high-income consumers.[8] Fresh cassava roots show a similar but much weaker increase in consumption with rising income. Corn and gaplek consumption both decline after passing through a threshold at which calorie requirements are apparently met.

Evidence of consistency is also available in the comparisons between urban and rural consumers. The population distribution

[7]Susenas II data are omitted because the sample is small and the timing duplicates the Susenas I survey. No information is available from Susenas III (1967). See Appendix C for details.

[8]This behavior is consistent with Bennett's Law, which states that the starchy staple ratio declines with increases in income. Other food expenditure patterns are not examined here, however, so evidence on this point is not conclusive.

among income classes shows urban consumers to be wealthier on average than rural consumers.[9] The Engel curves for the urban consumers from each of the surveys reach plateaus more regularly. They are also uniformly lower than the curves for rural consumers, suggesting that urban consumers eat less rice and other staples. Earlier evidence (Table 3.3), however, showed a general tendency toward higher average consumption of rice by urban consumers. This discrepancy is resolved by the population distribution data. Because urban consumers are wealthier, they are clustered farther to the right on the Engel curves. Rural consumers are more concentrated on the left side of the curves. For example, in recent surveys, about 50 percent of the total rural population has been in the first three income classes.

These curves also reveal that consumers eat more fresh cassava and rice when they can afford them. The survey data suggest that consumption of cassava and corn declined from 1963/64 through the 1970's, especially among urban consumers. However, the earlier surveys were conducted just before the rice harvest (November to February and October to April), whereas the later ones covered an entire year. Thus, the earlier results may be dominated by the seasonal substitution of secondary staples.

Like the regional and seasonal analyses, analysis of the relationships between income and consumption of starchy staples highlights another dimension of cassava's importance in Indonesia. Low-income consumers derive a large share of their total calories from cassava—both as fresh roots and as gaplek. In each of the surveys, the poorest people in the rural areas consumed more kilograms of cassava than rice, although not more food calories.

Economic Parameters of Consumer Demand

The extent of price and income variation evident above in the Susenas data permits direct estimation of both price and income elasticities. Table 3.5 reports the aggregate average expenditure elasticities estimated from four Susenas surveys. The underlying equations indicate the relationship between the log of total expenditures and the log of consumption for each of the primary staples, and the re-

[9]The income range defining an income group varies from survey to survey because of inflation between survey dates. Detailed information on the differences between surveys is contained in Appendix C.

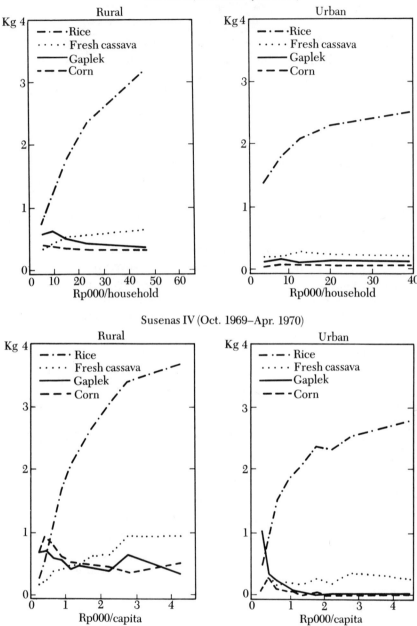

Figure 3.5. Weekly Per Capita Consumption of Rice, Corn, and Cassava by Income Group, Java and Madura

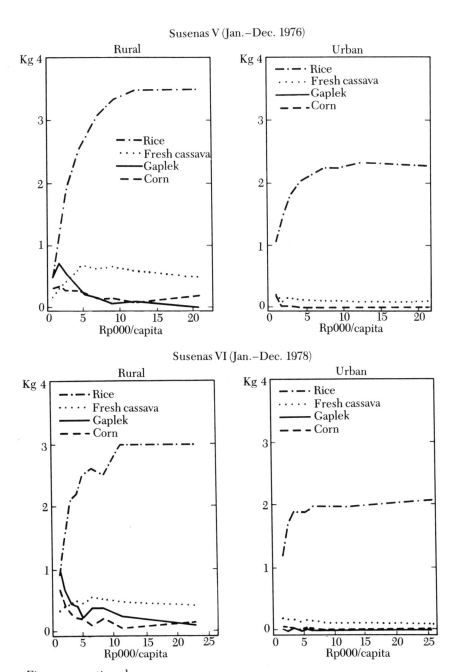

Susenas V (Jan.–Dec. 1976)

Rural

Urban

Kg 4

Kg 4

—·—· Rice
········ Fresh cassava
——— Gaplek
— — · Corn

—·—·Rice
········Fresh cassava
———Gaplek
— — Corn

Rp000/capita

Rp000/capita

Susenas VI (Jan.–Dec. 1978)

Rural

Urban

Kg 4

Kg 4

—·—· Rice
········ Fresh cassava
——— Gaplek
— — Corn

—·—· Rice
········ Fresh cassava
——— Gaplek
— — Corn

Rp000/capita

Rp000/capita

Figure 3.5 continued
For values of income group ranges, see note overleaf.

TABLE 3.5. *Average Expenditure Elasticities for Staple Foods, Java and Madura*

	Rice	Fresh cassava	Gaplek	Corn
Susenas I (Dec. 1963–Jan. 1964)				
Rural	0.71	0.34	−0.25	−0.15
Urban	0.25	−0.03[a]	−0.09[a]	−0.10[a]
Susenas IV (Oct. 1969–Apr. 1970)				
Rural	0.93	0.59	−0.29	−0.38
Urban	0.37	0.16	−1.48	−0.66
Susenas V (1976)				
Rural	0.68	0.53	−0.95	−0.45
Urban	0.15	−0.20	_[b]	_[b]
Susenas VI (1978)				
Rural	0.59	0.22	−0.76	−0.92
Urban	0.09	−0.23	_[b]	_[b]

SOURCE: Indonesia [75], Susenas surveys I, IV, V, VI.
NOTE: Log-linear form, significant at the 5 percent level except as noted.
[a]Not significant at the 10 percent level.
[b]No estimates were made because these categories contain no entries for most income groups.

sulting estimates give elasticities that are constant over the full range of incomes.

The signs and magnitudes of the estimated expenditure elasticities are remarkably stable over time. Rice elasticities are positive and large, whereas those for corn and gaplek are negative or zero. Expenditure elasticities for fresh cassava are positive and moderately large for rural consumers, but are small or negative for urban consumers. Given unequal expenditure elasticities for fresh cassava and gaplek,

---

NOTE TO FIGURE 3.5

The following table shows the income group ranges for Susenas I, IV, V, and VI. Income in Fig 3.5 is plotted as a midpoint of each income group.

		Susenas Survey		
Income group	I 1963–64 (rp/household)	IV 1969–70 (rp/capita)	V 1976 (rp/capita)	VI 1978 (rp/capita)
1	<6,000	<300	<1,000	<2,000
2	6,000–10,000R	300–500	1,000–1,999	2,000–2,999
3	10,001–16,000U	501–750	2,000–2,999R	3,000–3,999R
4	16,001–30,000	751–1,000R	3,000–3,999	4,000–4,999
5	>30,000	1,001–1,250	4,000–4,999	5,000–5,999
6		1,251–1,500U	5,000–5,999U	6,000–7,999U
7		1,501–2,000	6,000–7,999	8,000–9,999
8		2,001–2,500	8,000–9,999	10,000–14,999
9		2,501–3,000	10,000–14,999	>15,000
10		>3,000	>15,000	

R and U designate the rural and urban income groups that contain the fiftieth percentile of urban or rural population.

the aggregate expenditure elasticity for "total cassava" varies significantly by income group.[10] Low-income rural consumers who eat more gaplek and less fresh cassava have an income elasticity for cassava that is dominated by the gaplek elasticity. This combination apparently results in a strong, negative overall elasticity. Conversely, the income elasticity for all cassava at higher income levels is dominated by the fresh cassava elasticity and is positive.[11] These expenditure elasticities imply that the total demand for fresh and dried cassava will very likely decrease with increases in per capita income. It would take a major increase in incomes to have the positive income elasticity for fresh cassava outweigh the strong inferior-food characteristics of gaplek.

Gaplek and fresh cassava, however, do not represent the total food demand for all cassava products. Per capita consumption of gaplek flour and starch is substantial, much of it in processed foods such as cakes and krupuk. Accurate data on baked and processed foods are not available from most of the Susenas surveys; nevertheless, data on krupuk consumption from the 1978 survey provide some evidence that significant income-consumption relationships exist for starch products (Figure 3.6). Elasticity estimates for krupuk are 1.56 for rural consumers and 1.35 for urban consumers.

If starch demand is added to that for fresh cassava and gaplek, the average expenditure elasticity for all cassava must be modified. At low income levels, total cassava will still be dominated by the greater consumption of gaplek and its negative elasticity. The total elasticity may become positive at high income levels, and the change from negative to positive will occur at a lower income level when starch is included. The key point, however, is that the aggregate elasticity will vary significantly by income group. An additional factor, discussed below, may be important as well. Estimates of cassava-consumption functions using more detailed specifications and data show that the income elasticities themselves are not the same in all income groups, even for the separate cassava products.

[10]The aggregate elasticity is the weighted sum of the individual elasticities, where the weights depend on the relative consumption of the two foods at various income levels.

[11]A similar phenomenon was reported in Ghana by Polly Hill [66], leading her to enunciate a "cassava law" that rising incomes were associated with an increase in consumption of starchy staples. Jones [88] presents details of the relationship between income and consumption of fresh and dried cassava in Ghana that are similar to those reported by Susenas for low-income households.

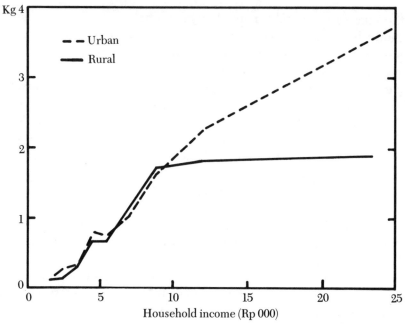

SOURCE: Indonesia [75], 1978 Susenas survey.

Figure 3.6. Weekly Per Capita Consumption of Krupuk by Income Group, Java, 1978

A Complete Demand Analysis

The income and price variations in the 1976 survey, the latest Su-senas survey for which detailed data were available at the time of this analysis, permit estimation of complete demand equations. Per capita consumption of the major staples was related to the price of each staple and to total expenditures. Following Timmer [138], the variables are in logarithms and the income function is quadratic to allow expenditure elasticities to vary by income groups. In addition to the primary demand factors, variables are included that allow shifts in the demand function for each region and for the different seasons (rounds) within each survey. Separate equations were estimated for urban and rural consumers.

With this demand formulation, both own and substitute prices were included as independent variables. In general, the measured effects of substitute goods' prices were not statistically significant, a common result in demand analyses using cross-sectional data. However, the signs of the cross-price terms were frequently positive, as expected. The estimated own-price elasticities shown in Table 3.6 are reasonable and statistically significant. Demand for rice, the major staple, is considerably more price elastic in rural areas than in urban areas, reflecting the lower incomes of the rural population. Wealthier city people are less likely to alter their consumption of rice in response to price changes. The same contrast is evident in the fresh cassava results, with a negative price elasticity for rural consumers and a smaller, positive elasticity for urban consumers.

The positive price elasticity for urban demand for fresh cassava may be a quality effect. If fresh cassava is consumed in cities as a delicacy rather than a staple and purchased by wealthier customers who buy better-quality roots at higher prices, the quantity sold will be positively correlated with price. Both the fresh cassava and the corn price elasticity in rural areas were significant only at the 10 percent level.

The log-quadratic specification for the expenditure variables permits the measured income elasticities to vary with income levels (Table 3.7). Except for corn, which was estimated linearly, the quadratic terms are significant. When evaluated at the overall mean of urban and rural incomes, these elasticities are very close to those estimated with constant elasticity equations. Rice and sweet potatoes are normal goods for both urban and rural consumers. Corn and gaplek are inferior goods in rural areas, and fresh cassava is normal for rural consumers and inferior for urban consumers.

Among both urban and rural consumers, however, each staple is both a normal good and an inferior good. For low-income consumers (approximately 50 percent of the respective populations), all staples except corn have positive income elasticities. Among middle-income consumers (the next 40 percent of the population), only rice and sweet potatoes are normal, with positive elasticities for both urban

TABLE 3.6. *Measured Own-Price Elasticities, 1976*

Staple	Urban	Rural
Rice	−0.484	−0.839
Fresh cassava	0.441	−0.813
Gaplek	−[a]	−1.855
Corn	−[a]	1.029[b]

SOURCE: Dixon [40].
[a]Equations not estimated because of insignificant levels of consumption.
[b]Not significant at the 5 percent level.

TABLE 3.7. *Expenditure Elasticity of Demand for Staple Foods, by Expenditure Group, 1976*

	Expenditure group			Weighted average
	Low	Medium	High	
Expenditure elasticities, rural				
Rice	0.780	0.491	0.159	0.564
Fresh cassava	0.744	0.133	−0.569	0.286
Gaplek	0.574	−0.970	−2.745	−0.582
Corn[a]	−0.547	−0.547	−0.547	−0.547
Sweet potato	1.390	0.417	−0.701	0.662
Expenditure elasticities, urban				
Rice	0.338	0.166	−0.043	0.166
Fresh cassava	0.107	−0.179	−0.526	−0.179
Gaplek	_[b]	_[b]	_[b]	
Corn	_[b]	_[b]	_[b]	
Sweet potato	0.487	0.013	−0.563	0.013
Susenas income group classifications				
Rural	1–3	4–6	7–10	
Urban	1–5	6–8	9–10	
Total expenditure ranges (Rp/capita/month)				
Rural	0–2,999	3,000–5,999	>6,000	
Urban	0–4,999	5,000–9,999	>10,000	
Percent of population				
Rural	53.0%	38.0%	9.0%	
Urban	45.9	37.1	17.0	
Average expenditures (Rp/capita/month)				
Rural	2,095	4,077	8,759	3,449
Urban	3,429	6,975	16,532	6,972

SOURCE: Data from Indonesia [75], Susenas V survey. Elasticities calculated from consumption function estimates reported in Dixon [40], Tables 20 and 21.

[a]Estimated from a log-linear equation.

[b]Equations not estimated because consumption insignificant.

and rural consumers. Finally, among high-income consumers only rice is normal and that only among rural consumers. These estimates imply a different view of the aggregate elasticity than that suggested by earlier formulations.

Calculation of aggregate elasticities by income groups requires both the individual commodity elasticities and the consumption levels for each commodity in each income group. In 1976, for example, average annual per capita consumption of fresh cassava in rural areas was 25.0 kilograms. The log-quadratic consumption function implies that rural low-income consumers averaged 21.9 kilograms per capita, medium-income consumers averaged 29.3 kilograms, and high-income consumers averaged 24.8 kilograms. These levels, when weighted by the relevant population shares, give the average per capita consumption of 25.0 kilograms.

Levels of consumption of each cassava product for each income group in both urban and rural areas are shown in Tables 3.8 and 3.9. These levels are derived from the weighted average per capita consumption levels (right-hand column in each table), which are those reported in the 1976 survey for both fresh cassava and gaplek. The reported figures for cassava starch (rural, 6.9 kilograms; urban, 0.7 kilograms) have been inflated to account for starch consumed as processed or prepared goods for which no direct data were available. The expenditure elasticity for starch was assumed in these derivations to be + 1.0 for all income groups, a conservative estimate based on the results for krupuk discussed earlier.

The variation in consumption levels between income groups is significant and mirrors the changes in the estimated elasticities. For example, fresh cassava consumption increased from low- to medium-income consumers, and the expenditure elasticities are both positive. However, for high-income consumers, the expenditure elasticity is negative and average consumption levels are lower. These consumption levels imply expenditure elasticities for all cassava as follows:

	Low Income	*Medium Income*	*High Income*
Rural	0.694	− 0.070	0.008
Urban	0.333	0.334	0.530

Among low-income consumers, cassava is a normal good. Among rural consumers, the aggregate elasticities decline significantly as incomes increase, the effect of sharply decreasing gaplek consumption among rural medium-income consumers. A decline in the aggregate urban elasticity would have been noted if gaplek had been a significant consumption item for these consumers. Finally, in both cases, aggregate elasticity increases for the high-income consumers with the increased share of starch in total cassava consumption.

Projections

The detailed estimates of expenditure and price elasticities are useful in evaluating the effects of policy options for the cassava economy on Java. Four are considered in Tables 3.8 and 3.9. First, per

TABLE 3.8. *Cassava Consumption at Various Price and Income Levels, Rural Java*
(kg/capita/year)

| | Expenditure group | | | | | | Weighted average per capita | |
| | Low | | Medium | | High | | | |
	Change	Level	Change	Level	Change	Level	Change	Level
Initial consumption levels[a]								
Fresh cassava		21.9		29.3		24.8		25.0
Gaplek		27.2		23.8		5.8		24.0
Starch		7.3		14.2		30.5		12.0
Total		56.4		67.3		61.1		61.0
All incomes increased 20 percent								
Fresh cassava	3.3	25.2	0.8	30.1	-2.8	22.0	1.8	26.8
Gaplek	3.2	30.4	-4.6	19.2	-3.2	2.6	-0.4	23.6
Starch	1.5	8.8	2.8	17.0	6.1	36.6	2.4	14.4
Total	8.0	64.4	-1.0	66.3	0.1	61.2	3.8	64.8
Incomes increased 40 percent for low group only								
Fresh cassava	6.5	28.4	0.0	29.3	0.0	24.8	3.5	28.5
Gaplek	6.2	33.4	0.0	23.8	0.0	5.8	3.3	27.3
Starch	2.9	10.2	0.0	14.2	0.0	30.5	2.1	14.1
Total	15.6	72.0	0.0	67.3	0.0	61.1	8.9	69.9
All cassava prices reduced 10 percent								
Fresh cassava	1.8	23.7	2.4	31.7	2.0	26.8	2.0	27.0
Gaplek	5.0	32.2	4.4	28.2	1.1	6.9	4.4	28.4
Starch	0.6	7.9	1.1	15.3	2.4	32.9	0.9	12.9
Total	7.4	63.8	7.9	75.2	5.5	66.6	7.3	68.3
All cassava prices reduced 30 percent								
Fresh cassava	5.4	27.3	7.2	36.5	6.0	30.8	6.1	31.1
Gaplek	15.0	42.2	13.2	37.0	3.3	9.1	13.2	37.2
Starch	1.8	9.1	3.4	17.6	7.3	37.8	2.9	14.9
Total	22.2	78.6	23.8	91.1	16.6	77.7	22.2	83.2

SOURCES: Data from Indonesia [75], Susenas V survey, and expenditure (group) and price elasticities reported in Table 3.7.

[a]Annual averages from the 1976 survey, except for starch, which has been inflated from the survey average (6.9) to reflect its use in baked goods. Consumption levels for each expenditure group have been derived from an overall average consistent with the log quadratic functional specification. Expenditure elasticity of starch is assumed to be +1.0.

TABLE 3.9. *Changes in Cassava Consumption Under Alternative Income and Price Changes, Urban Java*
(kg/capita/year)

| | Expenditure group | | | | | | Weighted average per capita | |
| | Low | | Medium | | High | | | |
	Change	Level	Change	Level	Change	Level	Change	Level
Initial consumption levels[a]								
Fresh cassava		7.4		7.2		5.3		7.0
Starch		2.5		5.0		11.9		5.0
Total		9.9		12.2		17.2		12.0
All incomes increased 20 percent								
Fresh cassava	0.2	7.6	−0.3	6.9	−0.6	4.7	−0.1	6.9
Starch	0.5	2.3	1.0	4.6	2.4	14.3	0.9	5.9
Total	0.7	9.9	0.7	11.5	1.8	19.0	0.8	12.8
Incomes increased 40 percent for low group only								
Fresh cassava	0.3	7.7	0.0	7.2	0.0	5.3	0.1	7.1
Starch	1.0	2.8	0.0	5.0	0.0	11.9	0.5	5.5
Total	1.3	10.5	0.0	12.2	0.0	17.2	0.6	12.6
All cassava prices decreased 10 percent[b]								
Fresh cassava	0.3	7.7	0.3	7.5	0.2	5.5	0.3	7.3
Starch	0.2	2.7	0.4	5.4	1.0	12.9	0.2	5.4
Total	0.5	10.4	0.7	12.9	1.2	18.4	0.5	12.7
All cassava prices decreased 30 percent								
Fresh cassava	0.9	8.3	0.9	8.1	0.6	5.9	0.8	7.8
Starch	0.6	3.1	1.2	6.2	2.9	14.8	1.2	6.2
Total	1.5	11.4	2.1	14.3	3.5	20.7	2.0	14.0

SOURCES: Data from Indonesia [75], Susenas V survey, and expenditure (group) and price elasticities reported in Table 3.7. Reported urban starch consumption of 0.7 in 1976 inflated to account for consumption in prepared foods.

[a]Annual averages from the 1976 survey, except for starch, which has been inflated from the survey average of 0.7 to reflect its use in baked goods. Consumption levels for each expenditure group have been derived from an overall average consistent with the log quadratic functional specification. Expenditure elasticity of starch is assumed to be + 1.0.
[b]Price elasticity of fresh cassava is set at − 0.4.

capita incomes are assumed to increase 20 percent.[12] Second, the incomes of only those consumers in the lowest income groups are allowed to increase—this time by 40 percent. Roughly 50 percent of the population is in the low-income group; therefore, this option represents an extreme "basic-needs" approach, with all income growth concentrated among the poorest consumers. Third, cassava prices are decreased 10 percent. Finally, prices of cassava products are decreased 30 percent. These last two price options bracket the probable effects of the potential 30 percent cost reduction in cassava production discussed in Chapter 2 and possible changes in European policy reviewed in Chapter 7.

In all four projections, total cassava consumption increases for both urban and rural consumers. This result is particularly important for the two income-change examples shown in Tables 3.8 and 3.9. With aggregate elasticities estimated to be near zero, previous studies suggested that cassava consumption would be unaffected by income changes. Disaggregation by group-specific consumption levels and elasticities shows that this conclusion may not be correct. Much of the total increase in consumption can be attributed to increased consumption of all cassava compounds by low-income consumers and to higher-income consumers' increased starch consumption, which more than offset declines in consumption of cassava in other forms. The former demand-for-calories effect is particularly clear when the income change is concentrated among the poorest consumers. In response to a uniform 20 percent change in incomes, for example, both rural and urban consumption of cassava would increase by about 6 percent. When a 40 percent income rise is concentrated among the poorest half of the population, cassava consumption would increase 15 percent in rural areas and 5 percent in urban ones. Tables 3.8 and 3.9 also show a similar sensitivity to changes in relative prices. Should cassava prices fall by 30 percent, domestic consumption would increase by about 36 percent in rural areas and by 17 percent in urban ones. The principal increases would be from expanded gaplek consumption in rural areas and from more starch use in the cities.

Although provocative, these results should be interpreted with care. For example, the effects of income changes are measured as-

[12] Under this option, average per capita incomes would be Rp 3,892 per month—an overall 13 percent growth, not quite the implied 20 percent. The difference stems from applying percentage changes to disparate income levels.

suming the elasticities are constant within income groups, although they are allowed to vary between income groups. Although this may be appropriate for relatively small changes in incomes, changes of 20 and 40 percent are not marginal changes.[13] Similarly, the present analysis used price elasticities estimated as constant over all income groups. There are both theoretical (Timmer [138]) and empirical (Timmer and Alderman [139]) reasons to suspect that the true price elasticities vary by income class. Finally, although the underlying analysis permitted average consumption levels to vary among regions, such variation was not permitted in estimating price and income elasticities.

Even with these caveats, however, the results in Tables 3.8 and 3.9 are important, especially the calculations showing change in income. Several previous analyses have concluded that cassava consumption was not responsive, in the aggregate, to income changes, since estimated average income elasticities were close to zero. These estimates are generally corroborated by this study.[14] This analysis also shows, however, the dangers of using average results for policy analysis when significant subgroup variation is expected. Total consumption of cassava will vary with changes in income, and the variations are more pronounced when the income change is concentrated among the lower-income, more responsive consumers.

New Product Forms

Changing economic parameters will clearly affect cassava consumption from month to month and year to year. These changes represent movements along a given demand curve. The possibility of shifting the demand curve to the right is also an intriguing prospect, especially in the long run. Development of new food uses or new forms of existing cassava foods would be especially important if the products could be produced in villages, could be stored, and were income elastic. If these attributes were combined with a reasonable price and attractive packaging, it would be possible to develop significant new markets for cassava products in both urban and rural areas.

---

[13] In this case, the derived consumption changes are somewhat overstated because of the difference in curvature between a constant-elasticity Engel curve and one that is log-quadratic within the income groups.

[14] The comparison would be closer if starch consumption, which is generally not included in other analyses, were excluded in the calculation of aggregate elasticities here.

Gaplek Flour

At present gaplek is usually sold in dried, sliced-root form in rural markets. The roots are then pounded by hand to produce flour, which is in turn made into *tiwul* or other products for consumption. There is some commercial production of gaplek flour (or cassava flour) for commercial baking, but the distribution system for gaplek flour is limited. Since gaplek flour has roughly the same caloric content as the other staples and could be processed, packaged in plastic bags, and sold for 40 to 60 percent of the cost of rice or wheat flour, it might be possible to expand rural and urban markets for this cheap source of calories. Key factors in the success of such an attempt would be attractive packaging and uniform, clean appearance of the product, which might offset the negative connotations associated with gaplek in its traditional forms. Gaplek flour may also be substituted for starch in some uses.

Admixtures

The addition of gaplek flour or cassava starch to wheat or rice flour might expand the use of existing cassava products.[15] Extensive experiments have tested admixture ratios and the quality of the finished products. The nutritional value of the admixture can be maintained or improved if a protein supplement (such as soy flour) is also added (Crabtree, Kramer, and Baldry [27], [28]; Crabtree and James [26a]; Nout [111]). It was once believed that a maximum 10 percent admixture of cassava with wheat flour was possible; at higher levels problems developed with the quality of the bread. Recently, however, much higher admixture ratios have proved possible by supplementing the gluten of wheat flour with other chemical binders. One common binder is glyceral monostearate (GMS), a substance made from glycerol and lard or a hardened vegetable oil (Jones and Akinrele [90]).

Indonesian bakers already mix gaplek flour with wheat and rice flour to a limited extent. With wheat grain imports of about one million tons a year resulting in approximately 750,000 tons of wheat flour, a 10 percent admixture would require 75,000 tons of gaplek flour or about 200,000 tons of fresh roots. It could result in cheaper breads, cakes, cookies, and noodles. Since these are all goods with

[15] An extensive literature exists on admixture technology (Tropical Products Institute [143], [144]; Dendy and Kasasian [37]) and on the manufacture of *gari* and *farinha de mandioca* (Kaplinsky [93]; Jones and Akinrele [90]; Baumer [9]; Hoopes [67]; Levi and Oruche [96]).

positive income elasticities and negative own-price elasticities of demand, a decline in price will lead to increased demand and, indirectly, increased demand for fresh roots.

Gari and Farinha de Mandioca

The search for new forms in which cassava can be consumed in Indonesia has focused on a cassava product widely consumed in Brazil and (in slightly different form) in West Africa. Known as *farinha de mandioca* in Brazil and *gari* in West Africa, this product is prepared by peeling and washing the roots, grating them into a pulpy mash, squeezing this to expel the juices, fermenting the resulting pulp for several days (for gari), and toasting it on heated plates.[16] The end product can be stored for several weeks and can be eaten dry, mixed into soups or stews, or made into a paste without further cooking to make an instant porridge. The product is lightweight, easy to prepare, and cheap. Tiwul, which resembles the synthetic rice developed in India, has some of the same attributes. Consumer acceptance trials of all these products would be worthwhile. All can be made in the villages with simple equipment.

Although these new food uses are appealing, none is as easy to implement as the admixture of gaplek flour with wheat flour. Brazil, for example, has had a law for many years that requires a 10 percent cassava flour admixture. The widespread introduction and acceptance of totally new forms of consumption (such as gari or farinha) will require greater concern with food and feeding by the government or a large private organization.

Summary

This chapter has shown the importance of cassava and cassava products in the diets of both urban and rural residents of Java. Urban demand is small and mostly for fresh roots, starch, and starch-based products; virtually no gaplek is eaten in urban areas. Rural demand per capita is about six times the demand in urban areas and is divided among three main product forms: fresh roots (about 40 percent), gaplek (about 40 percent), and starch and starch-based products (the remaining 20 percent).

Major differences are observed among rural regions and by season. Much more cassava is consumed in the upland areas of Java and

---

[16] The process is much the same as in making tapioca.

in those lowland areas where irrigation is difficult. People in West Java and on Madura rely heavily on fresh roots, whereas others eat a more equal combination of fresh roots and gaplek. The form of cassava consumption frequently reflects the harvest schedule of cassava and whether a substitute staple such as rice or corn is available at low prices.

Changes in demand for cassava will depend in part on changes in economic variables. Analysis indicates that a uniform rise in income across income groups will lead to some increase in per capita cassava consumption. The increase would come from more fresh-root and starch demand among middle- and upper-income consumers and from more gaplek consumption by poor consumers in rural areas. Major decreases in the relative price of cassava would likely lead to substantial increases in rural consumption of gaplek and to significant increases of fresh-root and starch demand in both rural and urban areas. In the longer run, new food uses for cassava roots or cassava products also hold some promise for expanding the domestic demand for cassava on Java.

4. Starch

Gerald C. Nelson

This chapter and the next deal with international trade and the domestic costs of making the two major cassava products—starch and gaplek products. Together, these chapters have three main goals: first, to convey an understanding of the world markets and of international price formation for these products; second, to describe the role of the processing industry in linking world and domestic markets; and third, to analyze the effects of government policy on the choice of technique and the utilization of domestic resources in processing.

If only a small portion of the potential for increasing cassava yields on Java is realized, farmers will have more cassava for sale (see Chapter 2). Domestic consumers, however, will probably not absorb all of the increased supplies even with substantial price declines, as shown in Chapter 3. The profitability of yield-increasing innovations, therefore, depends in large part on world markets for exported cassava products and on the capacity of domestic firms to process additional quantities of cassava.

During the 1970's, gaplek chips and pellets were exported from Indonesia in every year, whereas starch was exported in six years and imported in four. Because domestic markets for fresh roots, starch, and gaplek are linked by a reasonably efficient marketing system, export prices put a floor under domestic prices. During most of the 1970's, domestic cassava prices were at the floor (this is discussed in Chapter 6). In periods of food shortages, however, starch imports acted as a ceiling on domestic cassava prices. Understanding the determinants of world prices for cassava products is thus essential to an explanation of domestic price movements.

Historical Perspective

Before the Second World War, Indonesia (then the Netherlands East Indies) was by far the world's greatest exporter of processed cassava (Table 4.1). Its only rivals were Malaya, with exports of about

TABLE 4.1. *Annual Exports of Cassava Products, Indonesia,*
1925–40 and 1950–80
(000 tons)

Year	Gaplek	Starch	Year	Gaplek	Starch
1925	56	108	1957	43	–
1926	55	101	1958	21	1
1927	123	123	1959	145	1
1928	341	164	1960	102	3
1929	127	143	1961	80	–
1930	44	91	1962	6	3
1931	73	120	1963	94	7
1932	122	104	1964	n.a.	–
1933	48	124	1965	156	1
1934	32	113	1966	176	–
1935	41	116	1967	141	1
1936	108	177	1968	160	1
1937	194	223	1969	286	2
1938	106	157	1970	332	1.0
1939	65	221	1971	458	1.3
1940	44	194	1972	342	1.1
			1973	75	1.3
1950	71	18	1974	394	7.5
1951	76	24	1975	303	0.1
1952	–	–	1976	149	5.8
1953	21	11	1977	183	0.0
1954	141	3	1978	308	0.0
1955	174	8	1979	710	1.0
1956	17	1	1980	386	–

SOURCES: 1925–40, Dutch East Indies Statistical Dep't, *Exports of Agricultural Products* (annual); 1950–60, Indonesia, Central Bureau of Statistics, *Monthly Survey* (6/1958, 10–11/1960, 6/1961); 1961–80, Indonesia [71], [77].
NOTE: Starch includes tapioca flour, pearl, seed, flakes, and siftings. Gaplek may sometimes include ampas.

30,000 tons of starch, and Madagascar, with 30,000 to 35,000 tons of gaplek. Brazilian exports—all starch—varied from 5,000 to 15,000 tons (Scheltema [125]). Gaplek, then as now, went almost entirely to Western Europe to be used as animal feed. The principal market for cassava starch was the United States, which took one-half to three-fourths of the total exports of starch and tapioca.

In the 1970's, Indonesia remained Southeast Asia's largest producer of cassava, but it was no longer the largest exporter, that role having been usurped by Thailand. The Japanese occupation of the islands and the war for independence from 1945 to 1949 had stopped Indonesia's exports of cassava products, and it was not until the early 1950's that small amounts of Javanese starch again appeared on world markets. In the interval, Thailand filled the vacuum. Thai starch exports reached 30,000 tons in 1955 and 170,000 tons by 1970, peaking in 1976 at 241,000 tons (including 64,000 tons to Indonesia) (Table

TABLE 4.2. *World Exports of Cassava Starch and Starch Products, 1956–78*
(000 tons)

Years	Indonesia[a]	Thailand	Brazil	Malagasy Rep.	Malaysia[b]
1956–60[c]	1.3	117.0	20.2	8.9	14.5
1961–65[c]	2.8	152.0	16.7	7.2[d]	29.0[e]
1966–70[c]	1.2	158.0	–	0.4	20.0
1971–75[c]	2.3	169.5	29.3[f]	0.4	–
1976	5.8	241.2	1.8	0.1	28.8
1977	–	202.5	2.0	0.1	–
1978	0.3	235.0	4.2	–	6.4

SOURCE: National trade statistics for the countries included. Data for Indonesia from [77], 1956–78.
[a]Net exports.
[b]Excludes sago exports averaging about 2,000 tons per annum that may contain some starch products.
[c]Five-year average. [d]1960–64. [e]1962–65. [f]1972–75.

4.2). Thai gaplek exports increased 40 percent a year during the 1970's to a 1978 peak of 6 million tons.

The growth of Indonesia's population and income led to increased domestic demand for starch, and shortfalls in domestic production in the mid-1970's pushed prices up enough to make Indonesia a net importer. Imports reached a high of 64,000 tons in 1976. Domestic starch production, primarily in large mills built in Lampung (Sumatra), grew rapidly after 1976, and starch exports were resumed in 1979. In late 1982 and 1983, Indonesia imported sizable quantities of starch to make up for shortfalls in domestic starch production resulting from an increase in consumption of fresh roots and gaplek as food and the destruction of processing capacity by the eruption of Galunggung volcano.

Cassava and the World Starch Market

The greatest part of the world's starch requirements is supplied by corn and potatoes, with cassava a distant third (Table 4.3). Smaller amounts come from wheat, rice, and sago. Since the Second World War, characteristics of the natural starches have become less important with the rapid development of methods for modifying them.[1] Cassava starch, therefore, no longer enjoys sheltered markets of any size and must compete in price and quality with corn and potato starches.[2] To the extent that steady supplies of cassava starch can be

[1] For detailed accounts of the various methods of modifying starches, see Whistler and Paschall, eds. [160], vol. 2.
[2] Cassava starch still has a special place in Java, where it is the major ingredient of *krupuk*, a snack food. Indonesia exported about 1,000 tons of krupuk to Holland in 1980 (Indonesia [72]).

TABLE 4.3. *Estimated Average Annual Production of Corn, Potato, and Cassava Starches, by Major Producers*
(ooo tons)

Producer	Cornstarch[a]	Potato starch[b]	Cassava starch[b]
United States	4,000	–	0
Japan	720	160	0
European Community	2,200	909	0
Soviet Union	700	270	0
Thailand	–	0	400
Indonesia	0	0	660·

SOURCE: JETRO [87].
[a]Estimates for an average year between 1972 and 1975.
[b]Author's estimates for 1980.

marketed at competitive prices, it will probably share in the expanding world market for starch and its derivatives.

In addition to its place in bakeries and in the kitchen, starch has many industrial uses. A major derivative of starch, dextrose sugar, is widely used in food processing. The most prominent nonfood uses for starch are in the manufacture of adhesives and the sizing of yarns and textiles. Starch-based adhesives are used in corrugated and layered paper and cardboard, in heavy paper bags, in laminated fiberboard, in metal face lining, and in wallpaper. Starch is also used in making paper from wood pulp and in sizing paper. Dextrines derived from starch are used as binders in an expanding variety of fields ranging from core binding in foundries to making glass fiber. In the pharmaceutical industry, starch derivatives bind and coat medicines.

In the late 1930's, cassava starch provided almost all of the adhesives used in the American plywood industry and was widely used in the textile industry. Soon, however, the development of synthetic materials (for example, synthetic yarns and threads to which starches do not adhere) reduced demand in the traditional starch markets. At the same time, the increasing importance of starch-based sugars, initially dextrose and glucose, but now fructose as well, has brought starch into direct competition with cane and beet sugar. Despite this competition, the increasing demand for sweeteners in the United States and the development of economical methods of producing fructose sugar from starch has strengthened the competitive position of starch-based sweeteners (Jones [87a]). The fructose share of corn sweeteners has grown from zero in 1965 to almost 50 percent in 1980. Almost all fructose is now made from cornstarch, but the basic process for making fructose from cassava starch is similar, and several companies are advertising equipment for that purpose. In 1982, a parastatal corporation in Indonesia began operation of a cassava-based fructose plant that is expected to produce 7,500 tons annually.[3]

There is potential demand for starch, too, as a base for the manufacture of alcohol. Rising oil prices during the 1970's prompted additional interest in alcohol as a fuel, either alone or blended with gasoline. Although alcohol is much more expensive as a fuel than oil-based products at 1980 prices, a number of governments are subsidizing the production of alcohol from corn or sugarcane for use as a partial replacement for gasoline (Barzelay and Pearson [8]; World Bank [165]). It seems unlikely, however, that large quantities of cassava will be used for alcohol production in the near future unless the world price of petroleum rises rapidly and the costs of cassava-based alcohol are greatly decreased. Small amounts of alcohol might be produced economically from cassava, however, in remote areas where petroleum products are expensive because of high transportation costs.

Cassava Starch Importers

Japan, the United States, Taiwan, and Hong Kong account for the bulk of cassava starch imports today (see Table 4.4). Japanese imports increased gradually from about 30,000 tons annually in the late 1960's to about 90,000 tons in the late 1970's. U.S. imports, by contrast, dropped from about 150,000 tons annually in the late 1960's to less than 33,000 tons in 1979. Beginning when the Second World War disrupted trade in cassava starch, American production of potato starch and cornstarch increased. The share of imported starch in apparent American consumption[4] fell from 10 percent before the war to only 6 percent by 1960 (Bachman [5]) and is even less today. Taiwan has imported a moderate amount since the early 1970's, and Hong Kong's imports have slowly increased since the late 1960's to the level of 10,000 to 15,000 tons a year.

Trade barriers limit starch imports by two of the world's largest starch consumers—Japan and the European Community. Starch imports in Japan are subject to a 25 percent ad valorem tax and to an annual import quota based on the difference between estimates of domestic demand for starch at prevailing prices and supplies of do-

[3] Personal communication from the manager.
[4] Apparent consumption is production plus imports less exports.

TABLE 4.4. *Cassava Starch Imports by Major Importers, 1971–79*
(tons)

Importer	1971	1973	1975	1977	1978	1979
United States	82,564	64,341	38,422	37,641	35,057	32,886
Japan	46,952	71,799	71,105	94,206	90,622	69,355[a]
Taiwan[b]	–	12,642	65	11,921	15,159	–
Hong Kong	5,700	8,929	13,840	10,322[c]	14,454	11,162

SOURCE: National trade statistics for the countries included.
[a]Includes 10,326 tons from Indonesia, the first imports from Indonesia of the decade.
[b]Net imports of starch and starch products—classification codes BTN1106 and 190410.
[c]January through November only.

mestically produced potato starch and cornstarch (JETRO [87]).[5] In the European Community, a variable levy on starch imports set at 161 percent of the corn levy stops all but very small imports of cassava starch.[6] Trade barriers in these and other large potential markets have reduced the demand for internationally traded starch and increased the likelihood of price fluctuations. As a result, cassava starch is imported only to meet either residual demand after domestic supplies are used (as in the Japanese market) or specialized needs (as in Europe and to some extent the United States). In the long run, however, increased demand for starchy feedstuffs is likely to have a positive effect on international cassava starch markets by bidding up the world prices for other starch-containing commodities. The potential for new products made from cassava starch, especially fructose, also appears promising and should expand world demand.

Cassava Starch Manufacture

Cassava starch making, one of Indonesia's oldest industries, was well established by the early 1900's. Because starch making requires a plentiful supply of clean water, many starch mills were located in the hills. Several large estates on Java grew cassava and made starch for export (Brautlecht [16]), and numerous village factories produced starch for both export and domestic consumption.

The industry was severely damaged during the Second World War and the Indonesian war for independence. The large cassava plantations were expropriated, the land used for other crops, and the pro-

[5]Japanese corn imports depend on the political strength of the cornstarch and sweetener industry versus that of the potato farmers.
[6]The starch levy was implemented primarily to protect potato growers and starch firms located in depressed regions. For further discussion of European agricultural policies, see Chapter 5.

TABLE 4.5. *Number of Indonesian Starch-Making Firms by Location, 1974*

Province	Household	Small	Medium and large
West Java	1,671	246	90
Central Java	2,071	195	29
Yogyakarta	300	180	13
East Java	300	180	13
Lampung	0	30	7
Sumatra (except Lampung)	0	162	7
Others	0	17	2

SOURCE: Indonesia [74], 1974/75, adjusted in accordance with information from regional offices and personal surveys.

cessing equipment dismantled or destroyed.[7] After 1949, the void left by the decline of the large plantations was gradually filled by village starch mills, which expanded in number and to some extent in size.[8] Before 1940, the contiguous kabupatens of Tasikmalaya and Ciamis in West Java and Cilacap in Central Java were an important center of village starch production. After independence, starch making expanded there, and entrepreneurs from the region set up mills in other parts of West Java, on the north coast of Central Java near Pati, and in Kediri and Malang kabupatens in East Java.

The Distribution of Starch Production in Indonesia

Approximately 17 percent of the cassava grown in Indonesia was used in starch production in 1974/75, and that amount increased to more than 25 percent in 1979. Almost all Indonesian starch is made in Java and Sumatra (Table 4.5). In 1974/75, the year of the latest Industrial Census,[9] West Java led Indonesian starch production. Approximately 40 percent of the fresh roots harvested in West Java were made into starch in 1974 and almost 60 percent in 1979. Central Java ranked second in starch output in 1974 and third in 1979. The starch industry's share of cassava production there has remained fairly stable at 23 percent. In East Java, by contrast, the proportion of cassava processed into starch is low—only 5 percent in 1974 and 7 percent in 1979—and mills are primarily in Kediri and Malang kabupatens. Lampung province, across the Sunda Strait from West Java in south-

[7] One of the estates became a seed-multiplication station operated by the Ministry of Agriculture, and the buildings of another are used for a munitions factory.

[8] Village starch production refers to processing by "household," "small," and "medium" mills. Although these terms usually refer to mill capacity, they correspond closely to Central Bureau of Statistics classifications according to the number of employees: "household" mills employ fewer than five workers; "small" mills employ from 5 to 19 workers; "medium" mills employ 20 to 99 workers; and "large" mills employ 100 or more workers.

[9] Annual Industrial Surveys are more up-to-date, but do not present information on household and small mills.

TABLE 4.6. *Estimated Starch Production in Indonesia*
(tons)

Location	Starch[a] 1974	Starch[a] 1979	Fresh root equivalent 1974	Fresh root equivalent 1979
West Java	188,220	239,220	941,100	1,196,100
Central Java	126,020	149,180	630,100	745,900
East Java	33,300	57,780	166,500	288,900
Java total	347,540	446,180	1,737,700	2,230,900
Lampung (S. Sumatra)	27,750	150,750	138,750	753,750
North Sumatra	15,900	24,100	318,000	120,500
Riau	30,900	30,900[b]	154,500	154,500[b]
Other provinces	9,600	9,600[b]	48,000	48,000[b]
Total Indonesia	431,690	661,530	2,158,450	3,307,650

SOURCES: Indonesia [74], 1974/75, 1976, 1977, 1978; Ministry of Agriculture figures; and information from interviews and field visits. Sources are not consistent, and these results represent an attempt to select the numbers consistent with field observations.
[a]Generally, the production figures are derived by multiplying the number of mills of a particular size by an estimate of the quantity of starch produced by a firm of that size. Household mills are assumed to produce 200 kilograms of starch a day, 100 days a year. Small mills produce 3 tons of starch a day, 100 days a year. Medium and large mills produce 6 tons of starch a day, 150 days a year. Specific information on quantity produced was used where available, for example in Lampung for the large firms.
[b]No information is available on 1979 production, and it is assumed to be identical with 1974 production in calculating totals.

ern Sumatra, increased its starch production enormously in the 1970's. This increase occurred largely as a result of the doubling of root production betweeen 1974 and 1979, but also as a consequence of an increase in the share of cassava processed into starch from about 20 percent of the root crop to 70 percent (Table 4.6).

Almost all the cassava starch produced in Indonesia is consumed domestically, but little information on its end uses is collected. Field observations and discussions with industry officials indicate that kru-puk makers buy the largest share, perhaps as much as 65 percent annually (or around 430,000 tons, using 1979 production figures). Other food-processing firms probably buy about 15 percent (100,000 tons) for cookies and other snack foods. Textile manufacturers use about 10 percent (66,000 tons) annually, and glucose production, which grew rapidly from 1975 to 1980, probably uses 3 percent (20,000 tons). Direct household consumption and exports account for the remaining 7 percent.

Techniques of Starch Production in Indonesia

Three basic operations are performed to extract starch from cassava roots. First, peeled and washed roots are grated, releasing starch particles from the cells. This produces a mash or pulp containing starch and fiber. Next, the fibrous residue is filtered out, leaving a milky liquid containing the starch and wash water. Finally, the water is removed, either by allowing the starch to settle out and dry in the sun, or by centrifuging and heating. In Indonesia, these operations are performed differently in household, medium-scale, and automated large-scale starch mills.[10]

Household Production. With the very important exception of grating, which is now done mechanically, household starch making on Java has probably not changed much in 80 years. Freshly harvested roots arrive early in the day and are peeled, often by children or old women. The peelings—some 20 percent or more of the weight of the fresh roots—are sometimes fed to animals, and a household may process as much as 4,000 kilograms of fresh roots a day. Grating was formerly the most physically demanding part of the process, but now graters are almost always powered by a 3 to 7 horsepower portable diesel or gasoline motor. Freshly peeled cassava is forced between a rotating drum (mounted with rasping blades) and an opposing wall.[11] After grating, the mash is carried to the filtering equipment, which consists of a stand for the filter cloth and a number of clay pots or wooden boxes to catch the starch-bearing water. A few kilograms of the mash are placed in the cloth, water is added, and the mixture is agitated by hand. One or two women work at each filter stand, and each can filter the mash from 100 kilograms of fresh roots in about one hour. The work is almost always done by women, either family members or hired laborers. The starch water is sometimes refiltered to remove impurities, then allowed to settle overnight. The next morning the water is drawn off and the starch is removed from the bottom of the pot or box, broken up into small lumps, and placed on a bamboo mat in the sun to dry. If the weather is good, the starch will dry to about 14 percent moisture content within two days. If the weather is cloudy or rainy, more drying time is required and quality deteriorates because of microbial activity. Starch that has not dried within five days is of very poor quality.

Medium-Scale Production. The techniques of production used by medium-scale firms, which have an average daily processing capacity of 10 to 50 tons of fresh roots, also have changed little over the last 50

[10] See Grace [59] and Halleman and Aten [63] for extensive discussions of the technical aspects of starch processing.
[11] Variations include the use of an aluminum sheet around the drum with sharp-edged nail holes and a wooden drum with protruding nail points.

years.[12] Fresh roots are bought locally, either whole or already peeled by household labor, and brought to the factory in trucks. If whole roots are bought, women are hired to peel them at the factory. Next the roots are washed mechanically (a wooden screw drives them through a water bath), and then they are conveyed manually or mechanically to the rasper, a larger version of the drum used by household mills. The rasper is driven by the same diesel engine that powers all other operations.

After the mash leaves the rasper, it is filtered. The starch water that results then flows through a preliminary sedimentation area to remove heavy nonstarch particles and on into the main part of the settling tray, sometimes called the table. As the water flows along the tray, starch particles gradually settle out. At the end of the tray, the water is drained off, usually into a nearby river. Heavier starch particles settle out first, and grades of starch are identified by particle size and purity. After the starch settles, it is scraped up and carried to the drying area, broken into small lumps on drying mats, and placed in the sun.[13] This work and the unloading and carrying of fresh roots are the most labor-intensive parts of the medium-scale starch-making operation. They are usually done by women, who are paid according to the amount of starch they dry.

After sun drying, the output from household and medium-scale mills is a coarse, lumpy powder that must be ground and sifted (bolted) for most uses.[14] It is usually sent to a bolting mill that uses a disintegrater (a mechanical beater) to break up the lumps, producing powder that is passed through a fine mesh and bagged.

Large-Scale Automated Production. Large-scale, fully automated starch processing was introduced in Indonesia in 1975 and is responsible for the rapid growth of starch production in Lampung since 1976. In 1980, six plants using Thai equipment and having capacities of 40 or more tons of starch a day (200 tons of unpeeled roots) were in operation there (and a seventh was under construction). By 1980 also, three firms in East Java, using equipment designed in and imported from Taiwan, each had a capacity of about 30 tons of starch a day.

---

[12] Descriptions from the 1930's are still accurate. See Brautlecht [16].

[13] If the weather is not good or the available drying space is in use, wet starch is placed in a large cement collecting tank. According to starch makers, if covered with a plastic sheet to reduce exposure to the air, wet starch can be stored for one to three weeks without significant deterioration.

[14] Village krupuk makers, however, sometimes use coarse starch.

The Taiwanese and the Thai equipment process cassava similarly except at the stage where water is initially removed from the starch. With the Taiwanese equipment, settling trays similar to those used in medium-scale firms provide a preliminary reduction in water content. The Thai equipment uses a centrifuge for this purpose. In both methods, the moist starch is then "flash-dried"—lifted on a column of hot air that evaporates the water and allows the dry, finely powdered starch to fall back to be bagged. With Taiwanese equipment the entire process takes about five hours; with Thai equipment it takes only one. Both methods produce a uniform, pure starch.

Starch Quality

The quality of cassava starch is adversely affected by bacterial and particulate contamination of the wash water. Firms that use river water rather than well water often need water purification equipment to produce good starch. Sulfur dioxide or other bleaching chemicals are sometimes added to inhibit bacterial action and increase the whiteness of the starch. (To ensure whiteness, processing equipment is made of materials other than iron, because the hydrocyanic acid present in fresh cassava reacts with iron to produce gray or blue colors.) Starch can also be ruined by slow drying. The effect of clouds or rain on sun-dried starch has already been noted, but dust is also a problem because particles can be blown into starch drying outdoors. Indeed, the eruptions of the Galunggung volcano in 1982 stopped all production of sun-dried starch in West Java.

In general, starches from household and medium-scale mills vary greatly with water quality and weather conditions. The automated starch factories produce a more uniform product because of the speed of the process and the use of flash drying. Nonetheless, some processors claim that krupuk made only from flash-dried starch is inferior because it does not expand as well when fried.

Costs and Returns in Processing of Cassava Starch

Starch mills vary widely in their output, not only because they differ in size but also because the number of days a year they are in operation differs greatly. For example, a medium-scale mill may produce as much starch in a year as 50 household mills—or a large factory 800 times annually as much as a household. Table 4.7 details the costs and returns for the three different levels of starch production.

Comparison of unit costs of the three methods of making starch in-

TABLE 4.7. *Annual Output and Return of Starch Mills by Size and Type*

	Household	Medium	Bolting	Large
Output (*tons*)	12	500	3,960	8,298
Input (*tons*)	60	2,500	4,000	37,555
Invested capital (*million Rp*)	0.1	15	115	879
Operating costs and returns (*million Rp*)				
Revenues				
Starch	1.6	68	634	1,489
By-product (ampas)	0.2	9	–	41
Total revenue	1.8	77	634	1,530
Costs				
Raw materials	1.5	61	540	920
Labor	0.2	4	8	39
Fuel	–	1	3	61
Miscellaneous	–[a]	1	4	125
Taxes	–	2	38	17
Depreciation	–[a]	4	5	76
Interest paid	0	0	0	42
Total expenses	1.7	73	598	1,281
Net income	0.1	4	36	249

SOURCE: Nelson [105].
NOTE: Output of household and medium mills is coarse starch, of bolting mills and large mills fine starch. Input is fresh roots except in the case of bolting mills, where it is coarse starch. Bolting costs must be added to costs of household and medium mills for direct comparison with costs of large mills.
[a]Less than Rp 50,000.

TABLE 4.8. *Starch Processing Unit Costs and Returns*
(Rp/ton of fine starch)

	Processing technique		
	Household[a]	Medium[a]	Large
Roots	123,737	123,737	110,882
Labor	21,357	11,087	4,729
Fuel	663	3,049	7,386
Other expenses	3,661	3,156	15,045
Depreciation	2,950	8,444	9,218
Taxes	9,520	12,627	2,108
Cost of capital[b]	9,195	16,148	25,426
Total costs	171,083	178,248	174,794
Revenue	178,940	178,940	184,395
Starch	160,000	160,000	179,500
By-products	18,940	18,940	4,894
Rent	7,857	692	9,601

SOURCE: Nelson [105].
[a]Includes the costs of bolting.
[b]Private opportunity cost of capital invested in the firm, assumed to be 30 percent for the household and medium mills and 24 percent for the bolting and large-scale mills.

dicates that labor intensity per ton of starch decreases as factory size increases (Table 4.8). Fuel costs per ton also increase with firm size. Household processing uses only small amounts of fuel, in rasping and bolting, but fuel makes up 18 percent of the cost of processing in the large-scale factory, mainly because of flash drying.

Total processing and raw material costs per kilogram of starch are only 2 percent higher for the large mill and 4 percent higher for the medium-scale mills than for household mills. Taxes, however, are the lowest and rents (returns above the private opportunity cost of capital) highest for the large-scale firm because it receives exemptions from income taxes.

Government Policies

Government policies affect starch production in three principal areas: taxes, investment concessions, and fuel subsidies. Except for firms receiving tax holidays, the larger the firm, the more likely it is to pay taxes. Households usually do not pay national and provincial taxes, but operating fees undoubtedly are assessed by village officials. Medium and large starch firms must have a variety of trade and business licenses, and applications for them can attract the attention of tax collectors.[15]

Taxes actually paid by the large firm in Table 4.8, however, are much lower than taxes paid by firms using the other processing techniques. All large starch firms operating in 1980 received investment concessions consisting of duty-free imports of processing equipment and tax holidays of three to six years, which were still in effect in 1980.[16] A rough estimate of the annual value of the tax exemption for

[15] A special license is required of firms in industries such as cassava starch making that pollute the environment or otherwise disturb public well-being. After the plant is constructed, it is inspected by a team of officials from various local government offices. The certification procedure can be very time consuming and costly, although there have been recent improvements in some kabupatens.

[16] The tariff rates (import duties and import sales taxes) on imported processing equipment range from 10 to 40 percent. The rates depend on the individual items needed, which vary from plant to plant..The corporate profit tax, summarized in the following table, is between 20 and 45 percent depending on the level of profit and whether the accounts are audited.

Tax rates (percent)	Profit level (million Rp)	
	Not audited	Audited
20%	<25	<100
30	25-30	100-250
45	>30	>250

Firms that receive investment concessions must present audited accounts to the tax agency, but most other firms do not do so because they believe it is possible to negotiate lower tax payments.

the large firm in Table 4.7 is Rp 112 million (45 percent of net income). The decrease in the amount of capital needed because of the import duty and import sales tax exemptions might be as much as Rp 130 million (20 percent of the value of fixed capital). If both profits and import tax exemptions were removed, profits of the large-scale firm at 1980 prices would be somewhat less than the private opportunity cost of the capital.

The diesel fuel subsidy, roughly equal to the domestic price in 1980, also benefits starch-processing firms. Since the large processing techniques use more fuel, they benefit more from the fuel subsidy. If it were removed entirely, fuel costs of the household processing technique would increase by Rp 1.5 per kilogram of output, of the medium technique by Rp 3.0, and of the large mill by Rp 7.4.

Social Profitability

Government policies have two general effects on processing (and other economic activities). By changing the actual prices of inputs and outputs, they alter the distribution of the gains from processing and cause private and social profitability to diverge. This divergence means that some commodities are produced that are not socially profitable at the expense of others that would be socially profitable. To determine whether a processing activity should be expanded, a measure of its social profitability is needed. The measure of the domestic resource costs of foreign exchange (DRC) is defined as the ratio of the social opportunity cost of all domestic factors of production employed in the activity to the social value of the net foreign exchange earned by the activity.[17]

Formally, the domestic cost ratio is defined as:

$$DRC = \frac{\Sigma p_i Q_i}{p_1 Q_1 - \Sigma p_j Q_j},$$

where p_i is the social price of domestic factor Q_i,
p_1 the social value of output Q_1, and
p_j the social price of tradable input Q_j.

The world market provides a convenient measure of the social opportunity cost of domestic production. Most processing activities use domestic resources to make goods that can be imported or exported. An exchange rate can be associated with a particular prod-

---

[17] See Pearson, Stryker, and Humphreys [119] for an extended discussion of the DRC measure and additional references.

TABLE 4.9. *Domestic Resource Cost Ratios for Starch Making*

Type of production	DRC ratios at 1980 world prices	DRC ratios given a 10 percent decline from 1980 world prices	Break-even price decline[a]
Household	0.89	1.00	9%
Medium-scale	0.92	1.04	7
Large-scale	0.95	1.08	4

NOTE: This table assumes that a decline in the world price of starch has no effect on the social value of the cassava used in production.

[a] If the world price declined by this percentage and root prices did not change, the DRC would be equal to one.

uct; it takes a certain amount of domestic resources valued in rupiah (using social rather than private prices) to earn a dollar's worth of output. The DRC is then a ratio of the exchange rate of the product to the social exchange rate. If processing uses fewer domestic resources to earn a unit of foreign exchange than does the economy as a whole, the processing activity is socially profitable.

Household processing, with a DRC of 0.89, was somewhat more profitable than the other two levels of processing at 1980 social prices (Table 4.9). The medium-scale processing technique ranked second with a DRC of 0.92, and the DRC of the large firm was 0.95. These results are sensitive to changes in the world prices for starch. A 10 percent decline in the output price with no change in input prices makes the benefits of the household technique equivalent to the social costs (so that the DRC is 1.00), and neither medium-scale nor large-scale processing is socially profitable.[18]

Two factors not considered above increase the social profitability of the household technique. In the calculations, fresh roots are assumed to cost the same for all techniques. In fact, households often purchase roots at lower prices because they are closer to the fields and transport costs are lower. The extent of the savings varies, but it can be as much as three rupiah per kilogram of unpeeled roots. In addition, the conversion ratio used for the household and medium-scale techniques is 5 to 1, but for the large-scale technique 4.52 to 1. In practice, careful household and medium-scale processors can obtain higher yields. Thus the social profitability of the smaller processing techniques is often higher than is indicated above.

[18] In these calculations it has been assumed that the social profits earned in cassava growing and marketing are identical to the social costs. To the extent that positive net social profits are generated in these activities, the entire chain from farm to consumer has a lower DRC than that of the processing activity alone.

Labor Use

Recent discussions of industrialization strategies in Indonesia have focused on providing employment in the rural sector rather than drawing job seekers to the cities. Because starch mills are best located in the countryside, they fit nicely into such a strategy. Starch making also provides seasonal employment when other rural employment opportunities are scarce. Typically, starch making on Java starts in April or May and continues through September or October. During this period, farm work is scarce in the uplands where most processing is done; cassava is the last crop harvested, and land preparation for the next crop does not start until October or November (see Chapter 2).

Employment in the starch industry, however, depends on the processing technique used. A household starch maker uses roughly 40 days of labor to make a ton of starch, whereas medium-scale mills need only 20 days and large-scale mills less than 5. Wages comprised 12 percent of total costs in village manufacturing, 7 percent in medium-scale mills, and 3 percent in large mills. If all of the 1979 starch production had come from household mills, 26.5 million days of work or about 190,000 full-time workers during the five-month processing period would have been needed. By contrast, if all starch had been made by medium-scale mills, only 13.2 million days of work or the equivalent of 95,000 full-time workers would have been needed; and if all starch had been made by large-scale mills, only 3.3 million labor days or the equivalent of 23,000 full-time workers would have been needed. Roughly three-quarters of the workers in the household and medium-scale operations would have been women, whereas very few women would likely have been employed in the large mills. Consequently, incentives for using large or capital-intensive firms tend to reduce employment, and they especially reduce employment for women.

Growth in Household Processing

If increased employment at any cost were desirable, even more employment could be provided by returning to manual grating instead of using diesel-powered graters. The cost of the labor needed for grating, however, is approximately Rp 18 per kilogram of fine starch. By contrast, the cost of mechanical grating is only Rp 2.2. This large gap in costs is the major cause of the rapid growth of household starch manufacturing in the 1970's. Virtually without exception, small processors in East and West Java reported that the mechanized graters, first introduced between 1970 and 1975, have almost entirely displaced the older, more labor-intensive methods.[19] Owners of medium-scale firms also reported increased competition from household processing in the late 1970's.

A mechanical grater represents a major capital investment. Moreover, because it can process between six and ten tons of peeled roots a day, a substantial amount of working capital is needed to buy the roots necessary to maintain continuous operations. This is much more capital than is available to a typical household processor. Thus in order to utilize capacity more fully and spread fixed capital costs, sales of grating services, either at a central point in the village or door to door, have developed in some areas. The owner of the grater specializes in providing grating services, and households specialize in peeling, filtering, and drying. A capital-intensive innovation has thus combined with specialization in processing to make a small, marginally profitable processing activity much more profitable and to increase employment in the countryside substantially. If household processing tripled in the 1970's because of mechanical grating, the increase in employment directly attributable to mechanization is 50 percent. Mechanization of grating made household processing profitable, and the resulting growth of household processing increased the overall use of labor in making starch.

The Role of the Bolting Mill

On Java, seasonality in fresh root production hinders the development of modern factories, which need year-round supplies in order to spread large fixed capital costs. However, bolting mills provide marketing services—processing, blending, storage, and trading credits—that permit starch processing despite this seasonality. Since most starch consumers cannot use the coarse starch produced under the household and medium-scale methods without further milling, the bolting mill performs an essential function. It also buys starch of varying quality from many coarse starch producers and mixes it into a few standard blends that are marketed under a brand name. Consumers buy on the basis of the brand name and rely on a uniform product.

[19] A few households in East Java still use foot-powered pedal graters, but diesel engines of from 5 to 7 horsepower are now considered standard. Though much cheaper, 3-horsepower gasoline engines are not as popular: first, gasoline is three times as expensive as diesel fuel; and second, gasoline engines are said to wear out faster and be less reliable than diesel ones.

Bolting mills also sell to retailers on credit of 30 to 60 days, so in order to bridge the gap between the time coarse starch is purchased and payment is received from starch retailers, large amounts of working capital are needed. Working capital makes up 73 percent of the value of capital of the bolting mill in Table 4.7, compared with 18 percent for medium-sized mills and 25 percent for large mills. In essence, the bolting mill takes over the elements of processing and marketing that have economies of scale, leaving the more easily divisible processing activities to household and medium-scale mills. Without the bolting mill, much less starch would be made on Java, especially by households.

Potential Starch Demand

Although the starches produced by various types of mills are interchangeable to some extent, fairly distinct markets exist for each type in Indonesia. Sun-dried (coarse) starch contains more impurities—both particulate and bacterial—than the fine, flash-dried starch from large mills, and its chemical properties are somewhat different. The quality of sun-dried starch, however, is adequate for most domestic uses. Currently, most coarse starch is consumed by the krupuk industry, but some is also used in other food products and in the textile, paper, and glucose industries. Fine starch from the large mills can be used in all of the products mentioned above except krupuk, where it must be mixed with sun-dried starch. Some fine starch is also used in the pharmaceutical industry, and some is exported, mainly to Japan and Taiwan.

Prospects are good for the continued growth of the domestic paper and textile industries. Both industries should provide an expanding market for sun-dried starch. Consumption of processed foods using starch or starch products such as glucose and fructose is also likely to increase. Domestic production of fructose is beginning, and this industry may become a moderate user of starch if domestic sugar prices remain at high levels.

The American market for fine starch will also very likely grow, but the import restrictions of the European Community will probably not be relaxed in the near future. It may, however, be possible to expand exports to Japan as Thailand has done if special arrangements are made to protect Japanese potato growers. It seems improbable that there will be much international demand for coarse starch because of problems with its purity and quality, although high-quality krupuk could see a rapid growth in exports. Exports of high-quality starch will probably continue to increase, although perhaps not at the rapid pace of the late 1970's.

5. Gaplek

Gerald C. Nelson

One of the most interesting facets of agricultural trade during the 1970's was the large increase in imports of gaplek into the European Community (EC) for use as animal feed.[1] Imports increased from 1.3 million tons in 1971 to a peak of 6.5 million tons in 1978, only declining slightly from that level by the end of the decade. Three countries—the Netherlands, West Germany, and Belgium—accounted for 70 to 90 percent of these imports. (See Table 5.1.) To explain this growth in imports, it is necessary to understand how gaplek is used in livestock feed rations, how EC agricultural policies, especially toward grains, affect that use, and how animals and the animal feeding industry are distributed in the Community. With this information, an import demand function for gaplek can be estimated and the impact of European policies on Indonesian exports can be evaluated.

Livestock Feed Rations in Europe

Gaplek is used in the European Community as a component of compound animal feeds—a combination of ingredients designed to provide animals with an appropriate diet. Although many nutritional needs are considered when making a compound feed, energy and protein are the most important. Gaplek, with about 4,000 kilocalories per kilogram of dry matter, is an excellent energy source but contains very little protein. By contrast, the feed grains (barley, corn, wheat, oats, and sorghum) all have roughly 10 percent protein and about the same calorie content as gaplek. (See Table 5.2.) Soybean meal, which typically has about four times as much protein as feed grain for the same calorie content, can be mixed with gaplek in a ratio that provides the same nutrient value as feed grains, so that the feed compounder can use either grain or the soy-gaplek mixture depending upon relative costs. Since different species require different amounts of energy and protein, it is sometimes profitable to use gaplek in feed for one species but not for others, or to mix grain and gaplek.

[1] Early references include Phillips [121] and International Trade Center [84], [85].

TABLE 5.1. *Net Imports of Gaplek by Country, European Community,*
1971–80
(000 tons)

Country	1971	1972	1973	1974	1975
Netherlands	514	681	771	1,088	1,146
West Germany	522	429	334	431	507
Belgium and Luxembourg	274	293	204	394	480
France	38	139	159	164	147
United Kingdom	–	–	–	–	8
Italy	–	–	–	–	0
Denmark	–	–	–	–	0
Community total	1,348	1,545[a]	1,482[a]	2,121[a]	2,447

Country	1976	1977	1978	1979	1980
Netherlands	1,562	1,865	2,440	2,197	2,274
West Germany	680	959	1,482	1,480	1,464
Belgium and Luxembourg	590	704	907	870	849
France	176	203	715	571	372
United Kingdom	9	8	12	24	29
Italy	13	0	219	90	105
Denmark	8	57	127	82	55
Community total	3,243	4,032	6,461	5,877	5,613

SOURCES: 1971–74 country figures, International Trade Center [85]; 1972–74 totals and 1975–80 figures, EUROSTAT [129].
  [a]Totals reflect unspecified additional imports.

In addition to nutritional coefficients, compounders must consider technical constraints on the maximum amount of gaplek that can be used in a feed. For example, if poultry feed is more than about 15 percent gaplek, it tends to be dusty and unappetizing. Swine rations permit the highest percentage of gaplek—up to 40 percent. Cattle rations typically are limited to 15 to 25 percent, and poultry rations to 7 to 15 percent.[2] As a result, gaplek is used first in pig feeds, then in poultry, dairy, and beef-fattening rations as its price declines relative to that of grain.

Animals and Animal Feeding in the Community

The European animal population is spread widely throughout the Community, but there are several national concentrations. (See Table 5.3.) West Germany has almost one-third of the EC pigs; West Germany, France, and the United Kingdom have two-thirds of the cattle; and France, Italy, and the United Kingdom have more than

  [2]Depending on the country, these restrictions either have the force of law or are recommendations from the agriculture ministry or other agency.

TABLE 5.2. *Nutrient Values of Cassava, Soybean Meal, and Selected Feed Grains, on a Dry Matter Basis*

Feedstuff	Protein (pct.)	Digestible energy (Kcals/kg)
Cassava	2.84%	4,000
Barley	13.03	3,467
Corn, dent yellow	9.89	3,961
Wheat, soft red winter	11.86	4,254
Soybean meal, expeller	47.33	3,870

SOURCES: Cassava, Muller, Chou, and Nah [104]; other commodities, U.S. National Research Council [149].

TABLE 5.3. *Livestock in the European Community, by Country, 1978*
(000 livestock units)

Country	Pigs	Cattle	Chickens	Total[a]
Netherlands	2,295	4,158	851	7,399
West Germany	5,655	11,441	1,406	18,985
Belgium and Luxembourg	1,298	2,378	373	4,109
France	2,718	18,162	2,255	25,015
United Kingdom	1,949	10,620	1,894	16,688
Italy	2,283	6,555	2,473	12,926
Ireland and Denmark	2,384	7,231	300	10,317
Community total	18,582	60,545	9,552	95,419

SOURCE: EUROSTAT [130], 1975–78.
NOTE: Livestock units (LU) are computed on the basis of animal type, size, and sex. For example, male cattle two years or older are equal to 1.0 LU, sows 50 kilograms or more are 0.5 LU, and laying hens are 0.014 LU.
[a]Totals include all species—for example, sheep and goats.

half of the poultry. Not all animals are fed purchased feeds, and the feed industry is distributed somewhat differently than the livestock population. Total feed production in the Community in 1979 was 77.9 million tons, and the three major gaplek-importing countries—the Netherlands, West Germany, and Belgium—manufactured 46 percent of the total animal feed although they had only 32 percent of the livestock.

One-year figures conceal remarkable changes in animal numbers and feed use that occurred simultaneously with growth in imports of gaplek and other nongrain feed substitutes. Swine in the Netherlands, West Germany, and Belgium increased by 6.7 million head (21.8 percent) between 1970 and 1979, while the number of pigs in the remaining countries declined slightly. The composition of compound feeds changed as well, especially in the three major gaplek-importing countries (Table 5.4). Between 1974 and 1978, the share of grains in compound feeds in the Netherlands dropped from 32 percent to 18 percent (FEFAC [47]).[3] West Germany and Belgium experienced declines of 9 and 8 percent, respectively.

Four regions contain 40 percent of the Community's pigs (Table 5.5 and Figure 5.1). The southern half of the Netherlands, the northern half of Belgium, and the German areas bordering the Netherlands in the state of North Rhine–Westphalia contain the largest single concentration of feeding capacity in Europe and roughly 25 percent of the EC pig herd.[4] This region is interwoven with canals, most of which are large enough for the standard barge used to transport commodities unloaded from ocean-going vessels. According to industry sources, the transport costs from Rotterdam, Amsterdam, and Antwerp rarely account for more than 5 dollars per ton of "at mill" costs. The industry estimates that gaplek use in this region in 1980 was about 2.5 million tons for swine and chicken feed and another 0.6 million for cattle feed. In 1978, the year of record gaplek imports, 3.5 to 4.0 million tons of gaplek were used. The availability of cheap gaplek and by-product feeds has been a major cause of the rapid increase in animals in this region.

The second region is located in northern West Germany around the ports of Bremen and Hamburg and has about 9 percent of the European Community's pigs. Feed mills here probably used 700,000 tons of gaplek in 1980 and as much as one million tons in 1978. Transport and unloading costs for gaplek are higher in this region, primarily because smaller ships must be used (30,000 to 50,000 tons in the Bremen and Hamburg ports, as opposed to 60,000 to 120,000 tons in the Dutch and Belgian ports), and the gaplek must be moved into silos and then to rail cars or trucks.

The southern German state of Bavaria is the third area of large-scale pig feeding. Because of its distance from ocean ports and proximity to a large grain-producing area, less compound feed is used here than in the first two regions. Industry sources estimate that a north German pig eats 367 kilograms of compound feed a year whereas its south German cousin eats only 90 kilograms and obtains the rest of its feed from locally grown grains (Neville-Rolfe et al. [108], p. 109). The distance from Atlantic ports to Bavaria is such that CIF gaplek prices must be much lower than barley prices if apprecia-

---

[3] In the Netherlands in 1977/78, 77 percent of the gaplek consumed was used in pig feed, 14 percent in feed for cattle, goats, and sheep, and 9 percent in chicken feed (Netherlands [107]).

[4] These estimates are based in part on interviews with major European traders and feed-milling concerns.

TABLE 5.4. *Raw Material Used in Compound Feeds, European Community, 1978*
(000 tons)

Country	Cereals		Gaplek		Oilseed cakes and meals		Corn gluten feed		Other		Total	
	Amt.	Pct.	Amt.	Pct.	Amt.	Pct.	Amt.	Pct.	Amt.	Pct.	Amt.	Pct.
West Germany	4,506	30.3%	900	6.1%	4,900	33.0%	670	4.5%	3,876	26.1%	14,852	100%
Netherlands	2,470	18.3	1,904	14.1	2,349	17.4	1,152	8.6	5,597	41.5	13,472	100
Belgium	1,724	35.1	618	12.6	1,055	21.5	0	0	1,518	30.9	4,915	100
United Kingdom	5,578	49.4	0	0	1,377	12.2	0	0	4,336	38.4	11,287	100
France	5,862	44.1	710	5.3	2,500	18.8	200	1.5	4,028	30.3	13,300	100
Community total	27,643	38.0	4,557	6.3	15,793	21.7	1,717	2.4	22,961	31.6	72,671	100

SOURCE: FEFAC [47], 1978, Table 15.
NOTE: Gaplek imports and the share of gaplek in total Community compound feeds were at record highs in 1978.

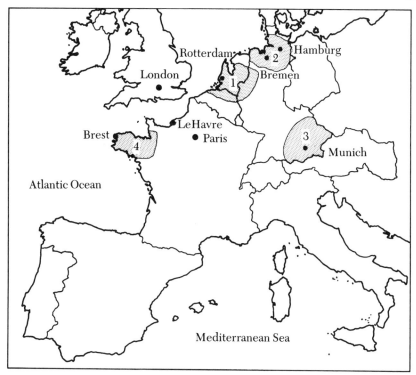

Figure 5.1. Regional Centers of Swine Feeding

ble amounts of gaplek are to be used as feed. Large quantities of gaplek (more than 100,000 tons) were probably used there only in
1978.[5]

Most of France's imports of 715,000 tons of gaplek in 1978 were
probably consumed in Brittany, the fourth major EC pig-raising region. However, port facilities for gaplek are inferior to those farther
north, making landed gaplek more expensive than in the Netherlands, Belgium, or West Germany. Furthermore, large amounts of
grain are produced nearby, so that a situation exists much like that in
Bavaria.

Policies of the European Community

Four goals guide EC policies in the field of agriculture. The two
most important objectives are adequate income for the farm sector
and a high degree of agricultural self-sufficiency, to be achieved by
remunerative and stable prices for agricultural products. The third

[5]This area is often supplied with imported feedstuffs via Bremen or Hamburg rather than
Rotterdam because of a subsidized German rail freight rate.

TABLE 5.5. *Distribution of Swine by Feeding Region*
(ooo head)

Region	December 1973	December 1977
Region 1		
Netherlands	6,889	8,429
Belgium	4,720	4,935
North Rhine–Westphalia	4,349	4,834
Region 2		
Bremen, Hamburg, and Lower Saxony	5,869	6,323
Region 3		
Bavaria	4,080	4,115
Region 4		
Brittany	3,885	4,251
Four-region total	29,792	32,887
Community total	70,567	72,130

SOURCES: EUROSTAT [131], [132].
NOTE: The figures are for the political regions that most closely approximate the animal feeding regions.

goal is common prices for agricultural commodities among countries, to be achieved by uniform support prices throughout the Community. In practice, however, national prices have been allowed to diverge, and this divergence has an important effect on the import demand for gaplek. The fourth goal, Community (rather than national) financing of Community agricultural policies, has played a central role in debates that began in 1978 about restricting imports of cassava.

Two policy instruments are used to implement the goals of increased farm income and stable and common prices—the intervention price and the variable levy. The Community stands ready to purchase domestic grains at an annually determined intervention price. If market prices drop below the intervention level, farmers can sell their grain to the Community. The intervention price thus provides a price floor for domestic cereals. The variable levy on imported grain is equal to the difference between the "threshold" price (somewhat higher than the intervention price) and the world price (see Table 5.6). To shelter domestic prices from fluctuations in world prices, the amount of the levy varies from day to day. The threshold price puts a ceiling on the domestic price and together with the intervention price creates a narrow band within which Community market prices move.[6]

---

[6] Community policies for livestock are similar to those for grains. All of the major livestock products receive variable-levy protection. Intervention prices also exist for dairy and beef

TABLE 5.6. *Administrative Prices for Corn and Barley, European Community*
(Units of account per ton)

Crop	1972	1974	1976	1978	1979[a]	1980[a]
Corn						
Threshold price	99.55	112.05	135.10	144.25	178.90	189.50
Intervention price	83.25	94.03	112.20	121.57	149.17	155.88
Barley						
Threshold price	102.00	113.25	135.10	144.25	178.90	189.50
Intervention price	95.70	101.43	116.00	121.57	149.17	155.88

SOURCE: FEFAC [47].
NOTE: Prices are for the crop year beginning in August of the calendar year indicated.
[a]European currency units per ton.

The first move toward achieving the Community's agricultural goals took place in July 1962, when threshold and intervention prices were instituted for all of the feed grains. Initially these prices were set at different levels in each of the countries, and additional levies were imposed on grain crossing national boundaries to eliminate intra-Community arbitrage. In July 1967, threshold and intervention prices were unified, and intra-Community border taxes on grains were abolished. Community regulations affecting cassava products became effective in July 1968, when, as part of the Kennedy round of trade negotiations, the levy on gaplek pellets and chips was bound at 25 percent of the barley level plus 0.25 units of account (UAs), but not more than 6 percent ad valorem.[7] With a few exceptions, the 6 percent rate has been the effective tax on cassava imports since that time.[8] The gaplek meal levy was not bound, and as a consequence meal imports dropped to zero.[9]

Green rates and associated border taxes called monetary compensatory amounts (MCAs) also influence gaplek imports and prices through their effect on national market prices of barley and other feed grains. The intervention price is initially set in ECUs, and then converted to national currencies using agricultural or green exchange rates between national currencies and the ECU. To establish

---

products, although not for poultry and pork. (Still, the EC does occasionally intervene to support their prices as well.) As a result, prices of poultry and pigs fluctuate more than prices of grain, dairy products, and beef.

[7]The unit of account (UA) was the Community's budget currency until 1979. It was originally set equal to the quantity of gold worth one U.S. dollar. Changes in exchange rates led to several changes in the budget currency during the 1970's, the most recent being the creation of the European Monetary System in 1979 and the introduction of a new budget currency called the European Currency Unit (ECU).

[8]In 1973 and 1974 world barley prices rose enough to make the levy on gaplek pellets and chips less than 6 percent of the import price.

[9]The African, Caribbean, and Pacific (ACP) countries affiliated with the Community receive some trade preferences on their exports to the EC, but they export little cassava.

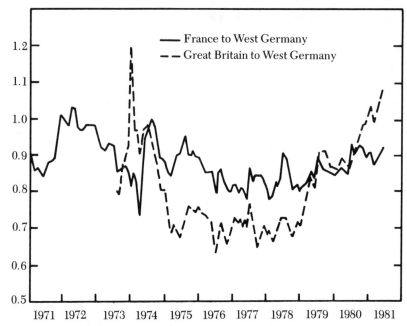

SOURCE: Wholesale prices in representative markets in each country, reported in various issues of *Agricultural Markets*, published by the Commission of the European Community.

Figure 5.2. European Barley Price Ratios, 1971–81

common agricultural prices within the Community, each country's green rate would have to be identical to its market rate.[10]

Uniform agricultural prices were achieved in all member communities in 1967, but they did not last long. Green rates differed from market exchange rates for most countries through most of the 1970's. As a result, prices were different in each country and MCAs were implemented to prevent arbitrage. For example, French and British wholesale barley prices were both lower than German barley prices during most of the late 1970's (Figure 5.2).

The Effect of EC Policies on Import Demand for Gaplek

Several variables identified in the preceding discussion interact to determine the CIF price of gaplek in Europe. The most important of these, the price of feed grains, is determined by EC price supports. In general, as the EC raises the price of feed grains, substitution of gaplek for cereals should pull the price of gaplek up.

The West German, Dutch, and Belgian national currencies have

---

[10]"Market rate" refers to exchange rates between currencies, including the UA or ECU, that are equivalent to those prevailing in the foreign exchange markets.

appreciated against the UA (or ECU), and MCAs allowed feed-grain prices to be generally higher in these three countries than in other Community nations. As long as gaplek is used in these countries, its price will be determined principally by these high feed-grain prices. Once the large markets of Regions 1 and 2 are exhausted, outlets must be sought in areas where transport and handling costs are higher and in countries where green rates reduce the price of feed grains.[11]

The price and the elasticity of demand should be initially high and then decline as gaplek moves out of Regions 1 and 2. Hence the relationship between prices and imports is nonlinear, and a quadratic function is used to approximate that relationship.

Because pig feed is the principal use of gaplek, the number of pigs in a region is the main variable determining the amount of gaplek that can be consumed there. The more pigs, the more mixed feed and the greater the possibilities of substituting gaplek-soymeal mixture for feed grains. Hence the number of pigs in Regions 1 and 2 and the quantity of gaplek imports determine the decline in the elasticity of import demand.

Since soymeal complements gaplek in animal feeds, as the soymeal price rises the price of a soymeal-gaplek mixture nutritionally equivalent to a feed grain also rises and the price of gaplek must fall if the mixture is to remain competitive.

Figure 5.3 is a stylistic representation of the EC import demand curve for gaplek. Curve A, which assumed a larger number of pigs in Region 1, is relatively elastic as imports increase to Q_A, whereas in curve B, with fewer pigs in the first region, demand becomes more inelastic by Q_B. Table 5.7 presents estimates of the coefficients of two forms of the import demand function. The dependent variable in each is the monthly CIF price per 100 kilograms of Thai gaplek pellets in northern European ports. Regression 1 includes dummy variables for 1977 and 1978, when imports increased by about 100 percent in two years. The European handling and distribution system could not yet manage an increase of this magnitude, and prices were pushed below what normally would have been obtained. Inclusion of the dummy variables improves the explanatory power of the regression, but scarcely alters the remaining coefficients, as shown in Regression 2. Monthly barley and corn prices are used to represent

---

[11] When gaplek prices fall sufficiently to allow significant quantities of imports into countries with low feed-grain prices, as happened in 1978, large profits result in the high-price countries.

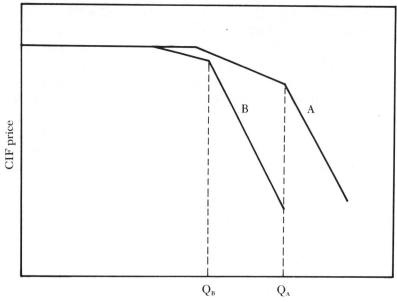

SOURCE: Text.

Figure 5.3. European Community Demand for Gaplek

feed-grain prices. Because monthly European gaplek import figures are not available, monthly exports from Thailand, lagged one and two months, were used as a proxy for imports.[12] All estimates have the expected sign. Coefficients of both feed-grain prices and the quantity of imports are statistically significant.[13] The sum of the coefficients on the barley and corn prices is almost one, indicating that an increase in the EC feed-grain support price causes an almost equivalent increase in the gaplek price.

To capture the effects of interaction between the number of pigs in the regions nearest the port and the quantity of imports, a composite term, "Pigs," is included, consisting of squared imports divided by the number of Dutch pigs. The squared imports component of "Pigs" captures the nonlinear effect of imports on price. As imports increase, their impact on price should become increasingly nega-

[12]The two-month lag is necessary because exports from Thailand arrive in Europe more than a month after departure. Greater lags were not statistically significant.
[13]It has been assumed that both the quantity of imports and the number of Dutch pigs are independent of the price of gaplek. Although Thai farmers (and Dutch pig farmers) are price responsive, they undoubtedly respond to prices with a considerable lag, probably a year or more. The regression results, however, are based on monthly data. Moreover, changing freight rates over the 1970's have reduced the correlation between European CIF gaplek prices and Thai FOB prices.

TABLE 5.7. *Import Demand for Gaplek, European Community*

	Regression 1		Regression 2	
Variable	Coefficient	*t*-ratio	Coefficient	*t*-ratio
Intercept	−7.41*	−1.86	−5.12	−1.00
Barley price[a]	0.42**	3.04	0.40**	2.58
Soymeal price[b]	−0.03	−1.62	−0.04	−1.60
Corn price[c]	0.56**	4.00	0.52**	3.33
Pigs[d]	−0.70**	−2.00	−0.75**	−2.19
D77[e]	−4.06**	−3.19	–	–
D78[f]	−4.94**	−3.39	–	–
Thai exports (−1)[g]	−0.80**	−2.80	−0.98**	−3.60
Thai exports (−2)[g]	−1.10**	−3.93	−1.11**	−3.94
R^2	0.75		0.61	

SOURCES: Prices of European grains and numbers of pigs from EUROSTAT publications; quantity of Thai exports from the Thai Ministry of Agriculture; CIF pellet prices from Alfred Toepfer & Co., a German importing firm, and Titapiwatanakun [141].

NOTE: There are 115 monthly observations beginning in January 1971. The coefficients have been corrected for first-degree autocorrelation and the *t*-ratios are only asymptotically valid.

[a] German wholesale price of barley per 100 kg, in Dutch guilders.
[b] Dutch wholesale price of soymeal per 100 kg, in Dutch guilders.
[c] Dutch wholesale price of corn per 100 kg, in Dutch guilders.
[d] Thai exports for the current month squared divided by the number of Dutch pigs (in thousands).
[e] Dummy for the year 1977.
[f] Dummy for the year 1978.
[g] Exports of pellets from Thailand, in hundred thousand tons. The numbers in parentheses are one-month time lags—i.e., (−1) is a one-month lag, (−2) is a two-month lag.
*Significant at the 10 percent level.   **Significant at the 5 percent level.

tive. The increase in the number of pigs in the Netherlands reduces this negative effect of gaplek imports, as larger amounts of gaplek can be consumed in the first region. The coefficient of "Pigs" has the expected sign and is significant in both equations.

The Politics of Imports of Nongrain Feed Ingredients (NGFI)

Three groups have been most affected by gaplek imports: Community officials, especially those in Directorate General 6 (DG 6), which is responsible for agriculture; French feed-grain and livestock growers; and German, Dutch, and Belgian traders, feed compounders, and feeders. Community officials have concerns on two interrelated grounds.[14] First, gaplek imports are the largest of a wave of imports of nongrain feed ingredients (NGFI) classified as processing wastes that pay low or no import taxes.[15] The share of NGFI (including soybean cake) increased from 54.6 percent of total compound feed consumption in 1974 to 62 percent in 1978. Oil cakes (imported duty free) currently make up more than half of the NGFI imports,

[14] It would be incorrect to imply that the whole of the Community bureaucracy is of one mind on the issue of gaplek imports or that all individuals within Directorate General 6 hold the views ascribed here to it.

[15] NGFI included gaplek, molasses, milling by-products, corn gluten, dried beets, oil cakes, and citrus pulp.

TABLE 5.8. *European Community Imports of Selected Nongrain Feed Ingredients* (000 tons)

Ingredients	1974	1975	1976	1977
Corn gluten feed (total)	694	930	1,147	1,486
(from U.S.)	(630)	(834)	(1,013)	(1,386)
Citrus pulp	339	490	666	985
Gaplek	2,121	2,447	3,243	4,032

Ingredients	1978	1979	1980
Corn gluten feed (total)	1,685	2,019	2,596
(from U.S.)	(1,639)	(1,983)	(2,525)
Citrus pulp	1,007	1,205	1,571
Gaplek	6,461	5,877	5,613

SOURCES: *Green Europe*, various issues; USDA [146]; *Agra Europe*, Aug. 21, 1981, and May 28, 1982.

but imports of citrus pulp and corn gluten, which have energy-protein ratios closer to those of grains than oil cakes do and thus compete directly with grains, have grown rapidly. Whereas gaplek imports increased roughly three times between 1974 and 1978 and then declined moderately in 1979 and 1980, citrus pulp and corn gluten imports not only grew almost as rapidly in the first four years but have continued to increase (Table 5.8). EC officials argue that imported NGFI enter through a loophole in the variable levy protection, thereby replacing domestically produced grains in animal feeds.[16] Second, the Community finances its operations, including intervention and export subsidy programs, with import levies and a share of the value-added tax revenues in each member country.[17] To the extent that free or lightly taxed imports of NGFI replace imports of more heavily taxed grain, there is a loss of revenue. Alternatively, NGFI imports raise the cost of the price-support program, because the grain purchased under intervention must then be sold at a loss on the world market.

At first glance, it might appear that French grain farmers should be unconcerned about gaplek and other NGFI imports because they can always sell their feed grains to the intervention program. They

[16] Corn gluten, a by-product of the wet milling process used in making both high-fructose corn syrup and alcohol, poses a special problem for Community officials. The major source of imports is the United States, and production there has grown rapidly with increased use of cornstarch in high-fructose syrup and alcohol production. Continued growth, however, depends on a rapid expansion of alcohol for fuel, which now appears unlikely. EC officials would like to prevent these exports from entering the Community, but the United States has repeatedly said that any restrictions on imports of corn gluten would be viewed unfavorably.

[17] See Fennell [51] for a discussion of Community financial resources.

have two reasons, however, for being unhappy about imports: they often find it more convenient to sell grain on the open market, where the subsidy is less obvious; and they see gaplek imports tending to push grain prices toward the lower end of the band set by threshold and intervention prices. French animal producers are also opposed to imports of NGFI, for a different reason. Because the Dutch and German port facilities are better than those in France, feed firms in the Netherlands, West Germany, and Belgium pay less for imported feedstuffs. This lowers the relative price for feed in these countries and makes it difficult for French meat products to compete. Consequently, the French government has been the strongest proponent of decreased gaplek imports.

By contrast, German, Dutch, and Belgian traders, feed compounders, and feeders rely on gaplek and other NGFI imports to maintain the competitiveness of their respective industries. The increased use of NGFI in these countries was a major cause of the rapid increase in animal numbers, and their governments have opposed measures to reduce gaplek imports.

Until 1978, proponents of continued free trade in gaplek were able to check efforts to restrict imports. Record imports of gaplek in that year, however, provoked the first systematic efforts at control. And because Thailand was by far the largest exporter of gaplek products (see Table 5.9), it was with the Thai government that those efforts be-

TABLE 5.9. *Exports of Gaplek Pellets, Chips, and Meal, Thailand, Indonesia, and China, 1965–80*
(000 tons)

Year	Thailand[a]	Indonesia			China
		Total	Lampung	Java	
1965	578	156	–	–	–
1970	1,097	332	71	261	–
1971	970	458	87	365	–
1972	1,111	342	101	240	16
1973	1,530	75	33	42	11
1974	2,030	394	199	187	4
1975	2,104	303	207	87	4
1976	3,316	149	138	10	7
1977	3,669	183	142	38	1
1978	6,041	308	194	98	1
1979	3,880	710	192	495	52
1980	–	386	161	220	336

SOURCES: For Thailand, Customs Department, Office of Commodity Standards, Board of Trade of Thailand; for Indonesia, [71]; for China, EUROSTAT [129].

[a]Includes exports of pellets, chips, and meal, but pellets made up more than 95 percent of the total by 1970.

gan. In November 1978, EC Commissioner for Agriculture Gunde-lach negotiated an informal agreement with Thailand to restrict ga-plek exports to Europe in 1979 and 1980 to 1978 levels. As it happened, Thai production declined in those years and the effective-ness of the agreement was not tested. Then in November 1980, Gundelach negotiated a second, longer-term agreement. The Thais agreed in principle to limit 1981 and 1982 exports to 5 million tons each year, plus a 10 percent (500,000-ton) margin to be used over the two years to handle unexpected fluctuations in supply; 1983 and 1984 exports were to be limited to 4.5 million tons a year, plus another 10 percent for the two years; and 1985 and 1986 exports were to be re-duced further. In exchange, the Community agreed to increase funds for a cassava diversification program set up as part of the first agreement and to prevent other countries from increasing their share of the European market at the expense of Thailand. [18]

The most commonly discussed mechanism for restricting the mar-ket share of third countries was an increased tax on EC imports from them. To increase the import tax, however, the General Agreement on Trade and Tariff (GATT) binding of the gaplek tariff to 6 percent had to be deconsolidated and new trade taxes applied in a discrimi-natory way. [19] This proved to be a difficult task. Early in 1980, the German, Dutch, and British governments expressed opposition to such a move, blocking deconsolidation. Agriculture Commission of-ficials responded by negotiating voluntary export restraints with other suppliers. An agreement was reached with the Indonesian gov-ernment in late 1981 to restrict 1982 exports to 500,000 tons and 1983 exports to 750,000 tons, but to permit larger amounts thereafter. Be-cause Indonesian exports exceeded 500,000 tons only once in the 1970's, the agreement will probably have no immediate impact on In-donesia, although the longer-run effects are far less certain (see Chapter 7).

After completing negotiations with the Indonesians, Commission officials reopened negotiations with the Thais in April 1982. In a new agreement, the 1983–84 limits were increased to 5 million tons an-

---

[18] The goal of the program was to identify alternative crops for the Northeast Region of Thai-land that would be more profitable than cassava. By the end of 1980, after extensive agronomic and economic research, no immediately profitable alternatives had been found.

[19] Tariff rate changes specified in a GATT negotiation are consolidated into a package that then supersedes previous tariffs. If a GATT-bound tariff is deconsolidated, it is removed from the package and higher rates can be applied. Tariffs can only be deconsolidated once every three years, unless it can be shown that a particular binding is causing hardship. In such a case, the binding can be waived and the importing country must compensate countries that are in-jured by the increased protection.

nually and the 1985–86 limits were set at 4.5 million tons (plus a 10 percent margin). The new agreement will commit the European Community to establishing a global tariff quota for other countries. By persuading the major exporters to "voluntarily" restrict their exports and accept a tariff quota, Commission officials have found a way to persuade the Council of Ministers to deconsolidate the GATT binding and restrict EC imports of gaplek.

Other Importers

Although the European Community has been the largest importer, other countries have occasionally imported gaplek. In 1973 and 1974, when world grain prices reached record highs, Japan imported sizable quantities. In most years in the 1970's, however, Japanese feed needs were met with imported corn that was rarely more expensive than an equivalent mixture of gaplek and soymeal.[20]

The Soviet Union purchased about 500,000 tons of gaplek from Thailand in 1980 and substantial quantities in 1981 (FAO [58]). According to some reports, the price paid was substantially above the market price. The motive behind such purchases is unclear, but Soviet relationships with countries in Southeast Asia and problems resulting from the U.S. grain embargo of 1980/81 were most likely involved. The potential market in Russia is large, but gaplek cannot compete with corn (at least at 1980 world market prices) unless political factors continue to play a part.

Hong Kong and Singapore import small amounts of gaplek for their domestic feedlots. Because of their size, though, neither is likely to develop a local livestock industry that will import large quantities of gaplek, regardless of price.

At current world prices for feed ingredients, substantial markets for gaplek outside the European Community will probably not develop. Because EC feed manufacturers have been willing and able to buy all exported gaplek at prices determined by their high domestic grain prices, other markets have not been able to compete.

The International Supply of Gaplek

Asked in the late 1950's to choose the Southeast Asian country that would be the world's leading exporter of cassava products in the late

---

[20] According to a Japanese importer interviewed in 1980, gaplek imports into Japan are hindered by a Japanese regulation prohibiting imports of feed containing excessive amounts of hydrocyanic acid (HCN). Although traded gaplek rarely contains HCN, Japanese traders and feeders prefer to use other foods when prices do not clearly favor gaplek.

1970's, an observer would probably have picked Indonesia. Yet Thailand's exports reached 6 million tons by 1978, whereas Indonesia's largest gaplek exports were only 710,000 tons in 1979. Thailand's success was built on fortuitous external circumstances and a rapid response by merchants and farmers to new market incentives. It has already been noted how Thailand's cassava industry developed to fill postwar shortfalls in the starch export market created by Indonesia's slow recovery, but the introduction of the Common Agricultural Policy (CAP) by the European Community opened a sizable new market for gaplek exports. At the same time, Thailand's road network, especially in the northeast, expanded significantly with external assistance during the Vietnam War. The subsequent addition of feeder roads by the Thai government further improved transport links between previously isolated areas and the ports.

Exchange rate movements in the 1970's also added to domestic incentives for the production of cassava in Thailand. With the Thai baht tied to the dollar, the gradual depreciation of the dollar against the German mark during the 1970's meant that Thai domestic gaplek prices increased more rapidly than did CIF European prices in German marks. It also meant that the rapid appreciation of the dollar in late 1980 pushed down baht prices at a time when mark prices were increasing.

The response to higher domestic cassava prices and reduced transport costs in Thailand was to expand the cultivation on newly opened lands. In central and northeastern Thailand the area under cassava increased from 90,400 hectares in 1960 to 952,000 hectares in 1978 without any decline in the area devoted to other crops.[21] Yield increases played no part in the increase in output; in fact, as cassava hectarage increased, average yields declined from 18.5 tons per hectare in 1952 to 14.9 tons per hectare in 1978/79 (Thailand [135]).[22]

Improvements in cassava processing and marketing reduced costs. Upcountry chipping capacity expanded greatly. Pelleting equipment introduced in 1967 helped reduce shipping costs by making the product more dense.[23] Finally, major private investment in port facilities at two locations on the Gulf of Thailand created the ca-

---

[21] See Nelson [105a] for a more extended discussion of the development of cassava production, processing, and exports in Thailand.

[22] This decline was probably the result of soil fertility depletion not offset by the use of chemical fertilizers, and of the extension of cultivation to less productive soils.

[23] Because dried cassava is not eaten in Thailand, roots are not peeled before drying and pelleting. This results in further cost savings.

pacity to handle deep-draft, bulk carriers (up to 100,000 tons). By substantially increasing loading capacity, these facilities also reduced costs associated with time in port.

The external forces that encouraged production of cassava in Thailand were also present in Indonesia. Indonesian exports are sold to the high-priced European market, and the rupiah is tied to the dollar. Total Indonesian cassava export figures, however, indicate a weak overall response to favorable market conditions, although this obscures dissimilar developments on Java and in Lampung, on southern Sumatra. On Java, available arable land was already intensively cultivated, and production increases for cassava could only occur through crop substitution or yield improvement. The amount of land under cassava did not expand through substitution because, despite the increase in gaplek prices on Java in the 1970's, other crops remained more profitable. What production growth did occur on Java resulted from yield increases of about 3.5 percent a year after 1973 (see Chapter 2).

Uncultivated land exists off Java, but in the 1970's only Lampung had an infrastructure favorable to the rapid growth of production (Suryana and Daud [134]). With the renovation of the trans-Sumatran highway in Lampung—completed by the beginning of the 1970's—the transportation system became adequate to allow profitable cassava production for export. High prices for gaplek paid by pelleting mills in the southern port of Panjang encouraged the rapid expansion of cassava production in areas previously under shifting cultivation. Planting materials were readily available for greater production by smallholders because immigrants from Java were already growing cassava for small starch mills and their own consumption.

Cassava production in Lampung increased by 14 percent a year during the 1970's, with cultivated area expanding at 9.7 percent annually and yields improving at the same rate as on Java. Fed by this striking production growth, gaplek exports from Lampung increased from about 71,000 tons in 1970 to 207,000 tons in 1975. They remained below 200,000 tons thereafter because starch processors took an increasing share of Lampung production.

Government policies in Thailand had almost no impact on cassava production and trade, but the same cannot be said for Indonesia. The Indonesian government levied a 5 percent export tax on gaplek chips until January 1982 (gaplek pellets and starch have always been exported free), and there is also a 40 percent import duty and a 10 percent import sales tax on cassava starch.[24] And government investment policy made new pelleting and starch firms eligible for investment concessions. These policies encouraged capital-intensive processing techniques but have probably had little impact on the quantity of exports.

A ban on gaplek exports from July to November 1973—part of a general ban on exports of food commodities—had more long-lasting effects. The ban was intended to contain gaplek price increases, but it was put into effect during harvesttime when gaplek prices were already declining, pushing them even lower. The ban not only ended plans to build special loading facilities in Lampung, but discouraged later investments in cost-reducing processing or loading facilities.

Future Export Supplies

The growth of Thai exports in the 1970's was based almost entirely on increased plantings, often on land in forest reserves where it was—and remains—officially illegal to plant commercial crops such as cassava. Until the late 1970's little was done to enforce the regulations, but a 1979/80 survey that revealed a significant decline in forest areas caused the government to commit additional resources to enforcement. It is unclear whether these efforts will be effective, but some individuals in the Thai cassava industry believe they will contribute to slower expansion in the future. Since major yield increases in the near future are also unlikely (Welch and Titapiwatanakun [159]), the period of rapid growth of Thai exports is probably over. Furthermore, normal fluctuations in yields caused by weather will cause declines in production and exports in some years that will no longer be offset by the general trend of increasing area.

Besides Thailand and Indonesia, only China has sold significant quantities of gaplek on the world market in recent years. Chinese exports, all of which are to the EC, have been very erratic, fluctuating between 1,000 tons in 1978 and 336,000 tons in 1980, as shown in Table 5.9. Little information is available about the reasons for these fluctuations or the likelihood of continued Chinese exports of gaplek. In the past, Tanzania, the Malagasy Republic, Ghana, Brazil, and Nigeria have also exported small quantities of gaplek, but although these countries grow large quantities of cassava, it seems unlikely that they will be significant exporters of gaplek in the near fu-

---

[24] Since 1977, the duty has been charged not on the CIF price but on the check price, which remained at $170 per ton through 1981. The import sales tax is charged on the check price plus 5 percent. For a discussion of the consequences of these tariffs on domestic prices, see Chapter 6.

ture. Inadequate infrastructure and inflation have led to high domestic prices in most of these countries, and overvalued exchange rates make domestic prices too high for profitable export.

Gaplek Processing

About 1.7 million tons of gaplek are made each year on Java, using 50 percent of the cassava crop.[25] Another 250,000 tons are made in Lampung province. The bulk of gaplek produced in Indonesia goes into food products such as *tiwul* and *oyek*: between 50 and 90 percent of all gaplek made on Java and 20 to 40 percent of all gaplek made in Lampung is used for this kind of home consumption. Most of the rest is exported as gaplek chips and pellets.

Gaplek is made by peeling and splitting cassava roots into pieces about 15 centimeters long and two centimeters in diameter, and then by drying these pieces in the sun. The entire process is generally done by hand on Java, usually in the field or farmyard. Drying takes four to six days in the dry season. Gaplek chips are made by breaking up large chunks of gaplek into smaller pieces one to two centimeters on a side. This is usually done by hand, but in 1979 mechanical chippers were introduced into the countryside in East Java.[26] Pellets are made by grinding gaplek into a coarse meal, steam heating the meal, and extruding it through a die to form a cylinder about five centimeters long and one centimeter in diameter. Some of the starch gelatinizes under the heat and pressure and binds the pellet together.[27]

The Growth of Pelleting

The first pelleting mill in Indonesia, a joint venture with a German trading company, went into production in Cirebon, West Java, in 1968. Shortly thereafter, plants were built in Surabaya, Panjang (the port of Lampung), and later in Cilacap, Banyumas, Malang, Kediri,

[25] The conversion ratio of unpeeled roots to gaplek ranges from about 2.5 : 1 to 3 : 1, depending on moisture content and skill in peeling. The ratio of peeled roots to gaplek is about 2 : 1. Peels make up 20 percent or more of the root weight.

[26] Although the end product is about the same (chips from Indonesia are slightly larger than chips from Thailand), the process of making chips in Thailand differs considerably from chip making in Indonesia. In Thailand, fresh unpeeled roots are sliced (or chipped) mechanically and then sun dried. With this process, less weight is lost since the peel remains with the chips, but extensive drying floors are needed; if Thai chips were dried in the fields (as is common for gaplek in Indonesia), large quantities of dirt would be mixed in. The starch content of Thai gaplek is also reduced by retention of the peel. Because most Indonesian gaplek is destined for human consumption, peeling is almost universal. There are only a few instances where exporters have ordered shipments of unpeeled gaplek.

[27] More details on processing gaplek can be found in Grace [59], Ingram [83], Thanh et al. [136], and Weber et al. [156].

Semarang, Probolinggo, and Palembang. After a rush of factory openings in the early 1970's, two crises led to factory closings—the 1973 ban on gaplek exports, and a decline in cassava production and gaplek exports in 1976. Several new pelleting plants started production in 1980, and in 1981 sixteen plants were active.

Fixed costs make up a large share of pelleting costs, and by storing raw material the processing season can be extended and these costs spread over a larger volume. In a year of good supplies, enough gaplek can be purchased during the harvest and stored to provide material for four months of pelleting. Extended storage, of course, increases requirements for working capital. Output can also be increased by pelleting materials other than gaplek, such as rice bran, copra expeller and extraction cake, and wheat bran. Indeed, for several pelleters on Java, gaplek pellets are no longer an important product. Three firms built in the late 1960's and early 1970's primarily to make gaplek pellets have now installed chemical extraction units to remove oil from rice bran and copra expeller cake and to pellet the waste.

Almost all pelleting plants are located in ports to minimize postprocessing costs. The cost of transporting pellets from the factory warehouse to the hold of a ship ranges from Rp 1.5 to Rp 5 per kilogram, depending upon port facilities and congestion. (In 1980, it cost Rp 1.5 per kilogram to keep a 15,000-ton vessel in the harbor for five days—a short stay in Indonesia.) Ex-factory-gate costs, not including losses from theft, can be as much as 10 percent of the value of the pellets. A port location is crucial in order to oversee loading operations and to minimize these costs. The few firms that are located outside ports usually sell their pellets to a pelleter-exporter located in a port rather than exporting pellets directly.

Private Costs of Processing

The cost of making gaplek is usually borne by the cassava grower or harvester (see Chapter 6) and consists almost entirely of wages. Typically, the work is done by family members or women who are hired on a piecework basis. Sometimes the work is divided into peeling and splitting, but most workers do both and are paid for each quintal (100 kilograms) of fresh roots peeled and split.[28] In the 1980 harvest season, the East Java rate was about Rp 150 per quintal, and the average worker could process between two and three quintals a day. Watchmen to guard the gaplek during the four to six days and

---

[28] Peels are returned to the soil, given away, or sold as animal feed.

TABLE 5.10. *Costs and Returns to Processors of Gaplek Chips
and Pellets for Export*
(Rp/ton)

	Chips		Pellets
	Manual	Machine	
Purchased gaplek	60,674	60,674	60,674
Transforming into chips or pellets			
Labor	3,785	2,265	3,394
Fuel and maintenance	–	154	2,591
Transporting and loading	2,700	2,700	2,500
Depreciation and interest	37	89	1,858
Total costs	67,196	65,882	71,017
Total revenue	81,875	81,875	82,500
Net revenue before taxes	14,679	15,993	11,483
Income taxes[a]	1,965	1,965	3,445
Export tax[b]	4,094	4,094	–
Net revenue after tax	8,620	9,934	8,038
Opportunity cost of capital[c]	22	114	7,974
Profit	8,598	9,820	64

SOURCE: Nelson [105].

[a]Income taxes were collected in part as an export levy of Rp 15 per U.S. dollar (Rp 625 = 1 U.S.$ in 1979/80). Pellet exporters pay an additional levy to bring tax up to 30 percent of net income.

[b]Five percent of the FOB price of chips.

[c]Opportunity cost of capital used by chip makers is assumed to be 30 percent a year; of pellet makers, 20 percent a year.

nights of drying were paid Rp 400 to Rp 600 a day, making the cost about Rp 3.9 per kilogram of gaplek.

In 1980, the principal cost of making chips and pellets was the cost of the raw material, gaplek (Table 5.10). Processing costs were much higher for pellets than for chips—Rp 6,000 per ton for pellets as opposed to 2,400 to 3,800 for chips. Costs of pelleting are much higher than costs of chipping partly because of the higher wages earned by the manager, amounting to Rp 2,100 a ton in 1979/80, but more because of the cost of maintenance and fuel for the costly pelleting installation. Net returns before taxes show pelleting to be much less profitable than chipping, and this disadvantage is increased when taxes and capital costs are taken into account. Nevertheless, pelleting firms earn a net return of 20 percent a year.

Government Policies

Several government policies, including some discussed earlier, affect choice of technique and private profitability in gaplek processing. Working capital borrowed by pelleting firms is charged an interest rate of only 1 percent a month.[29] Diesel fuel is subsidized, with

[29]This is the rate for all firms producing for export. It was lowered from 1.25 percent in January 1975.

TABLE 5.11. *Domestic Resource Cost Ratios for Gaplek Processing*

Type of production	DRC ratios at 1980 world prices	DRC ratios given a 10 percent decline from 1980 world prices	Breakeven price decline[a]
Manual chipping	0.785	0.867	26%
Machine chipping	0.771	0.852	28
Pelleting	0.936	1.039	6

NOTE: The table assumes that a decline in the world price has no effect on the social value of the gaplek used in production.
[a]If the world price declined by this percentage, the DRC would be equal to one.

the domestic price roughly half the world price. Income tax prepayments are deducted from exports of both chips and pellets at a rate of Rp 15 per dollar of exports. Any additional taxes owed are supposed to be collected at year's end, but pelleting firms are more likely to make year-end payments than chippers.[30] Many pelleting firms now in operation received investment concessions such as duty-free imports of capital equipment, thus reducing the total domestic capital needed to purchase the processing equipment.

Table 5.11 presents the domestic resource cost measure (DRC) for the three processing techniques for gaplek exports in Table 5.10.[31] At 1980 world prices, all processing techniques are socially profitable, chipping more so than pelleting. The additional domestic factors of production used in pelleting are not offset by the additional foreign exchange earned by exporting pellets instead of chips. Chip prices would have to decline about 20 percent before the social profit generated by these activities would be the same.[32]

International trading firms report that most exports in the 1970's were pellets, despite the indicated private and social profitability of chips in 1980. There are no completely satisfactory explanations for this apparent contradiction, but a number of observations can be made. The difference between CIF prices for pellets and chips shipped to Rotterdam or Hamburg in 1980, roughly five dollars a ton in favor of chips according to industry sources, was not enough to off-

[30]The corporate profits tax is 20 percent for firms with profits less than Rp 25 million (not audited) or Rp 100 million (audited); it is 30 percent for firms with profits between Rp 25 and 30 million (not audited) or Rp 100 and 200 million (audited); and it is 45 percent at profit levels above these. Firms that receive investment concessions must present audited accounts to the tax agency, but most other firms do not do so because they believe they can negotiate lower taxes.

[31]See Chapter 4 for a discussion of DRC calculations.

[32]These calculations assume that the social profits from cassava growing and gaplek making are equal to social costs. To the extent that net social profits are generated in those activities, the entire chain, from farm to export, has a lower DRC than the processing activity alone. The social profitability measured above is only that earned in processing.

set the additional transport costs of 10 to 12 dollars for chips. Large quantities of Indonesian gaplek, however, were shipped to Belgian feedstuff firms that faced stricter controls on pollution than did Dutch and German firms and that were willing to pay a higher premium for chips because they cause less dust pollution in loading and unloading. Complaints about the quality of pellets from Thailand became stronger after 1977 and may have resulted in an increase in the chip premium.

The rough equivalence between chip and pellet prices in late 1980 may also have been an anomaly. In 1979, both prices increased rapidly during the buying season, and the difference between the two ranged from one dollar in favor of chips to 25 dollars in favor of pellets. In 1981, chip prices were three to six dollars lower than pellet prices.

In addition, if the pelleting firm were still receiving income tax concessions, its rent would increase from less than zero to more than Rp 3.5 per kilogram, narrowing the gap between the profitability of the two products by about 40 percent. Hence, the expiration of investment concessions in the late 1970's increased the relative profitability of chips. It appears that the volume of chip exports increased in 1979 and 1980 and that domestic traders in East Java were investing in chipping equipment, both indications that chips have become more profitable.

The available evidence suggests that the chip premium in Europe depends primarily on the quality of Thai pellets. The more pellets are adulterated or dusty on arrival in Europe, the larger the chip premium. If this is the case, current Thai efforts to increase the hardness of pellets will reduce the premium and reduce the relative profitability of chips in Indonesia.

One of the most important factors in the choice between chips and pellets is employment. If one woman can peel and slice 2.5 quintals of fresh roots a day, a ton of gaplek provides a day's employment for ten women. If 1.7 million tons of gaplek are made on Java annually, 17 million days of employment are generated, or two months of full-time work in the harvest for more than 300,000 women. Clearly, making gaplek is an important source of employment for women in the countryside, especially since it is done at a time when other jobs are scarce.[33]

[33] The 1976 National Labor Force Survey put rural employment on Java at 27.4 million persons; hence, more than 1 percent of the rural work force is employed for two months a year making gaplek. Much of the work is not paid labor.

Hand chipping employs slightly more than four woman-days per ton of chips made. The mechanical chipper employs only 0.15 man-days per ton. More labor—perhaps as much as 1.5 man-days per ton—is required for loading and unloading. Pelleting uses more than two man-days per ton of gaplek, mostly to move goods in and out of storage and to load and unload trucks. By encouraging pelleting, employment per ton of gaplek exported is cut in half, mainly at the expense of jobs for women. If all 700,000 tons of gaplek exports in 1979, the year of largest exports, had been handmade chips, the employment generated in chipping and export would have been about 12,000 man-years.

Summary

Since the introduction of the Common Agricultural Policy (CAP) of the European Community and the binding of the import tariff on gaplek chips and pellets to 6 percent, the European market has been the major determinant of international trade in gaplek products and starch. With a domestic floor price and variable levy protection from imports, the CAP raised domestic feed-grain prices well above world market levels. Gaplek could be imported with a low fixed tariff and combined with duty-free imports of protein concentrates such as soybean cake to substitute for feed grains. Its price was therefore higher than if it had been determined freely in international markets.

Thailand and Indonesia are the main exporters of gaplek, but their responses to the price effects of the CAP have been very different. Whereas exports from Thailand increased about 40 percent a year during the 1970's, Indonesia's exports fluctuated widely and showed no discernible trend. Thai exports benefited from the development of excellent roads, and all increases in output came from expansion of the area planted to cassava. In Indonesia, there was little opportunity for expansion of the area cultivated on Java, the main cassava-growing island, and the CAP-driven price increases were not sufficient to cause extensive switching from other crops to cassava. Inadequate transport and port facilities inhibited the growth of cassava exports from the outer islands, except in Lampung Province, where adequate roads and ports led to the rapid growth of cassava exports for a few years. A government ban on exports in 1973 reduced the private incentives to invest in cost-reducing processing and transport facilities.

The rapid growth of gaplek imports from 1970 to 1978 stimulated opposition from several groups within the Community: French farmers, who claimed that gaplek imports depressed domestic grain prices; French meat producers, who said they could not compete with producers in other countries using cheap nongrain feed ingredients; and EC Commission officials, who viewed rising imports of NGFI as a principal cause of increased EC expenditures on price supports. The Thai voluntary export limitation agreements of 1978 and 1980 were not binding, and limits in the Indonesian agreement of late 1981 were considered too high to affect exports in the short run.

In 1982, however, the EC Commission persuaded the Council of Ministers to accept restrictions on gaplek that may impair imports from Indonesia. More restrictive controls seem likely to pass the Council with less trouble than the first set, so the prospects for future growth in exports to the EC have become much less certain. Furthermore, any restructuring of the CAP would have a negative effect on gaplek imports (Josling and Pearson [91]). The implications of such a change are reviewed in Chapter 7.

Since cassava starch and gaplek share a common raw material, the CAP-induced increase in gaplek prices also pushed up the price of cassava starch on world markets. Cassava starch competes with cornstarch sold at U.S. prices, so demand declined. New markets for starch-based products, especially sweeteners, have developed, however, and demand for starch has increased. If European restrictions reduce gaplek exports and prices, world starch markets should take up part of the slack.

In addition, world manufacturers of animal feeds will buy gaplek if the price falls enough. If Indonesia had sold gaplek to the United States for animal feed in 1981, a task not unlike carrying coals to Newcastle, the FOB value would have had to be roughly half the price then paid in Europe. Other potential markets closer to Indonesia—Japan, for example—have higher domestic corn prices and would have paid more for gaplek.

Finally, it is important to remember that changes in apparently unrelated variables can affect Indonesian cassava prices. Currency fluctuations in late 1980 caused changes in domestic cassava prices of the same order of magnitude as would be caused by an import ban in the EC.

6. Marketing and Price Formation

Laurian J. Unnevehr

The internal marketing system transmits world prices to domestic cassava markets and allocates cassava production among its various domestic and international uses. The efficiency of the marketing system helps to determine incentives to cassava producers and final costs to consumers of cassava products. This chapter examines several facets of pricing and marketing efficiency and evaluates the capacity of the marketing system to handle increased supplies of cassava products.

The Geography of Trade on Java

On average, approximately two-thirds of Java's cassava production moves through commercial channels, but there is a high degree of regional variation in commercial trade of cassava products. Farmers sell cassava either as fresh roots or as gaplek, and both products are sold to industry as well as to domestic food consumers. Fresh roots find their outlet at starch factories and in urban and rural markets. Gaplek is sold at the pelleting plants of exporters or to rural consumers.

Fresh roots are sold to consumers throughout Java, both in local retail trade and in urban markets. Local sales are particularly important in the rural areas of Madura, southeast West Java, and southwest Central Java, where trade flourishes over the short distances between villages and kabupaten (county) centers. Urban markets draw roots from more distant supply areas. Fresh roots for the Jakarta market normally travel 60 kilometers from Bogor, and sometimes 150 kilometers from Sukabumi. Surabaya is supplied by Ampelgading, about 125 kilometers away (Figure 6.1).

Gaplek is found in large quantities only in markets of the principal consuming and producing areas of southern Central and East Java. It is not important in West Java or in any urban markets. Most gaplek is sold in village markets and retailed in nearby kabupaten (county) or kecamatan (township) retail centers. Wonogiri, Pacitan, Ponorogo, and Trenggalek import gaplek from other regions, however—principally Malang, Madura, and such smaller producing areas on the north coast as Tuban, Situbondo, and Probolinggo.[1]

Starch is made throughout West Java, but 70 percent of Java's production comes from areas near Tasikmalaya, Ciamis, and Cilacap. Malang and Kediri in East Java and the areas near Pati on the north coast account for most of the rest. From 50 to 80 percent of cassava grown in these starch-producing areas is made into starch. Starch mills in each area also buy cassava from other regions. West Java occasionally draws roots from Central Java; Kediri-Malang starch producers purchase roots from Madiun to the west and Pasuruan to the north; and firms in Pati sometimes buy from Tuban to the east.

Two-thirds of Java's gaplek exports are from the East Java ports of Surabaya and Probolinggo; the ports of Cilacap and Cirebon handle the rest.[2] Important supply areas for Surabaya are Madiun, Ngawi, Ponorogo, Malang, Kediri, Tuban, and Madura. Probolinggo is supplied from Malang and from smaller nearby producing areas in Pasuruan, Situbondo and Bondowoso. Cilacap obtains its exports from Banjarnegara, Gunung Kidul, and Ciamis; and Cirebon draws its exports from West Java.

Marketing Channels

First sales of fresh roots and gaplek are similar, but from that point they move through different marketing channels on their way to the consumer.[3] Because they are bulky and perishable, fresh roots change hands less often and more quickly. Gaplek is handled by more agents and may be stored for three or four months.

Cassava trade is conducted principally by two groups—assemblers, who trade in villages, and wholesalers, who are based in trading centers.[4] Assemblers buy from farmers and sell to wholesalers, starch factories, and urban retailers. They trade in both fresh roots

[1] Wonogiri, Pacitan, Ponorogo, and Trenggalek constitute a subset of a six-kabupaten region where gaplek is consumed in large amounts. Formerly Gunung Kidul imported gaplek, but increases in marketed quantities during the late 1970's have satisfied local demand.

[2] Estimates are based on 1979 figures from the Ministry of Trade. The sole Semarang exporter went out of business in 1980.

[3] Information about channels and costs was obtained in interviews with 170 market participants between October 1979 and October 1980. Respondents included assemblers, wholesalers, retailers, petty traders, starch factory managers, exporters, transporters, and farmers in five producing areas (Malang, Kediri, Trenggalek, Garut, and Sumenep), eleven wholesale centers (Pasuruan, Dampit, Tulungagung, Kediri, Ponorogo, Ngawi, Tuban, Solo, Gunung Kidul, Banjarnegara, and Tasikmalaya), four ports (Surabaya, Probolinggo, Cilacap, and Semarang), and two urban markets (Surabaya and Jakarta). Interviews included questions about market flows, contracts, information, credit, prices, costs, and returns.

[4] Most wholesalers are of Chinese origin, whereas assemblers are usually indigenous Indonesians. Some wholesalers are indigenous traders who have accumulated enough capital over the years to invest in warehouses and trucks and to trade on a large scale.

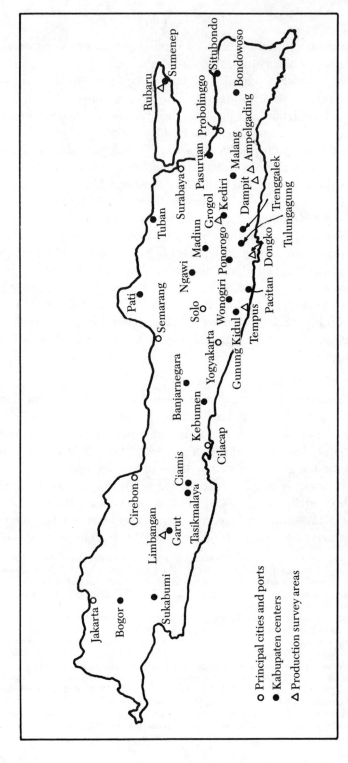

Figure 6.1. Cassava Trading Centers and Market Survey Areas

and gaplek. Assemblers' scales of operation vary from buying a few tons directly from farmers and transporting their purchases in rented trucks to buying from many smaller assemblers and owning their own trucks. Wholesalers trade cassava exclusively in the form of gaplek and often trade in other food and export commodities as well.[5] They typically own or rent a shop or warehouse in town, buy gaplek from 10 to 50 assemblers, deliver it to exporters in the harvest season, and store it for the off-season. A third group, retailers and peddlers, conducts small-scale retail trade in rural markets and villages.

First Sale

The grower sells cassava in one of three ways: either the roots are harvested and hauled fresh to a local market or roadside collection point for sale to assemblers or retailers; or the roots are harvested, peeled, sliced, and dried, and then sold as gaplek in the same way; or else the standing crop is sold in the field (*tebas*) to an assembler who harvests the roots and transports them to market.

Sale of the crop shortly before harvest is becoming more common because it reduces harvest and transport costs and transfers price risks to the traders.[6] Because they can guarantee regular employment, traders can hire laborers at wage rates somewhat lower than those paid by farmers, who offer only one or two days' work at a time. An assembler may also have more favorable standing arrangements with trucking companies. Where the final end-use market is for fresh roots, sale before harvest allows traders to time their harvesting in accordance with market demand, thus reducing losses.

Preharvest purchases are only advantageous to traders under certain conditions. Yields must be sufficiently uniform to permit reasonably reliable estimates of a field's production. Plots and yields must also be large enough to make it worthwhile for traders to seek them out. When large quantities for sale are close to good roads, assemblers can take advantage of economies of scale in transportation. In south Malang Kabupaten, where roads are good and commercial sales are 80 to 90 percent of production, almost all cassava is sold before harvest. At the other extreme, in south Trenggalek Kabupaten marketed quantities are small and paved roads are a recent phenom-

[5] Wholesaler-retailers trade fresh roots in large urban markets, but this group is distinct from gaplek wholesalers.

[6] The price is usually based on the assembler's estimate of yield per unit of area, but sometimes payment is corrected based on kilograms of harvested cassava.

enon. Most Trenggalek farmers process their cassava into gaplek and carry it themselves to local assembly markets.

Exceptions within each area further demonstrate the influences of roads and final markets. In Tamansari village, Malang, which is inaccessible except in the dry season, only a few of the largest farmers sell their cassava before harvest, most farmers instead processing it into gaplek and carrying it to a nearby collection point. By contrast, large farmers in Cakul village, Trenggalek, have recently begun to sell gaplek by the roadside to traders who have already contracted for quantity and delivery date. The increasing frequency of preharvest sale and the decline in bulking and assembly at local markets are the outcome of improvements in transport and increases in units of sale. These changes reflect the response of the marketing system to opportunities for reduction of marketing costs.

Fresh Root Marketing Channels

Fresh roots move to starch factories through channels that vary with transportation conditions and the location of the factories. In West Java, where mills are of medium size but roads are poor, trucks from the mills circulate daily among collection points to which farmers or traders take fresh roots, often over long distances. In Kediri, where many small household starch mills are scattered through the producing area, farmers more often deliver roots directly to the mills. Sale before harvest and delivery by truck predominate in Malang Kabupaten, where good roads lead to a few large and medium-sized mills.

Fresh roots for direct consumption move through channels that vary with the distance the product travels. Deliveries to Jakarta from assemblers in producing areas are bulked in a wholesale market outside the city and then sold to retailers, who carry the roots to retail markets in the city. Most retailers in Surabaya and in small towns buy roots directly from a few assemblers with whom they have established trading relationships. In rural areas, farmers often sell directly to consumers in nearby markets, or peddlers carry roots from door to door.

Gaplek Marketing Channels

Gaplek is made either by the grower or by an assembler. When sold for export, it is assembled and bulked for delivery to a port. Assemblers haul it in small trucks from the farm or village to sell to wholesalers or sometimes directly to exporters. Wholesalers may dry gaplek further before selling it, and may sometimes chip it before sale to an exporter. Most gaplek exports are pellets made by an exporter-processor. Pelleting plants store gaplek to allow for processing beyond the end of the harvest season.

Gaplek for rural consumption is supplied either locally or from wholesalers' stocks. Local gaplek trade moves from farmers to consumers through retailers in rural markets or through assemblers who sell to retailers in nearby towns. Most gaplek is made during the dry season, when sun drying is easiest. During the rainy season, consumer demand, principally in the gaplek-consuming region extending from Gunung Kidul to Trenggalek, is supplied from traders' stocks. Wholesalers store gaplek for three or four months after the main cassava harvest, for sale either to retailers in the town or to rural assemblers who in turn sell to retailers or petty traders in rural markets. Some supplies also come from wholesalers outside the consuming region, who sell to traders within the region.

Marketing Costs

The costs of marketing services vary substantially among products and markets. Transport costs are important in most channels and particularly in supplying gaplek to ports or fresh roots to starch factories. One-half to two-thirds of the total margin between the farm-gate price and the factory or port price is transport costs (Tables 6.1 and 6.2). Physical losses make up the largest part of storage-related costs in supplying gaplek for sale in the off-season (Table 6.3). Costs, which determine the size of margins, are examined here to provide insight into price relationships and to show the effects of particular public investments.

Transportation

Road quality determines mode of transport, and costs vary accordingly—from Rp 1,000 per ton per kilometer for porterage to Rp 18 per ton per kilometer for an eight-ton truck on an asphalt road (Table 6.4). It can cost the same to haul gaplek 200 kilometers from a wholesale center to a port as to haul it 4 kilometers from a farm to an assembly point. As a result, farmers served by dirt roads receive much lower prices than those close to asphalt roads.

Improvements in roads and an increase in the supply of vehicles

TABLE 6.1. *Gaplek Marketing Margins, Farm to Pelleting Factory, 1980*
(Rp/kg)

	Trenggalek[a]	Gunung Kidul[b]	Kediri[c]	Malang[d]
FARMER PRICE	34.0	45.0	45.0	38.5
Harvesting and processing	–	–	–	2.5
Moisture loss	4.5	–	2.0	–
Transportation	5.0	2.0	1.5	2.2
Return to assembler	1.5	1.0	1.5	1.8
(Percent of cost)	(3.4%)	(2.1%)	(3.9%)	(4.2%)
ASSEMBLER SALE PRICE	45.0	48.0	50.0	45.0
Transportation and loading	6.0	5.5	3.7	6.0
Moisture loss	3.0	1.5	0.3	1.0
Return to wholesaler	1.0	1.0	1.0	1.0
(Percent of cost)	(1.9%)	(1.8%)	(1.9%)	(1.9%)
FACTORY-GATE PRICE	55.0	56.0	55.0	53.0
TOTAL MARGIN	21.0	11.0	10.0	14.5
(Percent of factory-gate price)	(38.2%)	(19.6%)	(18.2%)	(27.4%)
Distance between first and final sale	189.0 km	306.0 km	178.0 km	145.0 km

[a]The farmer harvests, processes, and sells partly dry gaplek in the rural market to the assembler, who delivers it to the wholesaler. Based on interviews of 5 assemblers, 3 wholesalers, and 4 exporters.

[b]The farmer harvests, processes, and sells dry gaplek in the rural market to the assembler, who delivers it to the wholesaler. Based on interviews of 8 wholesalers and 2 exporters.

[c]The farmer harvests, processes, and sells dry gaplek in the rural market to the assembler, who delivers it to the wholesaler. Based on interviews of 2 assemblers, 2 wholesalers, and 4 exporters.

[d]The farmer sells his crop before harvest to the assembler, who delivers it to the wholesaler. The farmer price is doubled to provide a gaplek equivalent. Based on interviews of 6 assemblers, 6 wholesalers, and 4 exporters.

reduced transport costs in the 1970's. Between 1970 and 1980, the Directorate of Highways increased expenditures tenfold on road construction, rehabilitation, and maintenance. Total kilometers of road on Java increased by a third during the 1970's, from nearly 30,000 to just under 40,000. And a 150 percent increase in the number of trucks on Java between 1973 and 1978 was concentrated in the smaller truck sizes, reflecting increased opportunities provided by an expanded road network reaching into new areas.[7] The greater supply of trucks has also increased competition in transport, to the advantage of farmers and smaller traders.

Anne Booth found evidence that the difference between average farm-gate prices for secondary food crops and average rural market prices on Java declined between 1970 and 1975 (Booth [13], pp. 50–51). Field experience in 1980 indicates that truck transport is now

[7] Railroads carry only a small amount of the goods shipped on Java and have carried almost no cassava in recent years. Wholesalers prefer to use trucks because they are fast and reliable. Railroad shipments are often more expensive because of bureaucratic delays at provincial borders and the costs of transferring on and off trucks.

TABLE 6.2. *Fresh Root Marketing Margins, Farm to Starch Mill, 1980*
(Rp/kg)

	Garut[a]	Kediri[b]	Malang[c]
FARMER PRICE	20.0	18.0	18.0
Harvesting	1.0	1.0	–
Porterage	3.0	–	
Transportation and loading	4.2	1.0	3.2
Moisture loss	0.4	1.1	0.7
Return to assembler	1.4	0.9	1.1
(Percent of cost)	*(4.9%)*	*(4.2%)*	*(5.0%)*
FACTORY-GATE PRICE	30.0	22.0	23.0
TOTAL MARGIN	10.0	4.0	5.0
(Percent of factory-gate price)	*(33.3%)*	*(18.2%)*	*(21.7%)*
Distance between first and final sale	45.0 km	1.5 km	15.0 km

[a]Preharvest sale to the assembler, who sells the peeled roots to a medium-scale starch factory. Porterage wage includes peeling of roots. Based on interviews of 7 assemblers and 6 starch millers.
[b]Preharvest sale to the assembler, who delivers the unpeeled roots to a household starch firm. Harvest wage includes loading. Transportation is by cattle cart. Based on interviews of farmers, 4 assemblers, and 5 starch millers.
[c]The farmer harvests and sells unpeeled roots at a roadside collection point to the assembler, who delivers them to a medium-scale starch factory. Based on interviews of 8 assemblers and 3 starch millers.

TABLE 6.3. *Gaplek Marketing Margins in Storage by Wholesaler, 1980*
(Rp/kg)

	Malang to Tulung Agung[a]	North Coast to Tulung Agung[a]	Gunung Kidul to local retail[b]
WHOLESALE BUYING PRICE	55.0	55.0	55.0
Storage losses	10.5	7.0	15.0
Transportation	2.5	4.3	–
Return to wholesaler	2.0	3.7	5.0
(Percent of cost)	*(2.9%)*	*(5.8%)*	*(6.7%)*
WHOLESALER SALE PRICE	70.0	70.0	75.0
TOTAL MARGIN[c]	15.0	15.0	20.0
(Percent of wholesale price)	*(21.4%)*	*(21.4%)*	*(26.7%)*
Distance between first and final sale	165.0 km	195.0 km	30.0 km

[a]The wholesaler in the surplus region stores gaplek and delivers it to a wholesaler in the deficit region. Based on interviews with 6 wholesalers in Malang and 4 wholesalers in North Coast towns.
[b]The wholesaler in the consuming region stores gaplek and sells it to a retailer in the kabupaten market. Based on interviews with 8 wholesalers.
[c]All margins assume three months' storage.

available between all kabupaten centers on Java, integrating the island into one market. Transport between producing areas and wholesale centers remains expensive, however, particularly in the remote uplands of southeast West Java and the Gunung Kidul–Trenggalek region.

TABLE 6.4. *Transport Costs by Type of Carriage, 1980*

Type of transport	Rp/ton/km	Average load per unit (tons)
Porterage	1,000	0.05
Cattle cart	750	1.00
Truck[a]		
Class V	71	1.50
Class IV	43	3.00
Class IIIA	28	5.00
Class III	18	8.00

SOURCE: Field interviews, 1980.
[a]Trucks are licensed according to the grade of road they are allowed to enter. Class V is the poorest grade of road. Average loads represent actual practice rather than official government limits.

Government-regulated fuel prices set by the petroleum monopoly, Pertamina, also affect transport costs. In 1980, gasoline prices were approximately equal to world prices, whereas diesel prices were subsidized and sold at about half of world prices.[8] Low diesel fuel prices throughout the 1970's subsidized larger commercial vehicles that use diesel.[9] This subsidy reduces private marketing costs between wholesale centers and ports, and increases farm prices throughout Java. It favors farms close to good roads, however, since only small gasoline-fueled trucks can use poor roads. If the subsidy were removed, transport costs for large trucks would increase by about Rp 2 per ton per kilometer.

Storage

Traders begin storing gaplek in about October and sell it from December to February. Gaplek is only stored for three or four months, rather than the full eight months between harvests, because its role in consumption is seasonal (see Chapter 3). Though cassava is the cheapest source of calories throughout the year, its advantage is even greater from November to March when rice prices are highest. After the corn and rice harvests, consumers shift to these staples and market demand for gaplek falls sharply. Traders' stocks that are unsold by April must be sold to exporters, usually at a loss.

Despite the short period of storage, gaplek storage losses are reported to be 10 to 20 percent, considerably higher than losses for grains. Gaplek that is improperly dried or that is rehydrated by high humidity is susceptible to mold. Furthermore, insects infest gaplek

[8]"World" diesel and gasoline prices are FOB Singapore.
[9]Kerosene is subsidized to provide cheap energy for low-income households; and to discourage substituting kerosene for diesel fuel, the latter is subsidized as well.

within three to six months under normal storage conditions in tropical countries.[10]

Returns to Traders

Returns to traders vary with markets. Retailers and peddlers reported total daily returns of Rp 100 to Rp 500, about the same as agricultural wages, which vary from Rp 200 to Rp 400 a day. The amount of capital in this type of trade is small—perhaps Rp 500 to Rp 3,000—and it is turned over quickly. Returns are primarily to the trader's labor, which may include transporting goods to rural households.

Considerably more working capital is required in assembly and wholesaling. Assemblers delivering 5 to 35 tons a week may have Rp 50,000 to 1,750,000 invested, and wholesalers, who deliver from 10 to 50 tons daily, require Rp 1.5 to 38 million for the one- to two-week turnover in shipping to exporters. Wholesalers who store gaplek require even more capital to hold 500 to 1,000 tons over a three-month period. Thus the cost of borrowing money and the speed with which funds are recovered are important in determining the cost of trade.

As a percent of capital invested, returns to cassava trade in starch or export vary from 1.8 (wholesaling gaplek for export) to 5.0 (assembling fresh roots for starch mills). Wholesalers' profits in storage are returns to capital invested over a three- to four-month period, and monthly returns averaged 2 percent in 1980, about the same as returns in other wholesale trade.[11] In general, returns to assemblers were higher than returns to wholesalers and higher in the fresh root trade than in the gaplek trade.

Competition in Marketing

A competitive market has five characteristics: participants who are economically motivated, numerous buyers and sellers, products that are divisible and fungible,[12] equal access to trade, and widespread knowledge of prices and trading opportunities. This chapter assumes that participants are economically motivated. Numerous buyers and sellers are found in all cassava markets with the possible

---

[10] See Ingram [83]. Little research has been done on improved methods for storing dried cassava products.

[11] Examples of returns in 1980 do not reflect an average of gains and losses over a period of changing prices and do not include traders who left the market. They are therefore probably higher than normal returns to trade.

[12] Fungibility is a measure of the degree to which one unit of a commodity can be substituted for any other.

exception of the gaplek export market. Exporters are few, but their market power is limited by the existence of many alternative markets for cassava; for example, they compete for cassava supplies with starch firms that also export their product (see Chapter 4).

Both fresh roots and gaplek are divisible and fairly homogenous products, with only small price differentials between industrial and food markets. All cassava sales are by weight, and moisture content is an important determinant of price variation in gaplek markets. Fresh roots are highly perishable and therefore not fungible over time once they have been harvested. Temporal arbitrage is possible, however, by varying the harvest date, and assemblers purchase standing crops so they can be flexible in timing fresh root deliveries. Starch factories and urban retailers prevent oversupply by contracting for delivery in advance. Conditions of competition are more complicated, however, with respect to price information and access to credit.

Price Information

Information about fresh root prices is obtained mainly by word of mouth. Assemblers in the starch areas are in daily contact with starch firms, and price information passes rapidly through the short marketing chain from factory to trader to farmer, aided by the decentralized location of starch firms. Within the producing areas where starch factories are concentrated, farmers or traders can go directly to the factories to learn prices. Farmers also learn about prices from their neighbors and from observation in local markets. Fresh root and vegetable prices in Jakarta and Surabaya are broadcast daily on the radio by the Ministry of Agriculture.

Information about gaplek prices must pass through a longer marketing chain. Wholesalers talk with exporters by telephone and relay price changes to assemblers in their regions. Farmers learn of gaplek prices from assemblers, from wholesalers, or in local retail markets. Wholesalers also communicate with each other by telephone about domestic markets for gaplek, and this communication between regional wholesale centers integrates markets throughout Java. Gaplek prices in Surabaya and the wholesale centers of Tuban, Kediri, and Dampit are broadcast by radio throughout East Java by the Ministry of Agriculture.

Information is thus transmitted quickly and cheaply in the most common cassava trading channels. Farmers and traders can take advantage of trading opportunities by buying and selling in different markets as prices change. For example, farmers sell gaplek at retail or directly to wholesalers if assemblers' prices are unattractive. The availability of information is thus sufficient to encourage competition.

Access to Credit

A substantial portion of the cassava trade is financed on credit among traders or between traders and farmers. These informal credit arrangements vary in the different product markets. Although there is often no explicit interest charged, the terms of these contracts determine the implicit costs of capital in trade and influence the bargaining positions of market participants.

Though the government is concerned about traders lending money to farmers and altering the farmers' bargaining positions, it often happens that farmers advance credit to traders. This practice was reported in 1953 by Dewey ([38], p. 107) and confirmed by this study in 1979/80. In the fresh root trade, assemblers often pay farmers only a part (typically half) of the purchase value when the preharvest contract is made. The rest is paid when the trader has delivered the roots to a starch factory or urban market and been paid for them. In this trade, quick turnaround allows the trader to repay the farmer within a week. The portion paid at purchase is negotiable, suggesting that farmers can bargain for a better price in exchange for granting credit.

A less common credit arrangement is the loan of working capital from medium or large starch mills to traders to finance preharvest purchases. The trader is paid the market price when he delivers the roots a few days later, and there is no explicit interest. A trader who borrows, however, might be obliged to deliver to the starch mill at a later time when supplies are scarce.

Another credit arrangement in the fresh root trade is the loan of roots from assemblers to household starch makers. This loan is repaid in cash after the household processes and sells the starch, which might be three days to a week later. Other traders sell starch on credit to krupuk firms. There is no explicit interest, but some of the returns to assemblers reflect interest on these short-term loans.

Credit moves up and down the fresh root marketing chain in a variety of arrangements. There are no explicit interest payments, but since the loans are repaid within a few days the absolute cost of working capital extended is small. These contracts stimulate the flow of trade, benefiting all market participants.

Similar informal credit contracts facilitate gaplek marketing, but the credit is supplied in only one direction, from buyer to seller: European shippers advance funds to pelleters. A contract for forward delivery of gaplek is accompanied by advances of up to 80 percent of the value of the contract, as much as three months in advance of the contracted delivery date. The balance is paid when the goods are on the ship.

Pelleters in turn enter into forward contract with wholesalers for supplies and advance from 25 to 75 percent of the contract value. Prices are stipulated for the term of the contract, usually one or two months. There is no price difference between a contract with a cash advance and a contract without one, so accepting the advance appears to be costless to the wholesaler. A wholesaler risks losing money, however, if internal prices increase. Most gaplek wholesalers accept cash advances from exporters, but they have other sources of funds and can accept or reject formal contracts depending on their appraisal of future prices.

Wholesalers are the single largest source of credit to gaplek assemblers, not only passing along advances they have received from exporters, but normally providing capital of their own to assemblers as well.[13] Assemblers who have established connections with a wholesaler receive cash advances for delivery of a particular good within two weeks. Prices paid at delivery are the same for those who receive cash advances as for those who do not. It is quite common for wholesalers to pay assemblers the full value of a price increase and to split or cover the loss when prices decrease and the assembler has already purchased at a higher price.

Credit terms between wholesalers and assemblers are easy because wholesalers use cash advances to assemblers to assure themselves of supplies. They depend on a large volume of trade to cover their fixed costs. Availability of credit depends on how fast the assembler turns over the advance and delivers supplies to the wholesaler. Assemblers who use the cash advance in other lines of trade and are slow in delivering find future credit more difficult to obtain.

Credit arrangements can limit the ability of assemblers to bypass wholesale markets and deliver directly to the ports, thus inhibiting price competition between wholesalers and assemblers. The forward sales contracts that prevail between wholesalers and pelleters, however, enhance the effectiveness of price competition at that level.

[13] The following discussion of credit relationships between wholesalers and assemblers draws heavily on Zain [168].

TABLE 6.5. *Terms and Conditions of Loan Programs for Small Enterprises*

	Small investment credit (KIK)	Permanent working capital credit (KMKP)	Mini-Credit
Maximum loan	Rp 5,000,000	Rp 5,000,000	Rp 200,000
Annual interest rate	10.5%	12%	10.5%
Term	5 years	3 years	1 year
Grace period	4 years	_a	_b
Collateral (*percent of loan value*)	100%	100%	50%
Other requirements	Trading license	Trading license	Letter from village head

SOURCE: Bank Rakyat Indonesia, personal communication.
[a]Not applicable because the loan account is handled on an overdraft basis.
[b]There is no penalty rate.

Government Loan Programs

Government credit institutions in rural areas are beginning to provide an alternative to informal systems. Two kinds of government loan programs for small traders and businessmen are available in rural areas through local branches of government banks. The first, Mini-Credit, provides loans of up to Rp 200,000 to small unlicensed traders, half of the loan to be secured by property. The second program, which includes investment (KIK) and working capital (KMKP), provides 100 percent secured loans of up to Rp 5,000,000 for traders licensed by the Ministry of Trade (Table 6.5).[14] Many of the loans from these programs are to merchants or transporters. Interest rates are among the lowest in Indonesia—1.0 to 1.25 percent a month.

Indigenous wholesalers and large assemblers borrow working capital and funds to buy trucks from these programs. Small assemblers and retailers typically borrow working capital. Many assemblers borrowed from government programs for the first time in 1979 to expand following the boom in the gaplek export trade.

Government loan programs have grown rapidly since their inception in 1974, but the distribution of funds through them varies widely. Early in 1980, for example, only 36 small loan applications had been approved in Limbangen, Garut, whereas 402 loans had been approved in Dampit, Malang. This difference reflects not only local commercial potential but also the policy of the Dampit branch to promote awareness of the program in the village and to interpret collateral requirements liberally.

[14]A third program (KCK) providing loans of up to Rp 10,000 to retailers and peddlers is administered through the village cooperatives.

Despite the low interest rates on government loans, they were not economically attractive to all assemblers. Inflation in the wholesale prices of agricultural products between 1974 and 1979 totaled 162 percent, which reduced the real value of loans significantly. The Mini-Credit program, for example, offered loans limited to Rp 100,000 until 1980, only enough to buy two tons of gaplek at 1979 prices. This program did not meet the needs of village traders who wished to expand their operations, and access to larger loans was limited by the license requirement for the KIK/KMKP program. License fees are Rp 22,000 for an assembler, plus the travel costs and nuisance of the application procedures. Holders of trading licenses have also found it more difficult to avoid paying taxes, because licensing brings them to the attention of the tax office.

For the many assemblers who have access to interest-free working capital from wholesalers, government programs provide only supplemental sources of working capital. Loans from a wholesaler are quickly obtained and require no collateral, although they cannot be used to buy fixed capital. The government loan programs are more attractive for assemblers who wish to invest in trucks or warehouses or to trade in commodities other than those specified by the wholesaler.

The strength of informal credit institutions in a particular region can determine the demand for formal credit. The increased export demand for gaplek following the 1978 devaluation and rising world prices was accommodated by existing informal credit relationships in Malang Kabupaten, where cassava and other export crops were already traded extensively. In Trenggalek Kabupaten, however, only small commercial quantities of gaplek had been available earlier, and wholesalers had established credit relationships with only a few assemblers. In this situation, the government loan program enabled assemblers to expand their working capital, to purchase trucks and build warehouses, and in some cases to set up as local wholesalers.

Marketing Efficiency

Returns to wholesalers and assemblers identified in the discussion of costs may reflect the differences in capital availability in various product markets. Exporters borrow and lend at low international rates and provide much of the working capital in the highly seasonal internal gaplek trade. Readily available capital in the gaplek trade results in more participants, more competition, and lower returns. The fresh root trade is financed mainly by assemblers and growers with their own capital resources or credit from producers, since starch factories extend only small amounts of credit. Less capital is available to fresh root traders, and the higher returns in the fresh root trade reflect this relative scarcity.

Returns to successful assemblers are higher than returns to wholesalers because of differences in access to credit institutions as well as differences in product markets. For wholesalers, sources of credit include exporters and private banks that charge 2 to 4 percent interest monthly. Assemblers rely primarily on informal credit contracts within the marketing system. Market and village banks provide only small amounts of credit at interest rates of 5 to 10 percent a month. Government loans at 1.25 percent a month are still of limited importance in rural areas. Higher returns to assemblers are directly related to the higher costs of capital in rural areas that reduce entry into the trade.

Informal credit arrangements that facilitate marketing have developed as a result of the lack of formal credit institutions. Village traders have limited access to formal credit, but any trader who proves trustworthy to his suppliers or customers can borrow from informal sources. Although informal loans ease constraints on working capital, they do not provide for fixed capital investment in transport and storage facilities. In times of rapidly increasing demand or supply, therefore, these arrangements may prove to be inadequate.

Cassava Price Determination

Discussion in the preceding chapters has emphasized the importance of both domestic and international markets for cassava. Three connections between markets are important in domestic price determination: product price linkages in international markets, the transmission of international cassava prices to Java ports, and the price linkages between ports and internal cassava markets on Java. The strength of these linkages reflects how well the cassava marketing system integrates prices through arbitrage across time, space, and form.

International Product Price Linkages

International price determination for gaplek is fairly straightforward (see Chapter 5). One dominant importer, the European Community, sets its internal grain prices in European currency units (ECUs), and national grain prices are determined by translating the price into national currencies. The import price for gaplek is determined by its value as a substitute for the energy in high-priced European feed grains.

Price determination in international starch markets is less transparent because of the variety of starches made, the number of markets, and the restrictions on imports imposed by some countries. Corn prices in the United States, however, provide a useful standard against which to compare cassava starch prices. Corn is the largest single source of starch in the world, and prices and quantities of other starches are strongly affected by movements in corn prices.

For Thailand, the dominant cassava supplier, fresh root prices are largely determined by gaplek prices, and starch firms cannot offer less than gaplek makers are paying. Gaplek prices, therefore, put a floor under Thai starch prices, and how much starch is made depends on the markets in which this price is competitive. When world corn prices increase, cornstarch prices rise, the number of markets in which cassava starch is competitive expands, and more cassava starch is made. Falling world corn prices result in reduced cassava starch exports because starch prices fall below the price floor set by the gaplek market.

Bangkok wholesale starch and pellet prices moved together closely from 1971 to 1979, as indicated by a correlation coefficient of 0.93.[15] But cassava starch prices increased relative to gaplek prices when corn prices reached record highs in 1974. In that year Thai starch exports reached an all-time high. Starch exports were also influenced by gaplek price movements. In 1978 gaplek prices were very low and starch exports increased, but when gaplek prices rebounded to record highs in 1979, exports were half the previous year's level.

Transmission of International Cassava Prices to Java Ports

Cassava is exported from Java as gaplek and imported into Java as starch. In theory, cassava prices at Java ports cannot fall below the export price because excess supplies will be exported at that price. Similarly, increased imports will fill any shortfalls in quantities demanded when the domestic price equals the import price. Import and export parity prices put upper and lower bounds on domestic prices. The difference between these boundary prices is caused by international transportation costs.

Calculations of the import- and export-determined price bounds

---

[15] The correlation of the first differences, 0.54, is also significantly different from zero.

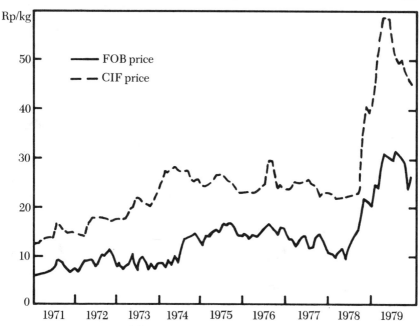

Rp/kg

SOURCE : CIF prices are Bangkok wholesale starch prices (Bank of Thailand, *Monthly Bulletin*) plus trans-portation costs (an index of freight rates between Japan and Indonesia multiplied by the actual freight rate from Thailand to Indonesia in 1979) and import tariff. FOB prices are CIF Rotterdam pellet prices (Alfred Toepfer & Co.)minus transportation costs (an index of rates between U.S. ports and Rotterdam multiplied by the acutal freight rate from Indonesia to Europe in 1979).
    [a]Assumes that 5 kilograms of cassava roots are required to produce 1 kilogram of starch and 3 kilograms to produce 1 kilogram of pellets. No other costs are considered.

Figure 6.2. FOB and CIF Cassava Prices at Java Ports, 1971–79 (fresh root equivalent)[a]

for cassava must take into consideration product form and trade taxes as well as transportation costs. Boundary prices for the 1970's are shown in Figure 6.2. The upper bound on domestic prices is established by the Thai starch price plus transportation costs to Java and import tariffs, and the lower bound is established by European gaplek prices minus transportation costs from Java.

The level of the band rose from 1971 to 1977, fell in 1978, and rose dramatically in 1979, following a rise in world cassava prices and the 50 percent devaluation of the rupiah. The width of the band varied from Rp 5 to Rp 28, averaging Rp 12.[16] Without the tariff on starch imports, the width of the band would have averaged Rp 4.

Evidence of movements in Java prices between the export price

[16]Changes in shipping rates account for some of this variation. Shipping costs doubled in 1973 from the 1971 base, fell back to the 1971 level from 1975 to 1978, and nearly tripled in 1979, partly as a result of devaluation.

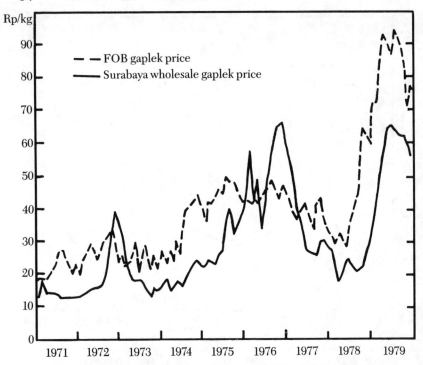

SOURCE: FOB gaplek prices are CIF Rotterdam pellet prices (Alfred Toepfer & Co.) minus transportation costs (an index of freight rates between U.S. ports and Rotterdam multiplied by the actual freight rate from Indonesia to Europe in 1979). Wholesale gaplek prices are from the Surabaya Brokers' Association.

Figure 6.3. Surabaya FOB and Wholesale Gaplek Prices, 1971–79

floor and the import price ceiling is found in the fact that changes in domestic prices correspond to changes in trade flows. From 1971 to 1979, gaplek prices in Java ports (as measured by Surabaya prices) were at the export price floor in most months (Figure 6.3). Surabaya prices generally followed the rising trend in European prices from 1971 to 1977, the fall in 1978, and the steep increase following the devaluation of the rupiah in 1978 and the rebound in world prices in 1979. In three periods in the 1970's, however, Surabaya prices rose sharply above export parity.

Comparison of yearly exports (Table 6.6) with Surabaya wholesale and export prices (Figure 6.3) and Jakarta rice prices (Figure 6.4) shows the degree to which exports responded to these price changes. Exports were high through 1973. They fell late in 1973, when prices rose, but recovered somewhat in 1974, declining again as rice prices rose in 1975. Domestic prices were at their highest relative to world prices in 1976, the year of record starch imports. In

TABLE 6.6. *Exports of Gaplek and Cassava Starch from Java, 1970–79*
(000 tons)

Year	Gaplek exports	Starch exports[a]	Total exports as percent of production[b]
1970	260.5	5.9	10.2%
1971	365.3	1.0	13.7
1972	240.0	2.3	9.2
1973	41.7	1.6	1.6
1974	186.6	9.3	6.3
1975	87.3	− 22.5	1.6
1976	9.5	− 64.1	− 3.3
1977	37.5	− 11.9	0.5
1978	98.2	− 0.4	3.1
1979	494.6	1.4	15.1

SOURCES: Indonesia [71], [72], [76].
[a]In some years starch exports include gaplek flour. Starch import data are total imports into Indonesia, since import data by port of destination are not available. In calculating net exports, it is assumed that all imports entered Java.
[b]Fresh root equivalent converted at 5:1 for starch and 3:1 for gaplek.

1978 and 1979 exports rebounded with the return of domestic prices to the export floor.

During the three periods when gaplek prices rose above the export price floor, real prices of rice also rose or cassava production declined. The first increase above export parity occurred in late 1972 when rice prices rose as a result of both poor crops in Indonesia and increases in world rice prices. After the 1973 rice and cassava harvests began, cassava prices returned to the export floor. The second increase came in late 1975. Domestic rice prices rose that year as the government reduced the subsidy on rice imports and allowed domestic rice prices to rise with the world market trend. Domestic rice prices remained high in real terms through the first half of 1976. In addition to the rise in rice prices, cassava production declined in 1976; gaplek prices rose above the export floor for the third time from mid-1976 to early 1977. In 1977 cassava production returned to its previous trend, rice prices stabilized, and gaplek prices returned to export parity. Because world cassava prices declined in 1978, Indonesian cassava prices fell sharply in their return to the export price floor.[17]

Gaplek Price Determination at Java Ports

Gaplek prices within Java are set by domestic supplies of staple foodstuffs and demand for cassava products, but they cannot be less

[17]This world price decline was caused in part by record Thai exports that drove European prices down. For further details, see Chapter 5.

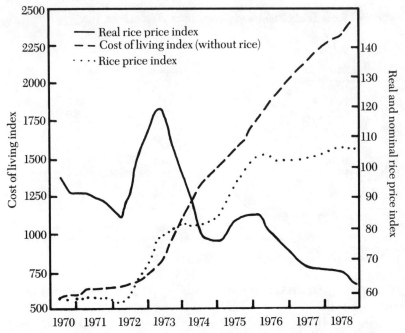

SOURCE: Mears [101], p. 233. Index base: 1966 = 100. Real rice price index is the rice price index divided by the cost of living index without rice.

Figure 6.4. Comparison of Real and Nominal Jakarta Rice Prices, 1970–79

than export parity. This implies that the total demand curve for cassava has two portions—a downward-sloping domestic curve and a perfectly elastic export floor. The total demand curve should be strongly kinked at the lower bound determined by export parity. Accurate estimation of domestic demand is not possible because marketed quantity series are not available for cassava or its principal substitutes, rice and corn; however, the change in price determinants between the domestic and export portions of the demand curve can be tested.

In the following model, principal domestic influences on the price of gaplek at Surabaya, represented by the wholesale price (P_i), are the availability of other staple foodstuffs as reflected in the retail price of rice (P_r) and the monthly quantity of cassava harvested on Java (Q) in hundreds of tons.[18] Export parity is defined as the FOB

[18]This formulation requires the assumptions (1) that the price of rice is fixed by Indonesian government policy and not simultaneously determined with the cassava price by demand for foods, and (2) that monthly cassava production represents gaplek supply. Because gaplek stocks contribute to marketed quantities during the off-season, this model ignores the simultaneity in determination of prices and quantities marketed.

price of pellets in Surabaya three months earlier (P_w).[19] A dummy variable (D) has a value of 1 when wholesale prices at Surabaya are at export parity ($P_i = P_w$) and a value of 0 when they are above export parity ($P_i > P_w$). Use of this variable allows the model to change the price determinants between the two portions of the demand curve. Variable P_w enters the equation only at the floor and variables DP and DQ test for changes in the relationship between cassava prices and domestic factors at export parity. The estimated equation follows, with t-statistics in parentheses (all estimates are significant at the 0.05 level).

$$P_i = 11.74 - 13.08D + 0.64DP_w + 0.29P_r - 0.27DP_r - 0.09Q + 0.10DQ \quad (1)$$
$$\quad (3.01) \quad (-3.15) \quad (12.22) \quad (10.50) \quad (-8.54) \quad (-2.82) \quad (2.86)$$

$R^2 = .91$ \hfill Durbin-Watson $= 1.72$

When prices are at export parity ($D = 1$), the coefficients of rice prices (P_r) and cassava production (Q) are not significant.[20] Gaplek prices depend on export prices alone.

$$P_i = -1.34 + 0.64P_w \quad (2)$$
$$\quad (0.2) \quad (12.2)$$

When gaplek prices are above the export price ($D = 0$), the coefficients of rice prices and cassava production are significant, and these domestic variables explain gaplek prices.

$$P_i = 11.74 + 0.29P_r - 0.09Q \quad (3)$$
$$\quad (3.0) \quad (10.5) \quad (-2.8)$$

The estimated demand curve shows the expected kink clearly and explains the total variation in internal gaplek prices quite well. When gaplek prices are at export parity only world prices affect them, and the elasticity of the Surabaya price with respect to the world price is very close to one (0.95).[21] Gaplek prices in Surabaya were at the world floor price during 84 of 108 months for 1971 to

[19]The wholesale gaplek prices were collected by the Surabaya Broker's Association. FOB gaplek prices are CIF Rotterdam pellet prices (from Alfred Toepfer & Co.) minus shipping costs. These prices are lagged three months because European landed prices are not immediately reflected in domestic prices. All price data are monthly observations from 1971 to 1979 in rupiah per kilogram. Cassava production equals area harvested monthly multiplied by average yields, which are reported for each third of the year in Indonesia [71].

[20]When $D = 1$ the coefficient of rice prices is the sum of the coefficients of P_r and DP_r, and similarly the sum of Q and DQ for cassava production. The t-statistics of these summed coefficients for P_r and Q are 1.3 and 0.9 respectively, indicating that they are not significantly different from zero at the 10 percent level.

[21]Calculated at the mean of observations at the floor.

1979, so that world prices are the most important price-determining factor.

Although the portion of the demand curve above the export price is misspecified, domestic factors, particularly the rice price, do seem to explain gaplek prices.[22] The quantity variable has a very small impact on price; the elasticity of the gaplek price with respect to quantity is 0.10 at the mean of observations on the domestic portion of the demand curve. The strong association between the price of rice and the price of gaplek indicates that the price of rice does affect cassava demand. The elasticity of the price of gaplek with respect to the price of rice is 0.85 when gaplek prices are above the floor.[23] These results are consistent with the view of gaplek as a "fallback" staple to which consumers shift when the price of the principal staple, rice, increases.

Transmission of Gaplek Prices to Producing-Area Markets

The lower export-determined boundary price in internal markets is reduced by additional transportation costs to the port. Producing-area prices should therefore reflect world prices in fewer months, and domestic demand and supply will influence prices more often. The number of months in which gaplek prices in 19 producing-area markets were at the export floor in 1971 to 1979 varied from 35 in Garut to 76 in Kediri, all less than the 84 months that prices were at the floor in Surabaya.[24] The degree to which internal market prices reflect Surabaya prices depends on whether internal prices are at the floor. When at the floor, prices in 14 markets are correlated above .90 with Surabaya prices, but when above the floor, no market prices are correlated above .90 with the port. Domestic demand and supply determine producing-area prices when they are above the floor; then these prices do not follow world price movements as reflected in Surabaya prices.

The integration among internal market prices also varies depending upon whether prices are at the floor or above it. When gaplek

[22] The Durbin-Watson statistic of 1.74 indicates that the errors do not show significant first-order autocorrelation. In spite of the misspecification of the domestic portion of the demand curve caused by excluding stocks and marketed supply, the effect of these missing variables on the residuals is not apparent. This fortunate result is probably due to the fairly small number of months when domestic demand determined prices in Surabaya.

[23] A true cross-price elasticity would measure the change in quantity of gaplek demanded in response to changes in the price of rice.

[24] The position of the floor is determined by visual inspection of the data and is defined as a percentage of the FOB price.

TABLE 6.7. *Correlations of Cassava Prices Among*
Nineteen Producing-Area Markets
(No. of markets correlated)

Correlation greater than or equal to	Prices above export parity price	Prices at export parity price
.80	102	149
.85	63	137
.90	27	106
.95	2	32
Total possible pairs	171	171

SOURCE: Indonesia, Ministry of Agriculture.
NOTE: Calculations are based on monthly retail prices, 1970–79, from 15 kabupaten markets representing major producing areas.

prices in producing-area markets are above the export floor, local demand and supply may cause prices to vary more independently among regions. To test this hypothesis, coefficients of correlation between gaplek prices in 19 markets were calculated separately for the months when prices in these markets were at the export price floor and the months when they were above it (Table 6.7). The number of market pairs correlated above .80 is 149 (out of 171) at the export floor and 102 above the floor.

In order to observe the structure of market integration when prices are domestically determined, market prices correlated at or above .90 when above the export price floor are mapped in Figure 6.5. The most striking result is the integration of markets in the principal consuming area from Gunung Kidul to Trenggalek. Tuban and Sumenep, wholesale centers where gaplek is stored, are also centers for market information.

The above discussion has focused on gaplek prices. The prices of fresh roots and gaplek are closely linked because any variation in relative prices will cause supplies to shift between product markets. Prices of fresh roots and gaplek are correlated above .90 in 15 of the 19 producing-area markets examined here, and above .80 in the remaining four markets.[25] Since fresh root and gaplek markets are linked, world market prices for gaplek also have an impact on fresh root prices, and the price determination model presented above appears relevant to both cassava products.

More generally, the price linkages between internal markets on Java and across product forms give evidence of a reasonably efficient

[25] For further discussion of product price linkages, see Unnevehr [151].

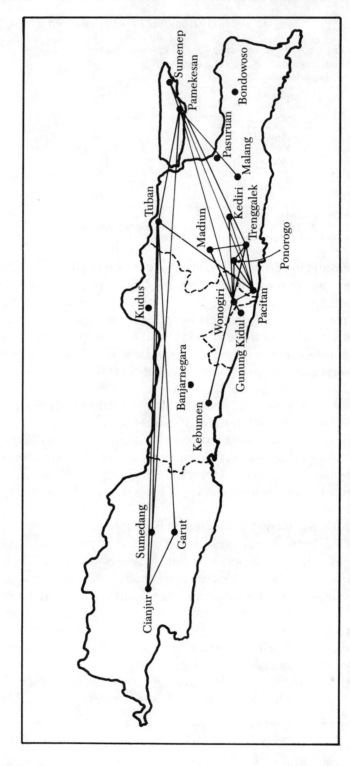

SOURCE: Retail price data collected by the Ministry of Agriculture. The lines connect market pairs with prices correlated ≥0.90 over the years 1970 to 1979.

Figure 6.5. Gaplek Price Correlations

marketing system. In addition, the strong links between cassava prices on Java and gaplek prices in Europe have important implications for the level and stability of cassava prices on Java, a point developed in Chapter 7.

Conclusions

The upland producers who sell cassava and the many poor consumers who rely on purchased cassava to meet calorie requirements are served by a reasonably efficient marketing system. Evidence of this efficiency is found in the market response to cost incentives, the degree of competition in cassava markets, and the integration of cassava prices. Nonetheless, improvements in efficiency or in the ability of the system to respond to change can still be made.

The correlation between place and timing of first sale and improvements in roads provides evidence that market participants respond to cost incentives. Where roads are poor, farmers transport cassava to market themselves and often process it into gaplek to reduce bulk. Improved roads allow traders to buy standing crops and take advantage of scale economies in harvesting and transport. Shifts to shorter, cheaper channels indicate that the marketing system is sufficiently competitive to encourage reduction of costs.

Evidence of competition is also found in the degree of access to markets. The greatly expanded road network and increased supply of small trucks to reach producing areas in the 1970's have provided greater access to markets for farmers and assemblers, most of whom can sell into several cassava markets or to a number of buyers. Price information is widely available and is transmitted quickly along marketing chains, allowing market participants to take advantage of trading opportunities.

A principal market imperfection was the poor access of assemblers to formal credit, which constrains rapid market expansion. Informal credit contracts provide working capital for assemblers, but these funds cannot be used to bypass wholesale markets or invest in fixed capital. Government loan programs have begun to provide credit to village traders, and further development of credit institutions would improve marketing by allowing village traders to expand their operations and make fixed capital investments.

The analysis of cassava prices confirmed that there are strong links between world and domestic prices on Java. Prices of cassava were seen to rise above the export-determined floor in response to shortages of domestic food supplies, however, as reflected by a rise in the real price of rice. Fluctuations in cassava prices are thus not the result of market inefficiency. The variations in prices from 1975 to 1980 can be traced primarily to government policy, world cassava prices, and changes in demand for cassava and its substitutes.

The results of the price analysis indicate which policy instruments are likely to be most effective in altering producer and consumer incentives. Export prices put a floor under domestic prices that is usually effective in the harvest season, when most producer sales are made. Trade-related measures, including tariffs, subsidies, quotas, and the exchange rate, can change producer prices. Rice prices and rice price policy also affect cassava prices. High cassava prices, imports of starch, and decreased exports of gaplek in 1975 and 1976 were adjustments to increases in the price of rice. If there had been no tariff on starch imports, they would have entered at a lower price and eased the pressure on cassava prices. This would particularly benefit those poorer consumers who shift to cassava when rice is expensive.

7. Cassava's Role in Food Policy

Walter P. Falcon, William O. Jones, and
Scott R. Pearson

Food policy discussions in Indonesia have typically started and ended with concern about rice self-sufficiency. The premise of this chapter is that a broader view of food policy, especially policy for cassava on Java, is now warranted. This need for a new perspective arises from past production successes rather than from previous policy failures.

Throughout the 1960's and 1970's there was understandable concern in Indonesia about the country's dependence on imported rice. This staple provides half the calories in the average diet, yet in five recent years imports were between 1.5 and 2.0 million tons—about 10 percent of Indonesian production and more than 15 percent of all the rice traded internationally (Table 7.1). In one critical period, 1972 to 1974, import supplies were difficult to obtain and import prices of rice tripled to more than $500 a ton. These troublesome events nevertheless had the positive effect of focusing attention on the food sector and on the need for programs and policies related to rice prices, investment, and research.

The growth in rice production that resulted from this attention has been impressive. Domestic rice production grew about 4 percent annually between 1968 and 1977, thereby contributing to the strong overall performance of the economy. Moreover, the 9 percent annual growth of rice production between 1977 and 1981 greatly reduced Indonesia's import requirements.

Yet Indonesia's food system can hardly be described as working perfectly. The FAO [54] estimates that 30 percent of Indonesia's population (39 million people) were moderately to severely undernourished in 1973. Yields of crops on Java other than rice remain lower than those of many neighboring countries (Table 7.2), in part because the upland cropping systems that provide much of the cassava, corn, soybeans, and peanuts have not been prominent on the government's policy agenda. In addition, the structure of food demand

TABLE 7.1. *Indonesian Rice Production and Trade, 1968–81*
(Million tons)

Year	Indonesian rice production	End-year government rice stocks	Indonesian rice imports	Total world exports	Rice price "Thai 5%s" (U.S. $/ton, FOB Bangkok)
1968	11.67	.50	0.707	7.942	$201.6
1969	12.25	.26	0.605	8.428	186.9
1970	13.14	.53	0.956	8.821	144.0
1971	13.72	.53	0.509	9.305	129.0
1972	13.18	.17	0.734	9.056	147.1
1973	14.61	.58	1.657	9.366	350.0
1974	15.28	.85	1.132	8.784	542.0
1975	15.18	.63	0.693	8.610	363.1
1976	15.84	.54	1.302	8.993	254.5
1977	15.88	.51	1.973	10.870	272.2
1978	17.52	1.18	1.842	9.686	367.5
1979	17.87	.81	1.922	11.856	331.3
1980	20.25	1.71	2.012	12.547	435.8
1981	21.67	2.50[a]	0.550	13.070	478.3

SOURCES: Mears [101]. Rice imports for 1968–80, FAO [52]; for 1981, World Bank [167]. Exports for 1968–79, FAO [52]; for 1980 & 1981, USDA [145], FG–19–82, June 15, 1982. Prices for 1968–79, World Bank [166]; for 1980 & 1981, FAO [58].
[a]Preliminary estimate.

TABLE 7.2. *Yield Comparisons for Six Basic Food Crops, Selected Countries, 1980*
(kg/ha)

Country	Rice (paddy)	Corn	Cassava	Sweet potatoes	Soybeans	Peanuts (in shell)
Bangladesh	2,032	773	–	10,890	–	1,160
Burma	2,643	1,250	9,115	4,075	679	941
China	4,163	2,980	13,016	8,231	1,042	1,249
India	2,049	1,103	17,568	7,111	970	853
Malaysia	2,698	1,327	10,192	9,474	1,579	3,758
Pakistan	2,400	1,365	–	4,565	514	1,245
Philippines	2,154	950	10,270	12,632	882	909
Sri Lanka	2,386	1,100	9,636	9,250	1,000	650
Thailand	1,968	2,017	13,300	9,876	778	1,083
Indonesia	3,187	1,241	9,366	6,750	769	1,500

SOURCE: FAO [57].

is changing rapidly as a result of the booming general economy, with consequent strains on the feed-livestock economy. These new food problems also create new opportunities for Indonesia's Fourth Five-Year Plan, which is scheduled to commence in 1984. Ironically, cassava's potential role in Indonesia's food policy is now greater than in earlier eras when concerns with food shortages were paramount.[1]

[1]A fuller description of how cassava could assist Indonesia in times of rice scarcity is contained in Afiff, Falcon, and Timmer [2].

Food Policy Objectives

Rice self-sufficiency, whatever its limitations as an economic concept, proved a powerful device for mobilizing a limited range of agricultural efforts within Indonesia during the 1970's.[2] Now that Indonesia is moving from being a low- to a middle-income country, policymakers seem determined to expand the array of food-policy objectives. A survey of food plans from around the world indicates that the following four objectives can be useful (Timmer et al. [140]): (1) efficient growth in the food and agriculture sectors; (2) improved income distribution, primarily through efficient employment; (3) satisfactory nutritional status for the entire population by providing a minimum subsistence floor; and (4) adequate food supplies to ensure against poor harvests, natural disasters, or uncertain world food supplies and prices. Whether or not these goals are adopted specifically by Indonesian planners, they are useful criteria for assessing the role of cassava on Java during the 1980's.

Efficient Growth of Income

The production analysis of Chapter 2 underscores the vital role of cassava in upland cropping systems and the potential of innovations to improve cassava yields. Cassava now contributes about 40 percent of the value of total food crop production in the upland systems, ranging from 25 percent in Garut to 60 percent in Kediri. It also supplies about half of total crop sales in these areas and about one-fourth of gross family income. In short, cassava is very important in the upland regions of Java that cannot produce irrigated rice.

Opportunities exist for increasing cassava yields from 25 to 100 percent and for doubling the total value of output from cassava intercropped systems. These gains would decrease the cost of producing a ton of cassava, but would increase the amount of labor used and its return. Whereas rice yields on Java are beginning to approach biological ceilings, cassava yield increases ranging from 2 to 8 tons per hectare are possible over widespread areas.

Two further aspects of the growth objective are important. First, cassava production in Indonesia is socially profitable. Cassava is exported in the form of gaplek and starch, and internal cassava pricing is at international levels. Even if the implicit fertilizer subsidy (relative to world prices) were removed, the suggested yield improve-

[2] See Mears [101] for complete discussion of rice policy.

ments would provide increased returns to land, family labor, and management in most upland cropping systems. Second, most of the upland areas of Java have been less a part of the development process than have the irrigated rice areas. The uplands contain many poor people; a focus on cassava can thus be justified by its contribution to regional equity as well as its potential for rapid growth.

Improved Income Distribution

Creating productive rural employment on Java to improve income distribution is a primary objective of Indonesia's planners. Sixty percent of the Indonesian labor force is in agriculture, and rural employment problems are especially severe on Java, where there is little unused arable land and modal farm size is only about one-third hectare. Moreover, the country's labor force is still growing at a rate of 2.5 percent annually, adding to underemployment in the countryside and creating additional pressure for migration and urbanization.

Irrigated rice production and rice milling have long been recognized for their positive employment effects. The use of 300 or more days of labor per hectare (per crop) of rice is common throughout Java, and extensive research has been done on the employment aspects of rice milling (Timmer [137]; Collier et al. [24]). However, little work has been done on the capacity of upland systems on Java to create additional jobs. The studies of cassava production reported in Chapter 2 demonstrate that there is substantial potential for increased employment in the upland areas.

Cassava is a hardy crop requiring little labor that is grown for food security in many parts of the world, to be harvested or not depending on prices and supplies of other staples. Although it is occasionally grown on Java in this manner, it typically is not. It is instead a dominant source of income and employment in complicated upland cropping systems that include corn, upland rice, peanuts, and soybeans. These systems are already labor-intensive, and acceptance of the agronomic recommendations of Chapter 2 would make them even more so.

Labor use on cassava varies substantially with location, soil, and production system. Most of the labor coefficients found in this study are in the range of 200 to 500 days per hectare per year, with about one-third of the labor typically supplied by women. In addition, with improved cropping systems such as those recommended by CRIA for Lampung, average annual employment could be increased on the intercropped systems from about 280 to 670 days per hectare. Furthermore, they would increase profits per hectare, improve daily returns to labor, and reduce costs of cassava production by 10 to 30 percent per ton.

The employment aspects of cassava go beyond farm production. A total of about 20 million days of labor are created annually by the starch industry on Java and Lampung. More than 65 percent of this amount is in household and small-scale starch firms on Java, with women holding a predominant share of the jobs. Although the rural starch industry is seasonal, it operates mainly during periods when there are few other job opportunities. Therefore, an expansion of the cassava processing system would also generate additional employment.

Three conclusions important for development planning can be drawn from these employment data. First, the use of labor in cassava production and processing is efficient because the products are competitive internationally. These jobs are neither make-work activities nor tasks created by inefficient industries behind high protective tariffs. Second, government policy, especially as it affects minimum wages, subsidies to capital, and tax concessions, can have an important bearing on labor intensity, especially in processing. Third, the creation of additional employment in rural areas is essential in the fight against hunger. In an important sense, the goal of development is to relieve individuals of hard work and drudgery, but relief can come only if jobs exist. Many of Java's hungry are undernourished because they are underemployed and cannot afford to eat well enough to meet recommended daily allowances of nutrients. Creating productive jobs is thus the most efficient means of redistributing income, for in this way individuals can solve their own nutrition problems. Cassava is now much more important on Java for its capacity to generate additional employment and rural income than for its ability to supply more food. Because income rather than food supply is the primary hunger issue, it matters little whether cassava products are consumed domestically or exported.

Adequate Nutrition

No single food causes diets to be poor. Diets may be unbalanced by lack of protein even if the primary staple is a good source of amino acids. Conversely, balanced diets can be achieved with low-protein staples. Widespread confusion about protein and HCN in cassava

has caused some analysts to be unduly negative about cassava, especially its use in the diets of poor people.

Cassava's best attribute is the cheap calories it supplies. The primary nutritional problem for the poorest 50 percent of the population on Java is inadequate calorie intake. Because cassava calories
cost less than half as much as calories from rice, poor people can consume more calories by eating cassava. This savings on calories means
that low-income consumers also have more cash to purchase other
goods, including foods high in protein. Without cassava, which supplies about 10 percent of total calories consumed on Java, the nutritional status of the population would be substantially worse, especially in the countryside. Rural consumers in 1978 ate a per-person
average of 57 kilograms of cassava (fresh root equivalent), composed
of 40 percent fresh roots, 48 percent gaplek, and 12 percent starch.
This total was roughly six times the amount consumed in cities.

Cassava has the deserved reputation of being a food of the poor.
The poorest 15 percent of the rural population eat 50 percent more
cassava than rice. Whether or not they would prefer to eat rice is important, but not determining. Their economic circumstances force
them to consume cassava. Cassava is also much more important
among middle- and upper-income groups than is commonly assumed. Consumption of fresh roots is significant in cities (10 kilograms per capita annually), and consumption of starch products,
such as krupuk, is highly elastic with respect to income in both rural
and urban areas.

Two important implications can be drawn from the consumption
aspects of cassava. First, the demand for cassava products, especially
among the poor, is sensitive to the price of cassava relative to the
price of other staples and to income levels. Income growth among
the poor would increase cassava consumption and decrease the incidence of hunger. A reduction in relative cassava prices would also affect consumption significantly. A 30 percent relative price decline,
for example, might increase the consumption of cassava by the poorest 50 percent in rural areas by about 40 percent. Second, new cassava products and increased use of existing food-processing techniques such as admixtures could shift long-run consumption patterns on Java toward locally produced goods and away from imports
such as wheat flour.

Food Security

There is a danger that the excellent rice crops of 1980 and 1981 will lead to complacency on food programs within Indonesia. These harvests were assisted by good weather, and lower rice production levels in the future are a possibility.[3] In addition to having uncertain weather, Java is also vulnerable to pest and disease attacks. In 1981, two-thirds of Java's irrigated rice was planted to one variety, IR 36. This variety has produced excellent yields and has adapted well to many ecosystems. Yet the dependence on one or two strains, which may prove susceptible to new viruses or pests, is risky. For the longer run, Indonesia has the capability to create and multiply new rice varieties. BULOG, the national logistics agency, is also much more able than before to handle shortfalls in rice output through its buffer-stock operations. Nevertheless, food security is still important, and for this goal too, cassava has a role to play.

In 1973, 1974, and 1976, cassava showed its potential as a flexible food source. As relative rice prices increased, consumers shifted to other staples, especially cassava. This shift gave policymakers additional freedom and reduced some of the difficulties with rice imports and with food-led increases in the cost of living. Cassava was particularly valuable in ameliorating hardships for the poorest groups whose standard of living is most harmed by rising food costs. This point was demonstrated again in 1983 when a two-month delay in the rains caused strains in the Java rice economy. Poorer rural consumers, as in the past, turned to cassava during the *paceklik* period.

Policy Priorities

If the potential of an improved cassava system is to be realized, a set of policy decisions is needed for cassava's production, consumption, marketing, processing, and trade components. One larger strategic issue—cassava pricing—may also require reassessment during the next few years.

Macro and Sectoral Policy

One of the contributors to Indonesia's agricultural and general economic success in the 1970's was innovative macro policy. Several

[3]The best assessment of production prospects for the 1980's is provided by the World Bank [167].

elements of that policy are worth noting, for they are in marked contrast to approaches taken in many other developing countries. One such element was a sensible exchange-rate policy, which had widespread effects on the food sector. The devaluation of the rupiah in November 1978, for example, was carried out not because Indonesia had a balance-of-payments crisis (Dick [39]) but because of concern about the continuing profitability of labor-intensive tradable goods from both industry and agriculture. A sound interest-rate policy was also important in promoting appropriate choices of techniques in processing industries. Many developing countries have fallen into the trap of negative real rates of interest, which results in excessive capital intensity and the displacement of productive jobs (McKinnon [99]). Indonesia, by contrast, maintained a rate structure close to the opportunity cost of capital (Patten, Dapice, and Falcon [118]; Dapice [35]; and Grenville [60]). These points, though dealt with here in very summary fashion, demonstrate the need for a continuation of strong macro policy, especially where interest and exchange rates are concerned. Economic decisions in the Central Bank, the Ministry of Finance, and the Planning Agency (BAPPENAS) can support or negate virtually any commodity-specific policies attempted by another ministry.

General sectoral policies on agriculture also affect cassava in important ways. Fertilizer distribution and investments in irrigation are two examples of the sensitivity of the cassava system to other agricultural developments. The decision to expand fertilizer distribution in the early 1970's was important to all of Java's agriculture. Prior to that time, urea was not available in some rural areas or was available only through government programs such as BIMAS. The decision to permit broadened fertilizer distribution through the cooperatives and private trade, though intended mainly to support the rice-production programs, was also the key element in increased cassava yields.

Other agricultural programs had an opposite impact on cassava. The large government allocations for rice research and for irrigation projects on Java affected rice positively but cassava negatively. A high percentage of the scientific talent working in agriculture has been oriented only toward rice, causing research and field testing of other crops to lag. Similarly, renovated irrigation projects on Java expanded the area in which rice could be grown, but partly at the expense of acreage in other crops.

These examples illustrate the interconnected nature of food policy across commodities and agencies. Some of the most important decisions, such as devaluation, are made for reasons largely unrelated to food generally or cassava specifically. The examples also illustrate the difficulties in suggesting policy changes that are necessary or sufficient conditions for improving a particular commodity system.

Production

A significant increase in cassava production on Java can be an important component of an improved food system in the 1980's. For production to expand, however, the government will have to alter its approach to commodity policy. Fortunately, there are important lessons in Indonesia's own experience of the last 15 years. What is needed for cassava (and for the entire array of upland systems) is a government commitment comparable to that recently given rice. This commitment would embrace varietal research and testing, extension work, production credit, and investments. An integrated program for upland areas would be an effective means of ensuring future growth and improved equity on Java.

The greatest need in the production component of the system is for a set of decentralized variety-and-fertilizer tests.[4] There exists no specific cassava variety or technology package that can be borrowed directly from ongoing work at international research centers, but there are promising locally improved varieties, such as Adira I, that need to be tested under a range of soil and moisture conditions. There are also significant variations in the productivity of existing field varieties. The potential contribution that can result from identifying and distributing cuttings of superior existing varieties can be great and the cost modest. Theft of Adira cuttings from the collection at Bogor confirms farmers' willingness to experiment with new clones. Additional breeding experiments at Bogor and elsewhere may eventually produce superior varieties. At present, however, basic varietal research is more advanced than regional test trials under both experimental and farm conditions.

A sound regional testing program should have several dimensions. Variety and fertilizer tests of the response of individual varieties to diverse soil conditions are urgently needed. Research in Indonesia to date has shown that cassava responds more to nitrogen and less to phosphorus and potassium than has been the case in many other

---

[4] See Jones [89] for a discussion of this point.

countries. Confirming these initial results and developing a set of area-specific recommendations are therefore fundamental. This decentralized field testing should also include testing of fungicides on planting materials. Research at CIAT has emphasized the impact that this inexpensive technique can have on the creation of vigorous plant stands.

Decentralized field experiments would have several advantages. They would confirm the economics of recommendations drawn from experiment stations, serve as useful demonstration plots to local farmers, and provide a sounder basis for an expanded cassava-based credit (BIMAS) program. The present technical basis for cassava credit and technology programs on Java is questionable. Two years of varietal and fertilizer testing at 8 to 10 sites would provide the necessary background for a sensible upland program. The results of the tests would be directly transferable, at least to situations where cassava is now planted in pure stands or in existing mixed-crop systems.

For new and more complicated intercropped systems, the necessary research must occur over a longer time. Little local work has been done on the development of improved seed varieties for peanuts, corn, soybeans, and other legumes suitable for upland systems. Many of these are high-value crops, but they are also very risky because of pest and other problems. Hence the necessary research, extension, and credit programs for improving the full intercropped systems will be much more difficult to establish.

These long-run difficulties need not stand in the way of constructive first steps. Improving fertilizer and variety recommendations for cassava could make an early impact on production without huge investments in either money or manpower. The testing involved will also be instrumental in determining a regional strategy and in selecting the particular areas in which the production potential of cassava can be achieved most easily. Testing is also needed to determine whether the current fertilizer distribution system, which emphasizes urea but not phosphorus and potassium, is adequate for the upland regions.

Consumption

One of the major obstacles to improved cassava policy is the negative image of the commodity in the minds of policymakers. This image can be traced in part to cassava's association with poverty, to concerns about cassava's protein content, and to the large-scale forced consumption of gaplek during the Second World War. If basic mis-conceptions can be cleared away about who eats cassava products and why, the government might wish to pursue two consumption policies (in addition to pricing).

The most promising short-run action is increasing the use of cassava in admixtures. The centralized nature of wheat-flour milling in Indonesia provides an excellent opportunity for mixing cassava and wheat flours into a 20 percent blend that would be cheaper than pure wheat flour. Wheat imports currently are in excess of one million tons a year, and the blending of cassava flour would be an import substitute that should cause little or no loss in the flour's baking and cooking qualities. Some mixing in of cheaper cassava flours is occurring already in bakeries and noodle factories, so the idea of mixtures is not new. Systematic blending at the mill level, however, would standardize cassava flour quality and increase demand for it.

Increased government support for food-technology experiments with cassava could be a second line of policy activity. Indonesia is unusual in the forms in which cassava is eaten. Other cassava-producing countries in South America and Africa have developed techniques of processing the root that result in a staple food that is more convenient to use, has a longer shelf life, and is more income elastic than gaplek. Adapting simple household techniques in use elsewhere to make these products suitable for local tastes and food preferences on Java could augment the demand for cassava in the longer run. The costs of completing these experimental activities through several universities and institutes would probably be small.

Additional experimentation with gaplek or other dried forms would be useful for another purpose. If the government wished to develop a subsidized food-distribution program for the needy—a topic whose full treatment is beyond the scope of this volume—some form of gaplek would be a good staple to use.[5] The poor, particularly in rural areas, would accept a gaplek ration, whereas middle- and upper-income families would not have a strong demand for the product. The commodity would thus "self-target" among the most vulnerable groups, and the resource costs and leakages would be much less than if rice were used. Gaplek would probably have to be laced with chilies (to deter its use as animal feed) and possibly with vege-

[5] See Timmer, Falcon, and Pearson [140], Austin [3], and Austin and Zeitlin, eds. [4] for discussions of targeted consumption programs.

table protein or oil supplements to meet nutrient requirements other than calories. Such a food distribution program would complement an effective employment program, although it would be a major undertaking and one that has met with only limited success in other countries. Clearly, however, a first step in such a program is experimentation on the most appropriate form of cassava for distribution.

Marketing

The cassava marketing system on Java is very efficient. Recent investments in roads and trucks have helped reduce the real costs of marketing, and these reductions have been passed through to farmers. Price linkages between European ports, Java's ports, and interior Java markets are strong. Therefore, only three aspects of marketing policy require policy attention. The first involves roads. Because fresh roots and gaplek are bulky and transportation costs are still important determinants of farm prices, further investments in roads as a part of a broader strategy to serve the more isolated uplands would have a positive impact on farming systems, especially for cassava.

Second, more credit will be needed to expand the domestic cassava marketing system. Credit now moves from the port to the village and finances the gaplek export trade, but most of the informal credit system provides only short-term loans that do not allow for fixed capital investment. Several of the small government programs supply useful lines of credit that extend to village traders and provide funds for capacity expansion. Interest rates on these loans are low, however, and expansion of government programs must lead at some point to credit rationing. Government loan programs are good mechanisms for assisting market expansion, but only if they do not lead to unequal access to credit.

The final point on marketing policy is made with respect to Strauss's Law.[6] The success of BULOG's internal pricing and buffer-stock arrangements with rice has given impetus to the creation of similar arrangements for other crops, including corn. Such a program for cassava would be both unnecessary and costly. Fresh roots cannot be stored for more than a few days, and even gaplek's storage life is limited to a few months. These technical problems with buffer

---

[6] Named after the former U.S. Special Trade Representative, Robert Strauss: "Don't fix it if it ain't broke!"

stocks suggest that government price support schemes for cassava would be disastrous. Furthermore, seasonal price movements for gaplek are relatively small and the price policies discussed below can be carried out with trade policy alone.

Processing

Although most Indonesian cassava undergoes little industrial processing before consumption, about one-third is made into gaplek pellets or cassava starch. The cassava industry has rarely been singled out for special industrial policies; however, several macro policies—including interest rates, tax concessions, and operating subsidies on fuel—have influenced the choice of processing techniques in favor of capital-intensive ones. These policies have not had major effects on cassava processing profitability, but they have tended to reduce productive employment in cassava processing. Future industrial strategy for cassava involves mainly regional considerations. The domestic demand for household starch production on Java is strong, and this rural industry employs many unskilled workers; hence any special efforts to foster a "modern" capital-intensive starch industry on Java would not be socially profitable.

Trade

Exports of cassava products use about 20 percent of Java's cassava crop, and world prices put a floor under domestic cassava prices. Java's cassava farmers thus reap substantial benefits from higher and more stable farm prices set by a small cassava export trade. Future trade policy options appear limited for Indonesia. A properly valued rupiah exchange rate is the most effective export inducement. Consistency in policy—especially the avoidance of export bans—is also important. The 1973 ban on gaplek exports, for example, broke the price link with Europe, accentuated domestic price movements, and deterred investments in export facilities.

For the longer run, two sets of trade negotiations could have a great impact on Indonesia's cassava system. The arrangements on gaplek trade negotiated with the European Community in late 1981 and made formal in July 1982 set import quotas for all gaplek suppliers. Gaplek imports from Indonesia were limited to 500,000 tons in 1982, expanding to 825,000 tons in 1986.[7] If Indonesian trade ex-

---

[7] EEC Regulation No. 2646/82 provides information on 1982 quotas. The Council Decision of July 19, 1982, describes the formal exchange of letters between the European Community and the Republic of Indonesia.

pands, the Indonesian import quota into the EC could become a binding constraint. If so, the handsome rent that Indonesia reaps from the EC gaplek trade would be limited to the quota quantity. Moreover, if quotas from other countries were also binding, the world price for gaplek not imported by the EC would fall appreciably to bring its value as an animal feed much more in line with world corn prices. A 20 or 30 percent drop in price might be expected in this circumstance, and as described in Chapter 6, the decline would be transmitted (in most months) to Indonesian producers and con-sumers of cassava production. Lower prices for roots in Indonesia, in turn, might be an impetus to greater starch production.

Trade negotiations for starch could thus also become increasingly important. The U.S. market, because of its size and the lack of tariff restrictions, has the most potential for Indonesian starch exporters. There are few specific uses for which cassava starch is definitely su-perior, however, and in general, the American market entails diffi-cult competition with cornstarch. In Japan, by contrast, where high starch tariffs are imposed, direct negotiations may be more impor-tant. If the interests of high-cost Japanese starch producers can be accommodated, it might be possible for Indonesia to work out spe-cial arrangements for profitable starch trade with Japan.

Finally, Indonesian trade in cassava products will be determined in part by political and economic events within and among developed countries. For example, agricultural policy in the United States, es-pecially with respect to corn, could have a substantial bearing on starch prices. Potential movements in exchange rates are even more significant. Gaplek trade contracts are typically written in German marks, yet the rupiah is pegged (more or less) to the dollar. As a con-sequence, variations in the dollar-mark exchange ratio directly affect Indonesian cassava prices. The decline in Indonesian root prices during 1981 resulted principally from the 20 percent gain of the dol-lar against the mark, which significantly altered the costs (measured in rupiah) of importing gaplek into Europe. Thus for cassava, as with other products, Indonesia is part of a world trading system over which it has only limited policy influence.

Pricing Strategies

A fundamental dilemma of development planning is the pricing of staple foods. The high prices that will induce farmers' innovation and investment conflict with the political pressures of consumers and with the nutritional needs of the poorest segments of society. The prices of staples also play key roles in determining wages and the profitability of industrialization.

Pricing rice is the most difficult food-pricing issue in Indonesia. Because rice is so important in the diet, its price strongly influences the consumption of many other foods, including cassava. Even the pricing of cassava, however, is complicated by the competition between domestic and foreign uses, between cassava and other commodities in domestic demand and supply, and between cassava growers and consumers.

Cassava-Rice Price Relationships

The pricing of rice in Indonesia has been the central food-policy intervention of the Suharto government. Through the operation of BULOG, a complex program has been instituted that includes price guarantees to farmers, substantial storage and import operations, and defense of ceiling prices by releasing rice into the market (Mears [101]). Rice policy objectives have been clear and have been pursued consistently and effectively. Domestic prices were generally below international prices in the 1970's (Figure 7.1). BULOG-operated programs have also narrowed seasonal price movements in rice and reduced marketing margins between farmer and consumer. As part of this process, the government has taken on many of the rice marketing functions itself.

The effect of these policies has been to provide stable rice prices at a reasonable level for both producers and consumers. These actions, in turn, have caused more rice to be produced and consumed domestically and have probably caused more rice to be imported than otherwise would have occurred. Rice policies have also significantly reduced the domestic consumption of cassava roots and gaplek.

If Indonesia's 1982 rice self-sufficiency turns out to be temporary, and rice imports again rise to disturbing levels, raising rice prices is one policy alternative. Such a strategy would also have significant consumption effects on cassava. A 10 percent rise in relative rice prices, for example, would have about as much effect on total cassava consumed as would a 10 percent decline in relative cassava prices (see Chapter 3). This result occurs because the income effects of a change in rice price are particularly significant among poorer households.

If production continues to grow and international rice prices continue the downward trend of 1981 to 1983, lower real domestic rice

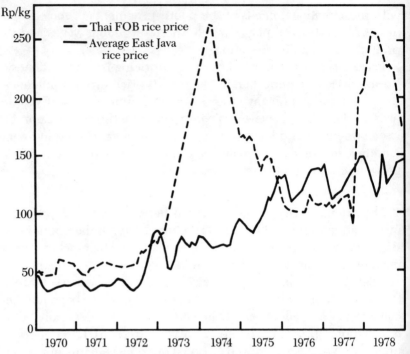

SOURCE: Rice Committee, Board of Trade, Thailand; Ministry of Agriculture, Indonesia.

Figure 7.1. Thai and Indonesian Rice Prices, 1970–78

prices might be in order. If the reverse prevails, however, raising relative rice prices is possible given the alternative sources of staple foods in Indonesia. It seems clear that, in the future, concerns about rice will continue to dominate concerns about cassava, and that domestic cassava demand and international trade will continue to be influenced by decisions on rice policy.

Cassava-Fertilizer Price Relationships

Subsidizing fertilizer is a common way in which developing countries increase incentives to farmers. Indonesia is no exception, and in 1981/82 the budget subsidy on fertilizer was more than $400 million. The low cost of fertilizer and its improved availability caused fertilizer use to increase by about 15 percent annually between 1970 and 1981. This increase added to farm profits and had a major effect on food production. The World Bank [167] indicates that about half the additional rice harvest between 1973 and 1981 was the result of additional fertilizer use.

The fertilizer pricing and distribution program on Java has been very successful, and one might again invoke Strauss's Law. However, budgetary pressures in 1982 raised serious questions within Indonesian financial circles about the wisdom of retaining urea prices at Rp 70 per kilogram. The logic of reducing or removing fertilizer subsidies in Indonesia depends on various premises. Subsidies were originally granted to accelerate farmer acceptance of fertilizer, a goal now largely accomplished in rice areas. Current application rates average about 250 kilograms of urea per hectare per crop on Java, which is high by Southeast Asian standards. One argument now being made is that farmers are accustomed to using fertilizer and will not cut back its use if prices are raised. Whether this proposition is correct depends on the existing profitability of fertilizer use and on the seriousness of working capital (credit) constraints among farmers.

Profitability analyses of the survey regions of this study provide partial answers for upland areas. Removing the subsidy and raising the fertilizer price from Rp 70 ($.12) to Rp 100 ($.17) per kilogram would add about Rp 9,000 ($15) per hectare to farmer costs.[8] Fertilizer at that price would still be profitable on cassava, returning three or four rupiah for every rupiah invested. Although upland farmers have had less experience with fertilizer than rice farmers, some reduction in the fertilizer subsidy should not seriously curtail its use. Higher farm prices for fertilizer will reduce fertilizer demand, and farm groups will oppose any price increase. Their case will be weaker, however, if the government continues the vigorous marketing of fertilizer in all kabupatens and introduces a differential subsidy by fertilizer type.

The rates of actual phosphate and potassium use throughout Java are lower than those recommended by the Ministry of Agriculture. Part of the difficulty may be with the recommendations themselves; however, the impact of potassium and phosphates is much less obvious to farmers than is that of urea. During the introductory phase, more financial inducements may be needed for these nutrients than for nitrogen. The availability and incentive pricing of potassium chloride could be especially important for cassava production in several regions.

[8] World fertilizer prices for urea were approximately $160 per ton in mid-1982.

Consumer-Producer Price Relationships

Indonesian trade policy regarding cassava, especially with respect to gaplek exports to Europe, affects the balance of payments and the level and variability of cassava prices on Java. Since 1971, domestic cassava prices have been largely determined by European grain prices. As explained in Chapter 5, Indonesia has received a rent transfer from cassava trade, and the link to Europe's administered prices has provided an effective price support system for Indonesia's cassava farmers.

The implications of this price link to Europe are extremely important also in determining price relationships between cassava producers and cassava consumers on Java. If the variable levy on grains did not exist in Europe, if Indonesia and Thailand faced binding import quotas for gaplek, or if a variable levy comparable to that on corn were placed on gaplek, a very different pricing situation would prevail in Indonesia. Instead of being tied to administered prices in Europe, gaplek prices would move much more in concert with world corn prices.

Under current trade circumstances, cassava producers in Indonesia are clear winners and consumers clear losers. It is distinctly possible, however, that the European gaplek market will become restricted. This could occur because of policy changes in Europe or because Indonesian gaplek trade reaches the currently agreed-upon EC import quotas. At such time, the price of cassava on Java would fall, making necessary a more consumer-oriented strategy.

Cassava demand and supply would be affected by such a change. If prices fell 30 percent, significantly more cassava would be eaten domestically. On the other hand, lower prices would destroy much of the current profit in cassava production. The exact effects would vary by region, but, in general, a drop in price of 30 percent would cause return above cash costs to fall by about 50 percent. At these lower cassava prices, the return to family labor would be less than market wages in about half of the systems analyzed in the three survey areas. Cassava production would probably stagnate or fall, although the exact outcome would also depend on prices of other crops in the intercropped systems.

The feed-livestock economy would also be affected by lowered cassava prices. The rapid growth of per capita income on Java has spurred the demand for poultry, eggs, milk, and beef. All of these items are very income elastic. As Indonesians become richer, the potential demand for gaplek as animal feed will increase greatly. In Brazil, the largest producer of cassava in the world, more than one-third of total production is now used as feed. On Java, as in Europe and Brazil, the feeding of cassava to livestock will be largely a matter of price. Hence, the future role of cassava as feed will be determined by feed grain supplies and prices as well as by the demand for animal products.

Even if Indonesia faces restricted European access for its gaplek, the situation is far from hopeless. Consumers on Java would gain through the price effects, and gaplek would be in a better position to serve a livestock industry that will probably expand greatly in the years ahead.

Summary

When this research on cassava began in 1979, it was motivated primarily by Indonesia's growing dependence on imported rice. The rice crops of the three succeeding years have relieved that import pressure, but this study has shown that cassava can also make an important contribution to income growth, improved income distribution through new employment, better nutrition, and food security.

Cassava is at the heart of Java's upland farming systems. Focusing on this crop and these systems is the next logical step for Indonesia's Fourth Five-Year Plan. The required changes in public policy are well within the financial and management capability of the relevant government agencies. Revision of government programs in the 1980's could do for cassava what national programs in the 1970's have done for rice.

Reference Matter

Indonesian Food Crop Production Statistics

Frederick C. Roche

The collection of farm statistics on Java is complicated by the large number of farms and the predominance of intercropping on rain-fed soils. Primary attention is given to irrigated rice in the data collection process, and estimates for *palawija* crops are, no doubt, less reliable. However, there is good reason to believe that the trends indicated by official time series accurately reflect events, although the absolute magnitudes of estimated areas and yields should be viewed cautiously.

Prior to 1973, the National Directorate for Agriculture (Dinas Pertanian) was principally responsible for production estimates. In 1973, the Central Bureau of Statistics (CBS) was assigned to supervise this process at the central level and to participate in data collection at the local level. Two major changes in data collection procedures occurred: the selection of locations for crop cuttings became the responsibility of CBS; and in many areas the most common size of plots for these cuttings was reduced from 10 meters square to 2.5 meters square. The basic responsibility for crop area estimates continues to rest with village officials who, in turn, report to local Dinas Pertanian offices. Because total production for a crop is simply the product of estimated yield and area, these procedural innovations could have caused a one-time change in yield and total production estimates but are unlikely to have produced spurious trends over time.[1]

The annual statistics do not distinguish between pure and intercropped stands, and it appears that no consistent method is applied for estimating crop areas in intercropping systems. When planting densities are no less than one-third of "normal" for a particular crop, the field is recorded as pure stand. The area for the crop is simply not recorded when the planting density is sparser. The definition of "normal" is left to the discretion of local officials and may be different in each area.

For example, a one-hectare field containing corn and cassava planted at one-half meter and one meter square spacing, respectively, would be re-

---

[1] A major change in the basis for reporting rice yields occurred in 1977, causing a sharp break in the time series for this crop. For more detail on Indonesian data collection procedures, see Mears [101].

corded as two hectares—one of each crop—in the production calculation. However, the spacing of corn is typically much wider when it is intercropped with both upland rice and cassava, with the result that corn may or may not be recorded in this system depending upon local practice. Since most cassava is planted at a density of one to one and a half meters square, the official estimates of cassava areas may be reasonably good, although these figures probably omit the small quantities of cassava planted on field edges, on sawah bunds, and in homestead gardens.

The crop cuttings used for yield estimates are often taken from pure-stand fields, but are applied in the total production calculations to areas that include both pure and intercropped stands. All things being equal, crop yields should be lower in intercropped fields because of interspecies competition. However, the field survey results and general field observations throughout Java suggest that fertilizer use and cassava yields may be higher in intercropping systems. Hence, the procedure for yield estimates does not necessarily produce upwardly biased results and may, in fact, lead to the opposite. It would be impossible, however, to ascertain the direction and magnitude of any error without careful field studies conducted at harvest time.

Costs and Returns Data from Garut, Gunung Kidul, and Kediri

Frederick C. Roche

Two measures of the profitability of alternative cassava cropping systems in the survey area during the 1978/79 crop year are calculated in Tables B.2–B.7. Profit I measures the net combined return to land, family labor, and management after all cash costs are deducted. Profit II measures the return to land and management after deducting the value of the family labor from Profit I. In addition, daily returns to land and total labor input (Daygain) are calculated, as are the costs of cassava production per ton in the various cassava systems. Input costs are valued at local market prices. For purposes of productivity comparisons, output prices are assumed to be the same in all survey areas. In fact, these prices do not vary greatly, either among or within areas, so the error introduced is minor.

Except for preparation of cuttings, planting, and harvesting, most production activities in an intercropping system are not specific to cassava. In this study, joint costs have been allocated in proportion to each crop's contribution to total value of output.

TABLE B. 1. *Input and Output Prices Used in the Profitability Calculations*

Input/Output	Price	
LAND (*average annual rental rate in Rp*)		
Garut (*tegal*, level or terraced)	75,000	
Gunung Kidul		
hillside *tegal* (terraced or unterraced)	0[a]	
level valley soil	100,000	
Kediri		
terraced hillside *tegal*	46,000	
level lowland *tegal*	146,500	
irrigated *sawah*	170,000	
LABOR (*daily farm wage rates in Rp*)[b]		
Garut		
women	400	(350–450)
men	500	(450–600)
Gunung Kidul		
women	150	(125–175)
men	200	(150–225)
Kediri		
women	600	(500–650)
men	600	(500–650)
FERTILIZER (*Rp/kg*)	70[c]	
BULLOCK RENTAL (*Rp/pair/day*)		
Gunung Kidul	1,500	
Kediri	1,750	
COMMODITY PRICES (*Rp/kg*)[d]		
cassava (fresh root equivalent)	20	
rice (dry, unhusked paddy)	115	
corn (dry seed)	75	
peanuts (dry unshelled)	125	
soybeans (dry seed)	270	
EXCHANGE RATE (1979/80)	U.S.$1.00 = Rp 625	

[a]Farmers lent this land to other farmers who cultivated it.

[b]Six-hour working day; modal wages paid during the 1979/80 crop year. The range of reported wages is shown in parentheses. Wages include the value of meals or snacks provided by employers.

[c]Urea or TSP. This price varied slightly both among and within survey areas because of differences in location and transportation costs.

[d]Similar modal crop prices were reported in all three areas. Variation in reported prices was roughly the same within and among areas. Minor legume crops grown in Garut and Gunung Kidul are valued at locally prevailing prices in the profitability calculations.

TABLE B.2. *Current Inputs and Outputs in the Principal Cassava Cropping Systems of Garut*

Inputs and outputs per hectare	Pure-stand cassava		Intercropped cassava, corn, upland rice, and legumes		Intercropped cassava, corn, and upland rice	
Soil type	Terraced hillsides		Terraced hillsides		Terraced hillsides	
Labor use per season (*days*)						
male	200.9		265.4		278.0	
female	99.4		119.1		161.6	
Percent labor hired[a]	34.4%		41.8%		39.9%	
Bullock power (*pair days*)	0		0		0	
Fertilizer (*kg*)						
urea	0		77.0		86.3	
TSP	0		44.5		82.5	
manure	143.3		1,530.0		1,370.0	
Nonlabor cash costs (*000 Rp*)[b]	0		20.8		23.5	
Yields (*00 kg*)[c]						
cassava	70.6	(75.8)	82.1	(83.2)	79.4	(84.1)
rice	–	–	6.2	(7.8)	7.2	(8.5)
corn	–	–	4.6	(4.6)	3.1	(3.5)
legumes	–	–	1.7	(1.7)	–	–
Total output value (*000 Rp*)	141.2	(151.6)	292.0	(312.0)	264.2	(291.4)
Profit I (*000 Rp*)[d]	85.8	(96.2)	181.6	(209.5)	146.7	(173.6)
Profit II (*000 Rp*)[e]	4.1	(14.4)	73.3	(98.8)	26.6	(52.3)
Daygain (*Rp/day*)[f]	470	(505)	705	(748)	547	(589)
Cassava production costs/ton (*000 Rp*)	30.0	(28.0)	16.7	(16.1)	18.4	(17.5)
Sample size	14		12		10	

NOTE: Yields and output values that farmers considered "normal" are in parentheses.
[a]Percentage of total labor input either hired for cash or employed under reciprocal labor-sharing arrangements. The former category was by far the most important in the survey areas.
[b]Total value of expenditures for seed, fertilizer, pesticides, bullock rental, and miscellaneous costs such as irrigation fees and land taxes.
[c]The following yield forms are used: cassava—fresh root equivalent; rice—unhusked paddy; corn—dry seed; peanuts—dry in shell; soybeans—dry seed. Various minor legume crops grown in Garut and Gunung Kidul are reported in dry seed form.
[d]Profit I is the return to land, family labor, and management after deducting all labor and nonlabor cash costs.
[e]Profit II is the return to land and management after deducting family labor input valued at appropriate local wage rates.
[f]Daygain is the average daily return to land and total labor input after deducting nonlabor cash input costs from gross output value.

TABLE B.3. *Current Inputs and Outputs in the Principal Cassava Cropping Systems of Gunung Kidul*

Inputs and outputs per hectare	Intercropped cassava and corn		Intercropped cassava, corn, and legumes		Intercropped cassava, corn, upland rice, and legumes	
Soil type	Unterraced hillsides		Terraced hillsides		Level vale soils	
Labor use per season (*days*)						
male	188.8		223.6		305.2	
female	157.0		138.7		246.4	
Percent labor hired[a]	0%		5.8%		14.8%	
Bullock power (*pair days*)	0		0		28.2	
Fertilizer (*kg*)						
urea	0		0.9		201.3	
TSP	0		0		40.2	
manure	0		174.0		3,520.0	
Nonlabor cash costs (*000 Rp*)[b]	1.6		3.5		59.2	
Yields (*00 kg*)[c]						
cassava	26.4	(26.4)	22.7	(22.7)	69.0	(75.0)
rice	–	–	–	–	4.6	(8.2)
corn	2.0	(4.3)	1.1	(2.7)	3.5	(4.7)
legumes	–	–	2.0	(2.7)	5.8	(8.3)
Total output value (*000 Rp*)	67.9	(84.8)	78.6	(97.4)	328.5	(438.6)
Profit I (*000 Rp*)[d]	66.3	(83.2)	71.7	(90.5)	252.7	(360.6)
Profit II (*000 Rp*)[e]	7.4	(8.2)	16.0	(31.3)	181.3	(258.4)
Daygain (*Rp/day*)[f]	192	(226)	207	(248)	488	(611)
Cassava production costs/ton (*000 Rp*)	17.3	(15.1)	15.8	(14.6)	15.8	(13.9)
Sample size	4		13		28	

NOTES: See Table B.2.

TABLE B.4. *Current Inputs and Outputs for Intercropped Cassava and Corn in Kediri*

Inputs and outputs per hectare	Intercropped cassava and corn		Intercropped cassava and corn		Intercropped cassava and corn	
Soil type	Level tegal		Terraced hillsides		Late season on sawah	
Labor use per season (*days*)						
male	203.0		292.1		202.1	
female	20.2		22.3		12.5	
Percent labor hired[a]	68.8%		38.5%		84.8%	
Bullock power (*pair days*)	18.8		4.5		28.7	
Fertilizer (*kg*)						
urea	356.8		386.0		398.0	
TSP	0		0		0	
manure	4,410.0		8,630.0		1,050.0	
Nonlabor cash costs (*000 Rp*)[b]	41.7		33.7		55.6	
Yields (*00 kg*)[c]						
cassava	195.0	(210.0)	120.0	(124.0)	165.0	(187.0)
rice	–	–	–	–	–	–
corn	9.0	(10.6)	6.1	(6.1)	9.3	(11.8)
legumes	–	–	–	–	–	–
Total output value (*000 Rp*)	457.5	(499.7)	286.0	(294.0)	399.5	(461.4)
Profit I (*000 Rp*)[d]	323.5	(368.7)	179.7	(187.7)	234.7	(290.0)
Profit II (*000 Rp*)[e]	281.8	(306.4)	63.7	(70.5)	215.1	(270.5)
Daygain (*Rp/day*)[f]	1,863	(1,913)	803	(823)	1,602	(1,801)
Cassava production costs/ton (*000 Rp*)	14.5	(13.9)	20.2	(18.7)	12.8	(11.7)
Sample size	16		11		11	

NOTES: See Table B.2.

TABLE B.5. *Current Inputs and Outputs in the Pure-Stand Cassava Systems of Kediri*

Inputs and outputs per hectare	Pure-stand cassava		Pure-stand cassava		Pure-stand cassava	
Soil type	Level tegal		Terraced hillsides		Late season on sawah	
Labor use per season (*days*)						
male	227.7		154.8		225.4	
female	9.5		7.0		1.8	
Percent labor hired[a]	81.4%		47.9%		91.8%	
Bullock power (*pair days*)	38.2		18.6		20.9	
Fertilizer (*kg*)						
urea	189.5		231.9		310.5	
TSP	0		0		0	
manure	5,560.0		4,960.0		0	
Nonlabor cash costs (*000 Rp*)[b]	43.1		35.7		44.1	
Yields (*00 kg*)[c]						
cassava	174.5	(183.0)	88.0	(93.0)	152.0	(152.0)
rice	–	–	–	–	–	–
corn	–	–	–	–	–	–
legumes	–	–	–	–	–	–
Total output value (*000 Rp*)	349.0	(366.0)	176.0	(186.0)	304.0	(304.0)
Profit I (*000 Rp*)[d]	190.1	(206.5)	93.8	(106.2)	134.8	(134.8)
Profit II (*000 Rp*)[e]	161.2	(177.6)	43.2	(55.0)	123.6	(123.6)
Daygain (*Rp/day*)[f]	1,290	(1,356)	867	(935)	1,149	(1,149)
Cassava production costs/ton (*000 Rp*)	20.0	(19.2)	21.1	(20.5)	17.7	(17.7)
Sample size	4		6		4	

NOTES: See Table B.2.

TABLE B.6. *Current Inputs and Outputs in Alternative Late-Season Crops on Sawah in Kediri*

Inputs and outputs per hectare	Pure-stand soybeans		Pure-stand peanuts		Pure-stand corn	
Soil type	Late season on sawah		Late season on sawah		Dry season on sawah	
Labor use per season (*days*)						
male	65.6		64.6		90.9	
female	19.0		49.2		9.1	
Percent labor hired[a]	75.2%		73.9%		76.0%	
Bullock power (*pair days*)	2.1		4.2		13.8	
Fertilizer (*kg*)						
urea	42.2		0		244.8	
TSP	0		0		0	
manure	0		0		0	
Nonlabor cash costs (*000 Rp*)[b]	30.8		68.6		33.6	
Yields (*00 kg*)[c]						
cassava	–	–	–	–	–	–
rice	–	–	–	–	–	–
corn	–	–	–	–	10.5	(12.5)
legumes	2.0	(7.7)	5.1	(16.2)	–	–
Total output value (*000 Rp*)	53.7	(208.8)	64.3	(202.1)	78.8	(93.4)
Profit I (*000 Rp*)[d]	– 7.5	(127.8)	– 54.7	(69.7)	– 0.3	(14.2)
Profit II (*000 Rp*)[e]	– 20.1	(114.0)	– 72.5	(44.9)	– 14.7	(– 0.2)
Daygain (*Rp/day*)[f]	270	(1,668)	– 37	(903)	453	(598)
Cassava production costs/ton (*000 Rp*)	–	–	–	–	–	–
Sample size	9		5		14	

NOTES: See Table B.2.

TABLE B.7. *Costs and Returns in Alternative Late- and Dry-Season Cropping Patterns on Sawah in Kediri*

Inputs and outputs per hectare	Intercropped cassava and corn	Soybeans-corn	Peanuts-corn
Soil type	Late and dry season sawah	Late and dry season sawah	Late and dry season sawah
Labor use per season (*days*)			
male	211.9	175.7	177.8
female	13.4	31.0	69.2
Percent labor hired[a]	85.6%	75.7%	73.6%
Bullock power (*pair days*)	28.7	15.9	18.0
Fertilizer (*kg*)			
urea	398.0	287.0	244.8
TSP	0	0	0
manure	1,050.0	0	0
Nonlabor cash costs (*000 Rp*)[b]	55.6	64.4	102.2
Yields (*00 kg*)[c]			
cassava	187.0	–	–
rice	–	–	–
corn	11.8	12.5	12.5
legumes	–	7.7	16.2
Total output value (*000 Rp*)	461.4	302.2	295.5
Profit I (*000 Rp*)[d]	290.0	142.0	83.9
Profit II (*000 Rp*)[e]	270.5	114.1	45.1
Daygain (*Rp/day*)[f]	1,801	1,288	783
Cassava production costs/ton (*000 Rp*)	11.7	–	–
Sample size	11	8/14	4/14

NOTES: See Table B.2.

The Susenas Household Expenditure Surveys

John A. Dixon

The data from the Susenas surveys (National Socio-Economic Surveys of Indonesia) are tabulated by expenditure subgroups and by urban-rural classifications for each province or group of provinces included. For example, data are available for twelve income subgroups by province and by rural and urban area for three separate rounds in 1976 (January to April, May to August, September to December) and for two rounds in 1969–70 (October to December 1969, and January to April 1970). Respondents were asked about consumption of foods from all sources—purchased, produced themselves, or received as gifts and loans. Unfortunately, quantities were aggregated in the published results and information about shares of own-production in total consumption is available only for the 1978 survey, Susenas VI. Expenditures were reported as actual cost; where no purchases occurred, estimates were made using local market prices for similar foods. The raw data consist of series of quantities consumed and rupiahs spent. Expenditure elasticities, seasonal variations, and implicit prices can be derived from this source. Table C.1 gives comparative information on the five available Susenas surveys.

Some underreporting of corn and cassava consumption seems to occur in the Susenas surveys, since corn and cassava are low-status foods and some people are reluctant to admit consuming them. There is some indication that subsistence production in urban areas is larger than previously thought (Evers [48]). The patterns of consumption between surveys are fairly consistent, however, and therefore comparisons of the Susenas surveys can be made to examine changes in staple food consumption over time.

Each of the successive Susenas consumption surveys has become broader and more sophisticated. The 1963/64 survey, Susenas I, had a sample size of 14,670 households, all on Java-Madura; the 1964/65 survey was larger, covering 21,305 households in all of Indonesia. No information is available from Susenas III conducted in 1967. Susenas V of 1976 covered some 54,000 households throughout Indonesia and Susenas VI of 1978 covered some 24,000 households. Although the last three surveys (Susenas IV, V, and VI)

TABLE C.1. *Comparisons of Susenas Surveys*

	Period	No. of households surveyed	Rounds	Coverage	No. of expenditure groups	No. of foods included
Susenas I	December 1963 to January 1964	14,670 (86% rural)	1	Java-Madura	5	20
Susenas II	November 1964 to February 1965	21,305 (81% rural)	1	All Indonesia Java-Madura Off-Java and by province	9	20
Susenas III	1967	–	–	–	–	–
Susenas IV	October 1969 to April 1970	–	2	All Indonesia Java-Madura Off-Java and by province	10	32
Susenas V	January to December 1976	ca. 54,000	3	Same as Susenas IV	12	over 100
Susenas VI	January to December 1978	ca. 24,000	4	Same as Susenas IV	12	over 100

SOURCES: Indonesia [75], various rounds of the Susenas surveys. All Susenas survey results are available for urban and rural areas separately. The division into expenditure groups is based on total rupiah expenditures per capita per month, except for Susenas I, for which the division is based on total rupiah expenditures per household per month. Some figures were not available from Susenas III and IV.

TABLE C.2. *Food Forms Reported in the Susenas Surveys*

Food	Susenas I	Susenas II	Susenas IV	Susenas V and VI
		Forms reported in:		
Rice	Open market Government- distributed	Open market Government- distributed	Open market Government- distributed Sticky rice	Total white rice Sticky rice Rice products
Corn	Grain	Grain	Ears Grain Corn flour	Fresh ears Dried ears Grain Corn flour
Cassava	Fresh Flour	Fresh Gaplek Flour	Fresh Gaplek Flour (starch)	Fresh Gaplek Flour (starch)
Other staples	Sago	Sago	Sweet potatoes	Sago Sweet potatoes Wheat flour Taro

are used most extensively in Chapter 3, a comparison of all of the available surveys gives a longer perspective of the staple food system and the changes in it. This information is especially useful for examining the distribution of consumption as well as the level of total consumption.

The Susenas surveys are not strictly comparable because of the way foods were reported, as is shown in Table C.2. The number of staple food forms reported increases from 6 to 14 over the course of the surveys, and confusion arises from definitional questions about cassava. A close examination of the data reveals a consistent pattern of total consumption when the assumption is made that all cassava forms have been converted to fresh root equivalents in Susenas I and II, but not in the later surveys. In Susenas IV, V, and VI, therefore, gaplek and starch need to be converted to fresh root equivalents using the appropriate conversion factors (2.5 to 1 and 5 to 1). Although this assumption allows these data to be used, the fact that Susenas II reported fresh roots and gaplek together (in fresh root equivalent) means that direct comparisons cannot be made of changes in the form of cassava consumption (fresh or dried) between Susenas II and the other rounds.

Estimating own-price and cross-price elasticities also presents difficulties. Prices are calculated by dividing expenditure on a good by the quantity of that good purchased. For some foods price variations reported during the course of the survey year are minor, and price elasticities cannot be measured. This is true for controlled goods such as sugar. For other foods there is more variation, and own-price elasticities are estimated. Since the prices used do not take quality into account, some of the variation in prices can be attributed to quality differences, not price changes. During any given subround the reported price of rice per kilogram may vary with quality. Poorer people generally buy cheaper rice and richer people buy more expensive varieties. Since richer prople also purchase more rice, this bias will dampen the value of the estimated own-price elasticity. This bias is minimized by the use of expenditure subgroups (low, medium, and high) in which the price variation owing to quality is lessened and the price variation caused by price changes for a given quality is more dominant. This same bias is found in own-price elasticity estimates of other foods.

The extensive nature of market activities for staple foods in rural as well as urban areas permits greater confidence in the implicit price estimates derived from the Susenas surveys and the own-price elasticities estimated from these data.

References Cited

[1] Ace Partadireja. 1974. "Rural Credit: The Ijon System." *Bulletin of Indonesian Economic Studies* (Canberra) 10, no. 3.

[2] Saleh Afiff, Walter P. Falcon, and C. Peter Timmer. 1980. "Elements of a Food and Nutrition Policy in Indonesia." In Gustav F. Papanek, ed.

[3] James A. Austin. 1981. *Nutrition Programs in the Third World.* Cambridge, Mass.

[4] James A. Austin and Marian F. Zeitlin, eds. 1981. *Nutrition Intervention in Developing Countries: An Overview.* Cambridge, Mass.

[5] Kenneth L. Bachman. 1962. "Report on Tapioca and Other Starch Imports." Working Paper, Trade Statistics and Analysis Branch, Development and Trade Analysis Division, USDA. March.

[6] K. V. Bailey. 1961. "Rural Nutrition Studies in Indonesia: Background to Nutritional Problems in the Cassava Areas." *Tropical and Geographical Medicine* 13, pp. 234–54.

[7] Bank of Thailand. 1971–79. *Monthly Bulletin.*

[8] Michael Barzelay and Scott R. Pearson. 1982. "The Efficiency of Producing Alcohol for Energy in Brazil." *Economic Development and Cultural Change* 31, no. 1.

[9] G. W. A. Baumer. 1962. "Processing of Gari and Tapioca in Rural Industries." FAB Report to the Government of Nigeria.

[10] Merrill K. Bennett. 1954. *The World's Food.* New York.

[11] G. G. Bolhuis. 1954. *The Toxicity of Cassava Roots.* Laboratory of Tropical Agriculture, Wageningen, Netherlands.

[12] Anne Booth. 1977. "Irrigation in Indonesia." *Bulletin of Indonesian Economic Studies* (Canberra) 13, nos. 1, 2.

[13] ———. 1979. "The Agricultural Surveys, 1970–75." *Bulletin of Indonesian Economic Studies* (Canberra) 15, no. 1.

[14] Anne Booth and Peter McCawley, eds. 1981. *The Indonesian Economy During the Soeharto Era.* Kuala Lumpur.

[15] Nyle C. Brady. 1974. *The Nature and Properties of Soils.* 8th ed. New York.

[16] Charles Andrew Brautlecht. 1953. *Starch: Its Sources, Production, and Uses.* New York.

[17] Brawijaya University. 1979. *Cassava Research Project: Progress Report 8.* Faculty of Agriculture, comp. and ed. Malang, East Java.

[18] Gerardus H. de Bruijn and T. S. Dharmaputra. 1974. "The Mukibat

System: A High-Yielding Method of Cassava Production in Indonesia." *Netherlands Journal of Agricultural Science* 22, no. 2.

[19] Barbara A. Chapman. 1980. "Traditional Food Systems and Development." Paper presented at the Ninth Annual Conference on Indonesian Studies. Univ. of California, Berkeley. June.

[20] A. H. Chisholm and R. Tyers, eds. 1982. *Food Security: Theory, Policy and Perspectives from Asia and the Pacific Rim.* Lexington, Mass.

[21] James H. Cock. 1982. "Cassava: A Basic Energy Source in the Tropics." *Science*, Nov. 19.

[21a] ———— . 1984. *Cassava.* Boulder, Col.

[22] James H. Cock, D. Wholey, and J. C. Lozano. 1976. *A Rapid Propagation System for Cassava.* CIAT. Series EE–20. Cali, Colombia.

[23] James H. Cock et al., eds. 1977. *Proceedings of the Fourth Symposium of the International Society for Tropical Root Crops.* IDRC. Ottawa, Canada.

[24] William L. Collier, J. Colter, Sinarhadi, and R. d'A. Shaw. 1974. "Choice of Technique in Rice Milling on Java—A Comment." *Bulletin of Indonesian Economic Studies* (Canberra) 10, no. 1.

[25] William L. Collier et al. 1982. "The Acceleration of Rural Development on Java: From Village Studies to a National Perspective." Agro-Economic Survey occasional paper no. 6. Bogor, Indonesia.

[26] Donald G. Coursey. 1973. "Cassava as Food: Toxicity and Technology." In Barry Nestel and Reginald MacIntyre, eds.

[26a] Joan Crabtree and A. W. James. 1982. "Composite Flour Technology: TPI's Experience and Opinions on the Planning and Implementation of National Programmes." *Tropical Science* 24, no. 2.

[27] J. Crabtree, E. C. Kramer, and Jane Baldry. 1978. "The Breadmaking Potential of Products of Cassava as Partial Replacements for Wheat Flour." *Journal of Food Technology* 13, pp. 397–407.

[28] ———— . 1978. "Use of Fresh Cassava Products in Bread Making." In Edward J. Weber et al., eds., *Cassava Harvesting and Processing.*

[29] CRIA (Central Research Institute for Agriculture [Bogor, Indonesia]). *Cropping Systems Research Reports.* Prepared by members of the Cropping Systems Working Group. Irregular.

[30] ———— . *Root Crop Progress Reports.* Prepared by the Root Crops Division. Irregular.

[31] ———— . 1978–79. "Cassava Breeding: Results of Trials." In *Research Progress Report* no. 10. Root Crops Division.

[32] ———— . 1979. "Growing Five Crops per Year on Upland Red-Yellow Podzolic Soils." Report of Cropping Systems Working Group.

[33] ———— . 1979. "The Research Design for Cassava Varieties Adira I and Adira II."

[34] T. W. G. Dames. 1955. *The Soils of East Central Java*. Contribution no. 141, General Agricultural Research Station. Bogor.

[35] David O. Dapice. 1980. "An Overview of the Indonesian Economy." In Gustav F. Papanek, ed.

[36] J. E. A. den Doop. 1937. "Groene bemesting, kunstmest en andere factoren in Sisal—en Cassave—productie" [Green manure fertilizers and other factors in sisal and cassava production]. *De Bergcultures* [*Upland Culture*] 2, no. 9; 2, no. 36.

[37] D. A. V. Dendy and Ruth Kasasian. 1974. *Composite Flour Technology Bibliography*. Tropical Products Institute Report G124, London.

[38] Alice Dewey. 1962. *Peasant Marketing in Java*. New York.

[39] Howard Dick. 1982. "Survey of Recent Developments." *Bulletin of Indonesian Economic Studies* (Canberra), 7, no. 1.

[40] John Dixon. 1982. "Food Consumption and Related Demand Parameters in Indonesia: A Review of Available Evidence." International Food Policy Research Institute, Working Paper no. 6. Washington, D.C.

[41] ———. 1982. "Use of Expenditure Survey Data in Staple-Food Consumption Analysis: Examples from Indonesia." Chapter 11 in Chisholm and Tyers, eds.

[42] Abunain Djumadias. 1979. "Nutritional Intakes in Indonesia." Paper presented at the Third Biennial Meeting of AESSEA, Kuala Lumpur, Nov. 27–30.

[43] Dutch East Indies Statistical Department. 1940. *Dutch East Indies Report, 1940*. Batavia [Jakarta].

[44] W. C. Edmundson. 1976. *Land, Food, and Work in East Java*. New England Monographs in Geography no. 4, University of New England, Australia.

[45] D. G. Edwards et al. 1977. "Mineral Nutrition of Cassava and Adaptation to Low Fertility Conditions." In James H. Cock et al., eds.

[46] Suryatna Effendi et al. 1980. *The Efficiency of Fertilizer Use by Non-Rice Crops*. CRIA. Bogor.

[47] European Feed Manufacturers Association (FEFAC). 1960–80. *Feed and Food Statistical Yearbook*. Brussels.

[48] H. D. Evers. 1981. "The Contribution of Urban Subsistence Production to Incomes in Jakarta." *Bulletin of Indonesian Economic Studies* (Canberra) 17, no. 2.

[49] Helen C. Farnsworth. 1961. "Defects, Uses, and Abuses of National Food Supply and Consumption Data." *Food Research Institute Studies* 2, no. 3.

[50] Paul L. Farris. 1965. "Economics and Future of the Starch Industry." Chapter 3 in Whistler and Paschall, eds., vol. 1.

[51] Rosemary Fennell. 1979. *The Common Agricultural Policy of the European Community: Its Institutional and Administrative Organization.* Montclair, N.J.

[52] Food and Agriculture Organization of the United Nations (FAO). 1950–80. *Trade Yearbook.* Annual.

[53] ———. 1972. *Food Composition Table for Use in East Asia.*

[53a] ———. 1973. *Energy and Protein Requirements.*

[54] ———. 1977. *The Fourth World Food Survey.*

[55] ———. 1979. *Fertilizer and Crop Yield Improvement in the Upper Solo River Basin.*

[56] ———. 1980. *Food Balance Sheets (1975–77 Average and Per Caput Supplies 1961–65 Average, 1967 to 1977).*

[57] ———. 1980. *Production Yearbook.* Vol. 34.

[58] ———. 1981. *World Rice Situation and Outlook, 1981–82.* Intergovernmental Working Group on Rice. CCP:R182/CRSI.

[59] M. Grace. 1971. *Processing of Cassava.* FAO Agricultural Services Bulletin no. 8. Rome.

[60] Stephen Grenville. 1981. "Monetary Policy and the Formal Financial Sector." In Anne Booth and Peter McCawley, eds.

[61] Donald H. Grist. 1965. *Rice.* 4th ed. London.

[62] John A. Guthrie and Joseph L. McCarthy. 1944. *Starch, Syrup, and Dextrose Sugar from Washington Wheat and Potatoes: Postwar Prospects for Industrial Development.* Olympia, Wash.

[63] L. W. J. Halleman and A. Aten. 1956. *Processing of Cassava and Cassava Products in Rural Industries.* FAO Agricultural Development Paper no. 54.

[64] Gillian Hart. 1978. "Labor Allocation Strategies in Rural Javanese Households." Ph.D. diss., Cornell University. Ithaca, N.Y.

[65] Yujiro Hayami et al. 1979. "Rice Harvesting and Welfare in Rural Java." *Bulletin of Indonesian Economic Studies* (Canberra) 15, no. 2.

[66] Polly Hill. 1957. "Some Puzzling Spending Habits in Ghana." *Economic Bulletin of Ghana,* June (Part 1), Nov. (Part 2), Dec. (Part 3).

[67] R. Hoopes. 1976. "Cassava as a Food Resource in Brazil." Agricultural Economics Staff Paper no. 76–18, Cornell University. Ithaca, N.Y.

[68] Reinhardt H. Howeler. 1980. "The Effect of Mycorrhizal Inoculation on the Phosphorous Nutrition of Cassava." In Edward J. Weber et al., eds., *Cassava Cultural Practices.*

[69] ———. 1980. "Soil-Related Cultural Practices for Cassava." In Edward J. Weber et al., eds., *Cassava Cultural Practices.*

[70] ———. 1981. "Mineral Nutrition and Fertilization of Cassava." CIAT, Series 09EC–4. Cali, Colombia.

[71] Indonesia. Central Bureau of Statistics. *Exports.* Jakarta, various years.

[72] ———. ———. *Imports.* Jakarta, various years.

[73] ———. ———. *Indonesian Food Balance Sheets.* Vols. for *1968–74, 1975, 1976, 1977, 1978, 1979.* Jakarta, various years.

[74] ———. ———. *Industrial Census.* Jakarta, various years.

[75] ———. ———. *The National Household Expenditure Survey of Indonesia (Susenas).* Jakarta, various years.

[76] ———. ———. *Production of Annual Food Crops on Java and Madura.* Jakarta, various years.

[77] ———. ———. *Statistical Pocketbook of Indonesia.* Jakarta, various years.

[78] ———. ———. *Survey Pertanian* [*Agricultural Survey*]. Jakarta, various years.

[79] ———. ———. *Vehicle and Length of Road Statistics.* Jakarta, 1978.

[80] ———. ———. *1973 Agricultural Census.* Vols. 1–7. Jakarta, 1977–79.

[81] ———. Ministry of Agriculture. *Annual Progress Report.* Non-Rice Crop Intensification Program. Jakarta, various years.

[82] ———. ———. *Summary of Realization of Intensification Targets for Rice, Non-Rice, and Vegetable Crops.* Jakarta, 1980.

[83] Jean S. Ingram. 1972. *Cassava Processing: Commercially Available Machinery.* Tropical Products Institute. London.

[84] International Trade Center. 1968. *The Markets for Manioc as a Raw Material for Compound Animal Feedingstuffs.* Geneva.

[85] ———. 1977. *Cassava: Export Potential and Market Requirements.* Geneva.

[86] Inu Ismail et al. 1979. *Cropping Systems Research in Transmigration Areas, South Sumatra, 1978.* CRIA. Bogor.

[87] JETRO (Japanese External Trade Relations Organization). 1978. *Access to Japan's Import Market, Tapioca.* Japanese Ministry of Agriculture and Forestry, comp.

[87a] Stephen F. Jones. 1983. *The World Market for Starch and Starch Products, with Particular Reference to Cassava (Tapioca) Starch.* Tropical Development and Research Institute Report G173. London.

[88] William O. Jones. 1959. *Manioc in Africa.* Stanford, Calif.

[89] ———. 1978. "Cassava in Indonesia: Preliminary Observations." Report to the Ford Foundation. Mimeo. Jakarta.

[90] William O. Jones and I. A. Akinrele. 1976. "Improvement of Cassava Processing and Marketing." Report to the National Accelerated Food Production Program. IITA, Ibadan, Nigeria.

[91] Timothy E. Josling and Scott R. Pearson. 1982. *Developments in the Common Agricultural Policy of the European Community.* USDA. Foreign Agricultural Economic Report 172.

[92] Keiji Dainuma. 1980. "Present and Future Prospects for Corn Utilization and Related Research in Japan." Working paper, National Food Research Institute, Japanese Ministry of Agriculture, Forestry, and Fisheries.

[93] Raphie Kaplinsky. 1974. "Innovation in Gari Production: The Case for an Intermediate Technology." Institute of Development Studies discussion paper no. 34. University of Sussex.

[94] M. Kikuchi et al. 1980. "Changes in Community Institutions and Income Distribution in a West Java Village." International Rice Research Institute, Research Paper Series no. 50.

[95] L. Koch et al. 1926. "Uitkomsten van eenige bemestingsproeven met cassave" [Effects of fertilizer on cassava]. Departement van Landbouw, Nijverheid en Handel, Korte berichten uitgaande van het Algemeen Proefstation voor den Landbouw [Department of Agriculture, Industry, and Trade, General Agricultural Research Station], no. 50. Buitenzorg (Bogor).

[96] S. S. Levi and C. B. Oruche. 1958. "Some Inexpensive Improvements in Village-Scale Gari Making." Federal Institute of Industrial Research. Lagos, Nigeria.

[97] J. C. Lozano et al. 1977. *Production of Cassava Planting Material.* CIAT. Series GE–17. Cali, Colombia.

[98] Jerry L. McIntosh and Suryatna Effendi. 1979. "Soil Fertility Implications of Cropping Patterns and Practices for Cassava." In Edward J. Weber et al., eds., *Intercropping with Cassava.*

[99] Ronald I. McKinnon. 1973. *Money and Capital in Economic Development.* Washington, D.C.

[100] Leon A. Mears. 1959. *Rice Marketing in the Republic of Indonesia.* Institute for Economic and Social Research and P. T. Pembangunan. Jakarta.

[101] ———. 1981. *The New Rice Economy of Indonesia.* Yogyakarta.

[102] Roger Montgomery and Sugito. 1980. "Changes in the Structure of Farms and Farming in Indonesia Between Censuses, 1963–1973: The Issues of Inequality and Near-Landlessness." *Journal of Southeast Asian Studies* 11, no. 2.

[103] S. Mortoatmodjo, Djumadias, Muhilal, Muhammad Husaini, and S. Sastroamidjojo. 1973. "Masalah Anemi Gizi pada Wanita Hamil dalam Hubungannya dengan Pola Konsumsi Makanan" (The problem of dietary anemia for pregnant women in connection with food consumption patterns). *Penelitian Gizi dan Makanan [Food and Dietary Research]* 3.

[104] Z. Muller, K. C. Chou, and K. C. Nah. 1974. "Cassava as a Total Substitute for Cereals in Livestock and Poultry Rations." *World Animal Review* 12, pp. 19–24.

[105] Gerald C. Nelson. 1982. "Implications of Developed Country Policies for Developing Countries: The Case of Cassava." Ph.D. diss., Stanford University, Stanford, Calif.

[105a] ———. 1983. "Time for Tapioca, 1970 to 1980: European Demand and World Supply of Dried Cassava." *Food Research Institute Studies* 19, no. 1.

[106] Barry Nestel and Reginald MacIntyre, eds. 1973. *Chronic Cassava Toxicity: Proceedings of an Interdisciplinary Workshop.* IDRC. Ottawa, Canada.

[107] Netherlands. Ministry of Agriculture and Fisheries. 1979. *Jaarsstatistiek van de Veevoeders 1977/78* [Annual fodder statistics]. Directorate-General of Agriculture and Food Prediction. The Hague.

[108] Edmund Neville-Rolfe et al. 1979. *Feed Use and Feed Conversion Ratios for Livestock in the Member Countries of the European Community.* Brussels.

[109] J. A. Nijholt. 1935. "Absorption of Nutrients from the Soil by a Cassava Crop." General Agricultural Research Station, Report no. 15. Bogor.

[110] Edgard S. Normanha. 1982. *Derivados da Mandioca: Terminologia e Conceitos* [Manioc products: Terminology and concepts]. Sao Paulo, Brazil.

[111] O. M. J. R. Nout. 1978. "Composite Flour Breads: More Questions Raised." *League for International Food Education Newsletter.* August.

[112] Rozany Nurmanaf. 1976. "General Picture of the Social and Economic Situation of Ciwangi Village, Sub-District Limbangan, Garut District." Report of the Rural Dynamics Project, Agro-Economic Survey of Indonesia. Bogor.

[113] Albert Nyberg and Dibyo Prabowo. 1979. "Status and Performance of Irrigation in Indonesia as of 1978 and the Prospects for 1990 and 2000." Report of the IFPRI/IRRI/IPDC Rice Policy Project for Southeast Asian Countries. Washington, D.C.

[114] L. H. Oldeman. 1975. "An Agro-Climatic Map of Java and Madura." Contribution no. 17, CRIA.

[115] I. C. Onwueme. 1978. *The Tropical Tuber Crops.* Chichester, Eng.

[116] H. A. P. C. Oomen and G. J. H. Grubben. 1977. *Tropical Leaf Vegetables in Human Nutrition.* Colonial Institute for the Tropics. Amsterdam.

[117] Gustav F. Papanek, ed. 1980. *The Indonesian Economy.* New York.

[118] Richard Patten, Belinda Dapice, and Walter Falcon. 1980. "An Experiment in Rural Employment Creation." In Gustav F. Papanek, ed.

[119] Scott R. Pearson, J. Dirck Stryker, and Charles P. Humphreys. 1981. *Rice in West Africa: Policy and Economics.* Stanford, Calif.

[120] People's Bank of Indonesia. 1980. "Summary Report on Bimas Credit by Planting Season up to June 30, 1980." Jakarta.

[121] Truman P. Phillips. 1974. *Cassava Utilization and Potential Markets.* IDRC. Ottawa, Canada.

[122] PRC Engineering Consultants, Inc. 1980. *The Citanduy River Basin Development Project: Feasibility Report.* Directorate General of Water Resources Development, Indonesian Ministry of Public Works. Jakarta.

[123] Frederick C. Roche. 1983. "Cassava Production Systems on Java." Ph.D. diss., Stanford University, Stanford, Calif.

[124] T. A. B. Sanders. 1977. "Food and Nutrition in Indonesia." *Plant Foods for Man* (London) 1, pp. 145–56.

[125] A. M. P. A. Scheltema. N.d. "World Production and Consumption of Cassava Articles." *The Netherlands Indies* 4, nos. 13, 14, 15.

[126] Rudolf Sinaga, Abunawan Mintoro, Yusuf Saefudin, and Benjamin White. 1977. "Rural Institutions Serving Small Farmers and Laborers." Report of the Rural Dynamics Project, Agro-Economic Survey of Indonesia, Rural Dynamics Series no. 1. Bogor.

[127] Soekirman. 1974. "Priorities in Dealing with Nutrition Problems in Indonesia." Paper prepared for the Division of Nutritional Sciences, Cornell University. Ithaca, N.Y.

[128] George F. Sprague, ed. 1955. *Corn and Corn Improvement.* New York.

[129] Statistical Office of the European Community (EUROSTAT). *Foreign Trade: Analytical Tables (NIMEXE).* Luxembourg, various years.

[130] ——— . *Yearbook of Agricultural Statistics.* Luxembourg, various years.

[131] ——— . 1974. "Livestock, Meat Production, Civil Year Balance Sheets." In *Yearbook of Agricultural Statistics.*

[132] ——— . 1978. *Animal Production, 1968–1977.* Luxembourg.

[133] Ann Stoler. 1978. "Garden Use and Household Economy in Rural Java." *Bulletin of Indonesian Economic Studies* (Canberra) 14, no. 2.

[134] Achmad Suryana and Lekir Amir Daud. 1981. *Study of Cassava Production and Marketing Systems in Lampung.* Agricultural Economics Research Center, Ministry of Agriculture. Bogor.

[135] Thailand. 1979. *Agricultural Statistics of Thailand, Crop Year 1978–79.* Agricultural Statistics Report no. 108, Ministry of Agriculture and Cooperatives. Bangkok.

[136] Nguyen Cong Thanh, M. B. Pescod, and Samorn Muttamara. 1976. "Technological Improvements of Tapioca Chips and Pellets Produced in Thailand." Asian Institute of Technology Research Report no. 57. Bangkok.

[137] C. Peter Timmer. 1973. "Choice of Technique in Rice Milling in Java." *Bulletin of Indonesian Economic Studies* (Canberra) 9, no. 2.

[138] ———. 1980. "Food Prices and Food Policy Analysis in LDCs." *Food Policy* 5, no. 3.

[139] C. Peter Timmer and Harold Alderman. 1979. "Estimating Consumption Parameters for Food Policy Analysis." *American Journal of Agricultural Economics* 61, no. 5.

[140] C. Peter Timmer, Walter P. Falcon, and Scott R. Pearson. 1983. *Food Policy Analysis*. Baltimore, Md.

[141] Boonjit Titapiwatanakun. 1980. *Feasibility Study on Regional Co-operative Arrangements in Tapioca*. Trade Cooperation Group, United Nations Economic and Social Commission for Asia and the Pacific. Bangkok.

[142] Julio C. Toro and Charles B. Atlee. 1980. "Agronomic Practices for Cassava Production: A Literature Review." In Edward J. Weber et al., *Cassava Cultural Practices*.

[143] Tropical Products Institute. 1975. *Composite Flour Technology Bibliography*. Report G89. London.

[144] ———. 1977. *Supplement to Composite Flour Bibliography*. Report G111. London.

[145] United States. Department of Agriculture. *Foreign Agricultural Circular*. Washington, D.C. Various issues.

[146] ———. ———. *Foreign Agricultural Trade of the United States*. Economic Research Service. May/June 1981. Washington, D.C.

[147] ———. ———. *Sugar and Sweetener Outlook*. Dec. 1981. Washington, D.C.

[148] ———. Department of Commerce. Bureau of the Census. *Statistical Abstract of the United States*. Washington, D.C. Various years.

[149] ———. National Research Council. National Academy of Sciences. *Nutrient Requirements of Swine*. 8th revised ed. Washington, D.C., 1979.

[150] United States and FAO. 1972. *Food Composition Table for Use in East Asia*. Washington, D.C.

[151] Laurian J. Unnevehr. 1982. "Cassava Marketing and Price Behavior on Java." Ph.D. diss., Stanford University, Stanford, Calif.

[152] A. G. van Veen, Lie Goan Hong, and Oey Kam Nio. 1971. "Some Nutritional and Economic Considerations of Javanese Dietary Patterns." *Ecology of Food and Nutrition* 1, pp. 39–43.

[153] M. S. van Veen. 1971. "Some Ecological Considerations of Nutrition Problems on Java." *Ecology of Food and Nutrition* 1, pp. 25–28.

[154] J. Wargiono et al. 1978. "Effect of Spacing and NK Fertilizer on the Yield of Grading Cassava Variety." Contribution no. 50, CRIA. Bogor.

208   *References Cited*

[155] ———— . 1979. "Long-Term Fertilization of Cassava." *Research Progress Report—Breeding—Agronomy Series for Cassava and Sweet Potatoes*. Report no. 10, CRIA. Bogor.

[156] E. J. Weber, J. H. Cock, and Amy Chouinard, eds. 1978. *Cassava Harvesting and Processing*. IDRC, Ottawa, Canada.

[157] E. J. Weber, Barry Nestel, and M. Campbell. 1979. *Intercropping with Cassava*. IDRC, Ottawa, Canada.

[158] E. J. Weber, Julio C. Toro, and Michael Graham. 1980. *Cassava Cultural Practices*. IDRC, Ottawa, Canada.

[159] Delane Welch and Boonjit Titapiwatanakun. Forthcoming. *Cassava Marketing in Thailand*.

[160] Roy L. Whistler and Eugene F. Paschall, eds. 1965, 1967. *Starch: Chemistry and Technology*. 2 vols. New York.

[161] B. White. 1976. "Population, Involution, and Employment in Rural Java." *Development and Change* 7, no. 3.

[162] Benjamin White and Makali. 1979. "Wage Labor and Wage Relations in Javanese Agriculture: Some Preliminary Notes from the Agro-Economic Survey." Unpublished ms. Bogor.

[163] C. N. Williams and K. T. Joseph. 1970. *Climate, Soil, and Crop Production in the Humid Tropics*. Kuala Lumpur.

[164] Gunawan Wiradi. 1978. "Rural Development and Rural Institutions: A Study of Institutional Change in West Java." Report of the Rural Dynamics Project, Agro-Economic Survey of Indonesia, Rural Dynamics Series no. 6. Bogor.

[165] World Bank. 1980. *Alcohol Production from Biomass in the Developing Countries*. Washington, D.C. September.

[166] ———— . 1980. "Price Prospects for Major Primary Commodities." Internal document, Washington, D.C. January.

[167] ———— . 1982. *Indonesia: Policy Options and Strategies for Major Food Crops*. Report no. 3686–Ind. Washington, D.C. May.

[168] D. Zain. 1980. "Peranan Kredit dalam Perdagangan Gaplek" [The role of credit in the trade of gaplek]. Brawijaya University, Malang, Indonesia. Mimeo.

[169] H. G. Zandstra. 1979. "Cassava Intercropping Research: Agroclimatic and Biological Interactions." In Edward J. Weber et al., eds., *Intercropping with Cassava*.

Index